Sex and desire in British films of the 2000s

Manchester University Press

Sex and desire in British films of the 2000s

Love in a damp climate

Nigel Mather

MANCHESTER UNIVERSITY PRESS

Copyright © Nigel Mather 2021

The right of Nigel Mather to be identified as the author of this work has been asserted by them in accordance with the Copyright, Designs and Patents Act 1988.

Published by Manchester University Press
Oxford Road, Manchester M13 9PL

www.manchesteruniversitypress.co.uk

British Library Cataloguing-in-Publication Data
A catalogue record for this book is available from the British Library

ISBN 978 1 5261 3923 8 hardback
ISBN 978 1526 1 8236 4 paperback

First published 2021

The publisher has no responsibility for the persistence or accuracy of URLs for any external or third-party internet websites referred to in this book, and does not guarantee that any content on such websites is, or will remain, accurate or appropriate.

Typeset by
Servis Filmsetting Ltd, Stockport, Cheshire

Contents

List of plates	vi
Acknowledgements	ix
1 Introduction: Relationships and intimacy in British films of the 2000s	1
2 From *The Happy Prince* to 'Lady Lazarus' and *Iris: A Memoir*: Writers in British society and tales of their private lives and personal affairs	18
3 'Diary of a somebody': Bridget Jones's journey from the 'edge of reason' to marriage and motherhood	51
4 'No sex, please – we're British?': Sex, sensibility and British cinema	85
5 'The way we live now': Narratives exploring relationships in modern British society	126
Afterword: 'We must love one another or/and die?'	197
Select Bibliography	206
Index	211

List of plates

1 *The Happy Prince* (2018). Bosie (Colin Morgan) and Oscar (Rupert Everett) reunite on foreign shores (BBC Films/Lions Gate UK Movie Management Corporation/Daryl Prince Productions/Casa Kafka Pictures/Raindog Films/Maze Pictures/Entre Chien Et Loup/Palamor Cine Plus Filmproduktion/Tele München Gruppe Proximus RTBF/Television Belge). Pictorial Press Ltd/Alamy Stock Photo.
2 *Sylvia* (2003). 'Till Death Do Us Part': Ted (Daniel Craig) and Sylvia (Gwyneth Paltrow) get married (BBC Films/Capitol Films/UK Film Council/Focus Features/Ruby Films). Pictorial Press Ltd/Alamy Stock Photo.
3 *Iris* (2001). Iris Murdoch (Judi Dench) and John Bayley (Jim Broadbent) face the future together (Miramax Films/Touchstone Pictures/BBC Films/Fox Iris Productions/Intermedia/Mirage Enterprises). Pictorial Press Ltd/Alamy Stock Photo.
4 *Bridget Jones: The Edge of Reason* (2004). Professional colleagues or potential partners in love? Rebecca (Jacinda Barrett) and Mark (Colin Firth) enjoy each other's company (Universal Pictures/Studio Canal/Miramax Films/Working Title Films/Little Bird Limited/Studio Canal). Photo 12/Alamy Stock Photo.
5 *Bridget Jones: The Edge of Reason* (2004). 'Was every look I ever gave you a lie?': Bridget (Renée Zellweger), Rebecca and the 'female gaze' (Universal Pictures/Studio Canal/Miramax Films/Working Title Films/Little Bird Limited/Studio Canal). Photo credit: Laurie Sparham: Universal File Reference #30735782THA: PictureLux/The Hollywood Archive/Alamy Stock Photo.
6 *Bridget Jones: The Edge of Reason* (2004). 'He really didn't stick up for me at the lawyers' supper': Bridget compares tales of woe with her fellow inmates (Universal Pictures/Studio Canal/

Miramax Films/Working Title Films/Little Bird Limited/Studio Canal). TCD/Prod. DB/Alamy Stock Photo.

7 *I Want Candy* (2007). 'I need someone to please help me': Candy Fiveways (Carmen Electra) seeks release from her chains (Ealing Studios and Thema Sa in association with Grosvenor Park Films/Sky Movies/A Fragile Film/UK Film Council). Allstar Picture Library Ltd/Alamy Stock Photo.

8 *The Look of Love* (2013). Paul Raymond (Steve Coogan) discovers the power of the 'male gaze' (Studio Canal and Film 4/Anton Capital Entertainment, SCA and Lipsync Productions/Revolution Films/Baby Cow Films). Photo 12/Alamy Stock Photo.

9 *On Chesil Beach* (2017). Florence (Saoirse Ronan) and Edward (Billy Howle) part company forever (Lionsgate/Number 9 Films/BBC Films/Rocket Science/Golan Films and Lipsync Productions). Moviestore Collection Ltd/Alamy Stock Photo.

10 *Animals* (2019). 'Isn't marriage part of the whole system we've been railing against all these years?': Laura (Holliday Grainger) and Tyler (Alia Shawkat) discuss the concept of the 'modern wedding' (Screen Australia, Screen Ireland/Fís Éireann/Cornerstone Films/Sarah Brocklehurst Productions/Closer Productions/Vico Films/Head Gear Films/Metrol Technology, Kreo Films/Adelaide Film Festival and South Australian Film Corporation). Pictorial Press Ltd/ Alamy Stock Photo.

11 *One Day* (2011). Emma (Anne Hathaway) and Dexter (Jim Sturgess) share an idyllic moment on holiday (Focus Features/Random House Films/Film 4/Color Force). Pictorial Press Ltd/Alamy Stock Photo.

12 *Unrelated* (2007). 'It's about making a bond with someone': Anna (Kathryn Worth) and Oakley (Tom Hiddleston) discuss sex, marriage and having children (Raw Siena). Everett Collection Inc/Alamy Stock Photo.

13 *Notes on a Scandal* (2006). Pupil and teacher interaction: Steven (Andrew Simpson) and Miss Hart (Cate Blanchett), his art teacher (Fox Searchlight Pictures/DNA Films/BBC Films/UK Film Council/A. Scott Rudin/Robert Fox Production/Ingenious Film Partners). Moviestore Collection Ltd/Alamy Stock Photo.

14 *Notes on a Scandal* (2006). Barbara (Judi Dench) gets the inside story on Sheba's shocking behaviour (Fox Searchlight Pictures/DNA Films/BBC Films/UK Film Council/A. Scott Rudin/Robert Fox Production/Ingenious Film Partners). Photo 12/Alamy Stock Photo.

15 *Closer* (2004). 'I've been here before': Dan (Jude Law) and Alice (Natalie Portman) revisit the past (Columbia Pictures/Inside Track 2). AA Film Archive/Alamy Stock Photo.
16 *Closer* (2004). 'It's not a war': Alice and Larry (Clive Owen) discuss sexual politics in the 'Paradise Suite' (Columbia Pictures/Inside Track 2). AA Film Archive/Alamy Stock Photo.
17 *Disobedience* (2017). 'That's my dad': Ronit (Rachel Weisz) and the Jewish community pay their respects (Film 4 and FilmNation Entertainment/Element Pictures/LC6 Productions/Braven Films Scope Pictures/Stage 6 Films). AF archive/Alamy Stock Photo.
18 *God's Own Country* (2017). Mutual disdain hiding mutual desire? Johnny (Josh O'Connor) and Gheorghe (Alec Secareanu) (British Film Institute/Creative England/Met Film Production/Shudder Films/Inflammable Films/Magic Bear Productions). Moviestore Collection Ltd/Alamy Stock Photo.
19 *Kidulthood* (2006). The teenage group about to tear itself apart (Revolver Entertainment/Stealth Films/Cipher Films/TMC Films/UK Film Council). AF archive/Alamy Stock Photo.
20 *Adulthood* (2008). Sam (Noel Clarke) and Lexi (Scarlett Alice Johnson) wonder whether they can trust each other (UK Film Council, Pathé and Independent present a Cipher Films/DJ Film/TMC Films and Limelight/Unstoppable Entertainment). Everett Collection Inc/Alamy Stock Photo.
21 *Pride* (2014). Members of 'Lesbians and Gays Support the Miners' commemorate the end of the strike (Pathé UK/CBS Films/BBC Films/Proud Films/Calamity Films/Canal Plus/British Film Institute). Entertainment Pictures/Alamy Stock Photo.
22 *Perfect Sense* (2011). Intimate encounters in a virus-ridden world: Michael (Ewan McGregor) and Susan (Eva Green) (BBC Films/Zentropa Entertainments/Scottish Screen/The Danish Film Institute/Screen Ireland/Sigma Films/Subotica Entertainment). Allstar Picture Library Ltd/Alamy Stock Photo.

Every effort has been made to identify copyright holders. Any omissions or corrections brought to our attention will be remedied in any future editions.

Acknowledgements

I am extremely grateful to the School of Arts and the Film and Media department at the University of Kent at Canterbury for kindly allowing me to be an Honorary Researcher while writing this book. The Templeman Library at the University has provided excellent computing facilities, invaluable IT help and assistance, and access to an outstanding collection of journals and periodicals which have been extensively drawn upon in my study. The library effectively and efficiently introduced measures so that it could reopen as soon as possible during the difficult year of 2020. Heartfelt thanks to everyone who made this possible.

Thank you to Professors Simon Kirchin, Peter Stanfield, Martin Hammer and Mattias Frey of the University of Kent for your much appreciated support and encouragement. Thanks also to Ann-Marie Fleming, a former Film Studies PhD student and Assistant Lecturer at UKC for her thoughtful and perceptive observations on sections of the book and for drawing my attention to the film *Perfect Sense*. With fond memories of those who have passed through the doors of the UKC Assistant Lecturer Film office at one time or another (Kat, Dominic, Maria, Zahra, Keeley, Pete, Frances, Alaina, Caleb, James, Barney and Gary). Thanks to all the staff at Manchester University Press, Bourchier Ltd and to Sixteen Films for generously granting permission for the beautiful image from *Ae Fond Kiss...* to appear as the cover for this book. Best wishes to Carolyn and Jeremy (with deepest thanks for their support and good humour), their daughter Libby, and to my sisters, Valerie and Francesca and their husbands, Jim and Kevin, and my nephews, Angus and Marcus.

This book is dedicated with love to the memory of my parents, Thelma and Derek Mather.

1

Introduction:
Relationships and intimacy in British films of the 2000s

To say 'I love you' to someone is always, inevitably, to be citing a well-known and well-worn phrase.[1] Thus, when speakers may want to be most authentic and personal, speaking deeply from the heart, they end up having to quote an unoriginal formulation of words, what Terry Eagleton has described as having to speak 'other people's lines'.[2] As the lovelorn Danny (Douglas Henshall) observes in *This Year's Love* (David Kane, 1999), the concept of 'love' contains 'Too many things in it for just one word.' In such circumstances, presumably what counts is having found someone to whom this phrase can be uttered deeply and sincerely. In *Alfie* (Lewis Gilbert, 1966), Gilda (Julia Foster), one of Alfie's many girlfriends, asks him if he loves her. 'Shall we say, I like you a lot,' replies Alfie, choosing his words very carefully so as to convey the precise nature of his feelings (and to avoid giving Gilda the impression that he might be willing to settle down into a monogamous relationship with her). Later, he observes in one of his asides to the film's audience (with a seemingly genuine air of confusion), 'I don't know what love is, the way you birds talk about it.'[3] When asked if he was in love with his bride-to-be as his wedding drew closer, Prince Charles famously – and somewhat notoriously – replied that he was in love, 'whatever that may mean',[4] an observation some have seen as indicating that his imminent marriage to Diana Spencer was built on shaky foundations and unlikely to last. The remark can, however, be read as evidence of Charles's recognition that the term 'love' in philosophical, emotional and linguistic terms was not one which could be unambiguously or definitively defined for all times, people or occasions. The novelist and philosopher Iris Murdoch described the act of falling with love with someone as a 'violent process', involving lovers becoming aware 'of an entirely separate reality',[5] creating a world which suddenly seems more enchanting and hopeful than it did previously. The term 'falling', however, does suggest that this can be a somewhat disorienting process, which may result in a painful 'landing' or an uncertain ending. The writer Laurie Penny, in her study *Unspeakable Things: Sex, Lies and Revolution* (2014), argues that 'romance' provides a welcome diversion from what she evocatively and memorably termed 'the grim, meat-hook reality of work and death'.[6] From such a perspective, the prospect of finding love and sexual fulfilment with one or numerous partners can be viewed as offering hope for new and optimistic stories to emerge in people's lives, creating appealing alternatives to what may otherwise seem to be depressing, uninspiring and unmemorable situations and ways of living.

The journalist Dolly Alderton's memoir *Everything I Know about Love* (2018) stresses the importance of approaching matters of relationships and sexuality in a positive manner, but the author is aware that the drive towards sexual happiness is not necessarily or straightforwardly satisfied by being directed at just one partner. Thus, she suggests (a little wryly) that 'It is important to have a lot of sex with a lot of people but probably no more than ten,' adding, 'It's a good idea to get married a bit later in life.'[7] Alderton is also conscious that no relationship can be viewed as exempt from a sudden and possibly unwelcome alteration leading to its demise: 'Everything will change. And it could happen any morning.'[8] Loved ones can suddenly develop a feeling of passion and desire for someone else, so that what seemed permanent may turn out to have been only temporary and provisional (and even the most loving of relationships are destined to end in the deaths of both partners).

Problems around finding and staying in work, earning money or partners who hold radically differing religious/cultural/political values can all create tensions within relationships, possibly resulting in lovers heading off in separate directions and never seeing each other again. In his study *After Theory* (2003), Terry Eagleton makes a distinction between what he terms the 'impersonal' sensually oriented 'ravages of desire' ('a monster at the heart of the self'), involving urges which are fundamentally self-regarding and self-seeking, and the more generous nature of unselfish and unconditional 'love' as a spiritual and material force which seeks to create the conditions for others to 'flourish' and prosper in a state of emotional and psychological well-being. Eagleton feels that the ideals associated with such forms of love also offer a 'model' of how 'a just society' might be organised and constructed in political and economic terms.[9] Sexual desire and unconditional love, the self and society might find themselves at odds in certain key ways when considered from such perspectives. Eagleton's intriguing formulations and distinctions will be important guiding lights when exploring the depictions and representations of sex, love, desire and society within a British cinematic and cultural context in this book. Eagleton's mentor at Cambridge University, Raymond Williams, once wrote of D.H. Lawrence being torn between 'thinking of the flame of life that can be kindled in a loving relationship' and a feeling that it was necessary to break 'away, from people and from society' in order to find true peace of mind and contentment. Williams concluded that Lawrence 'never really made up his mind about this final issue ... he kept trying to get it clear and right'.[10] One can similarly note that many of the characters in the films discussed in this study are similarly torn and troubled by doubts about to whom and to what they should pledge their true allegiance and commitment.

With regard to the medium of film and the significance of its particular depictions of love and desire, Thomas Wartenberg, in his book *Unlikely Couples: Movie Romance as Social Criticism* (1999), argues that films based around gay partnerships or couples whose liaisons meet with opposition from the society in which they unfold (for reasons pertaining to issues of class, race or culture) are capable of raising vital and important questions concerning love, sexuality and society in human relationships. What he designates 'unlikely' or untypical couples in films offer the possibility for assumptions about what is deemed natural, normal or desirable in characters' sexual and romantic behaviour within particular communities to be questioned, challenged and thoughtfully examined. Wartenberg suggests that the 'unlikely couple, by contravening a principle of hierarchy, portends social chaos and must be either be prevented ... or sanctioned in some way'.[11] Such narratives are therefore inherently dramatic and encourage audiences to reflect on the validity of arguments put forward by the 'unlikely' lovers for their relationship to prosper and also by characters who oppose or disapprove of the union in question. As a result, according to Wartenberg, spectators are encouraged to think more deeply about the role played by love, desire and sexuality in their own everyday experiences and aspirations, making the cinema both a valuable form of entertainment and a source of potential enlightenment and understanding.

In *Military Wives* (Peter Cattaneo, 2019), Kate (Kristin Scott Thomas) suggests to the assembled partners of army personnel present at a coffee morning event that they might convert the base's regular film night screenings into organised film seasons, where, as she puts it, they examine 'the body of an auteur'. Lisa (Sharon Horgan) speaks up for many of the women present by declaring that 'when we watch films, usually we like them to be fun'. *Sex and desire in British films of the 2000s: Love in a damp climate* will seek to illustrate that promising film writers and directors did emerge in British cinema during the 2000s, and that many of the films exploring romantic and sexual themes during this period might well appeal to Lisa and the women on the base as films which succeed in being both 'fun' and worthy of study and analysis. A thesis of the book is that the new millennium witnessed the release of a wide range of British movies capable of engaging in imaginative and creative ways with issues pertaining to sexuality,[12] desire,[13] society,[14] and the formation of romantic partnerships in a British context. Laurie Penny's *Unspeakable Things* calls for the 'creation of new narratives' exploring the subjects of love, desire, sex and relationships.[15] The 2000s in British film-making, indeed, witnessed treatments of these themes and topics in a range of generic forms, including the biographical/historical/literary picture, romantic comedy dramas, sexually oriented comedies, socially concerned narratives and adaptations of novels and plays, all of which will be explored in this book. Where possible, filmmakers operating within these various generic forms and modes of address also sought to draw inspiration from and expand upon significant previous engagements with the subjects of sex, love and desire in British films from earlier decades and periods (which the book will briefly consider in order to see how treatments of these themes in modern British cinema have developed and changed over time).

The writer, director and actor Noel Clarke emerged as a potential 'auteur' during the 2000s when he created and formulated an impressive trilogy of films about young people and their (often destructive or disruptive) drives and desires. *Kidulthood* (Menhaj Huda, 2006), *Adulthood* (Noel Clarke, 2008) and *Brotherhood* (Noel Clarke, 2016) engaged with the emotional and sexual interactions between British teenagers in a frank and fearless fashion. Alan Franks, writing in *The Times*, went so far as to compare the first film in the series, *Kidulthood*, with *Romeo and Juliet* (1597) for the stylised way in which it hurtles inexorably towards a series of tragedies, while engaging with such timeless and topical subjects as 'love, sex, pregnancy, jealousy, drug abuse, violence' and 'revenge'.[16]

If the 'hood' trilogy was fast paced, drawing upon the iconography of pop music videos and 'grime' culture, featuring characters who did not believe in repressing or restraining any of their desires for immediate physical gratification of a sexual or violent nature, *Unrelated* (2007), *Archipelago* (2010) and *The Souvenir* (2019) focused on very different kinds of characters and narrative events. In writer-director Joanna Hogg's exquisite film portraits, articulate, but rather unhappy men and women struggled to find the right words to express the emotions building up inside them, sometimes in the context of settings abroad (two of the films were set outside Britain and one features a deathly and uneasy trip to Venice). David Sexton, writing about Hogg's films in the *Evening Standard*, claimed that they offered 'a new way of seeing' in British film-making and succeeded in grappling with such themes as 'the power of family, the significance of childlessness' and the 'awkwardness of goodness'.[17] Both Noel Clarke and Joanna Hogg create portraits of difficult and intense relationships within diametrically opposed settings, situations and scenarios, making their depictions of modern manners and culture important in a study of relationships in British cinema of the 2000s.

The 2000s saw the release of impressive and moving accounts of complicated and complex relationships between male and female characters taking place in differing decades of British social history, the 1960s and the 1990s: *On Chesil Beach* (Dominic Cooke, 2018), *An Education* (2009) and *One Day* (2011), the latter two both directed by Lone Scherfig; and films exploring the pleasures and pains of same-sex attractions: *Imagine Me & You* (Ol Parker, 2005); *Pride* (Matthew Warchus, 2014); *Weekend* (Andrew Haigh, 2011) and *God's Own Country* (Francis Lee, 2017).

There were serious and uncompromising narratives depicting the ways in which religious beliefs, values and customs may create serious problems and obstacles for lovers and 'unlikely couples' who devoutly wish to be together: *Ae Fond Kiss…* (Ken Loach, 2004), *My Summer of Love* (Pawel Pawlikowski, 2004) and *Disobedience* (Sebastián Lelio, 2017). *Notes on a Scandal* (Richard Eyre, 2006) depicted the 'scandalous' sexual relationship of a couple who legally should not be together (a fifteen-year-old boy and his female art teacher, Sheba Hart), alongside the study of the uneasy friendship which develops between the art teacher and an older, woman colleague, whose silence about the affair is dependent on the art teacher entering into an intense emotional relationship with her. Emilia Clarke starred in two films which engaged with loving relationships imbued with a pervasive sense of loss – *Me Before You* (Thea Sharrock, 2016) and *Last Christmas* (Paul Feig, 2019). Feig's film (co-scripted by Emma Thompson), in particular, meditated on what kinds of values might be associated with 'Britishness' as the country worked towards extricating itself from the European Union in the drawn-out and contentious process which became known as Brexit.[18]

Two established American directors succeeded in producing dramas exploring Anglo-American relationships during a modern era. *Closer*, directed by Mike Nichols in 2004, was summed up by Robert Hanks as 'A love story for our times',[19] and Woody Allen's *Match Point* (2005) explored the tragic consequences of a former tennis player turned coach, Chris Wilton (Jonathan Rhys Meyers), being torn between his pleasant, kindly but somewhat baby-obsessed wife from a wealthy British background and his sexually seductive American lover, Nola (Scarlett Johansson), whom critic Tim Robey colourfully described as a 'chain-smoking mistress from hell'.[20] Allen's multi-character narrative about contrasting relationships in the city of London, *You Will Meet a Tall Dark Stranger*, was released in 2010 as a 'New Labour' government (in power since 1997) was voted out of office. The rather pessimistic mood of the four films Allen made about life, death and aspirations in Britain between 2004 and 2010 may, in part and indirectly, reflect something of the dimming of social optimism and belief in the 'New Labour' project under Tony Blair,[21] and Gordon Brown.[22]

In relation to representations of sexual intercourse on screen, one British film of the 2000s specifically sought to present sexual interactions between a man and a woman in a franker and more explicit manner than had previously been thought possible or desirable in British cinema – *9 Songs* (Michael Winterbottom, 2004). The same director was also responsible for *The Look of Love* (2013), a study of Paul Raymond (1925–2008), a pioneer in breaking down barriers regarding the depiction of female nudity on the printed page and a key figure in the emerging 'permissive society' in British culture during the 1960s and subsequent decades. Alongside these films, there were attempts to recreate and update the traditions of the 1970s British sex comedy film within quite different social, cultural and political contexts.

In a lighter and more comic mood, but still probing serious and important issues around romantic commitment and contentment in a determined and unblinking fashion, the 'Bridget Jones trilogy', a series of films released between 2001 and 2016, offered a constantly changing and engaging picture of one modern woman's search for sexual and emotional fulfilment within British culture and society as she reaches middle-age. These films (like the original diaries in novel form) aimed to 'tell the whole truth' about Bridget Jones and to see if the love of her life (Mark Darcy) would one day say that he liked Bridget just as she was, without preferring – as her friends put it – someone 'thinner ... cleverer, with slightly bigger breasts'. In fact, when Mark does eventually get around to stating that he wouldn't change anything about Bridget, best friend Shazzer admits that she is startled and amazed ('Well, fuck me,' she declares).

The subtitle of this book is taken from Raymond Durgnat's *A Mirror for England: British Movies from Austerity to Affluence* (1970), in which he headlined three sections of his study 'The Glum and the Guilty', 'Love in a Damp Climate' and 'The Lukewarm Life',[23] none of these headings seemingly presenting British culture or British cinema in the most alluring or seductive of lights. Durgnat expresses the view that when it comes to portraying passion and sexual desire in British feature films, even 'Marriage tends to be seen as a transcendent loyalty rather than as an expression of the erotic', with 'inhibition, shyness, melancholy and pessimism' pervasive and recurring features of the national cinema's 'way with erotic emotion'.[24] His book suggests in a regretful tone that directors and writers working within British cinema have by and large (with a few notable exceptions) failed to depict and explore the ebbs and flows of human relationships and matters of love, desire and sexuality in a spirit of uninhibited, unimpeded and productive enquiry.[25] He is not necessarily alone in this viewpoint. Jim Leach goes so far as to entitle one chapter of his study of *British Film* (2004), 'No Sex Please – We're British: Sex, Gender and the National Character'.[26] James Leggott, writing about British cinema in the period from 1997 to 2008, suggests that film-makers in Britain tend to treat 'sexual desire' in contrasting ways, which tend towards being either 'overly flippant … or joylessly earnest'.[27] I.Q. Hunter succinctly sums up his views on this topic by claiming that 'Britain, it is fair to say, is not renowned for its contribution to erotic cinema.'[28]

In taking such a view of British culture, society and sexuality, Durgnat, Leach, Leggott and Hunter can be seen as following in the footsteps of D.H. Lawrence, who in a 1930 essay 'The State of Funk', advised the 'English' from his European exile (in what would turn out to be the year of his death) to 'Conquer [their] fear of sex, and restore the natural flow', warning that if they did not, 'savage disaster' lay 'ahead'.[29] Defending and explaining the thinking behind his novel *Lady Chatterley's Lover* (1928), he declared that he could not envisage 'any hope of regeneration for a sexless England', concluding that 'An England that has lost its sex seems to me nothing to feel hopeful about.'[30]

My study will argue that such strictures and concerns about the evading of sexual themes and their exclusion from public and artistic life in British culture are not applicable to British film-making in the 2000s. I will aim to demonstrate that key films produced during this era explored many different aspects of relationships, including the joys and tensions of married and single life, the potential difficulties caused by couples splitting up and seeking divorces,[31] the complexities involved in finding the 'right' kind of partner at varying ages and the importance of sexual fulfilment in all kinds of relationships. The book does not suggest these are subjects which are in any way solely the preserve of modern British cinema or society; but I would want to claim that these are areas of universal human interest which were explored in dramatic and vivid fashion in a series of films emanating from British culture during the 2000s. This book will offer detailed readings and analyses of films viewed as particularly significant, aiming to make meaningful connections between texts and contexts, and giving serious consideration to the kinds of moral, emotional and political questions and dilemmas posed by specific films and directorial groupings of films (what Kate in *Military Wives* describes as the 'body' of an auteur).

Chapter 2 will seek to provide a historical/literary dimension and grounding for the more contemporary studies of love and desire in British film culture to be examined in subsequent chapters. This chapter will focus on the cycle of British biographical pictures from the 2000s that explore the lives and personal relationships of a varied set of writers in differing periods of British social history, in particular focusing on films exploring the legacies and lived experiences of three hugely important writers of the nineteenth and twentieth centuries: Oscar Wilde (1854–1900), Sylvia Plath (1932–1963) and Iris Murdoch (1919–1999). I will explore how the respective films in question – *The Happy Prince* (Rupert Everett, 2018), *Sylvia*

(Christine Jeffs, 2010) and *Iris* (Richard Eyre, 2001) – dramatise and dissect the extreme situations faced by these authors in their quests for creative fulfilment, satisfying romantic and sexual relationships, emotional happiness and psychological stability.

Chapter 3 will focus on the romantic and comic complications of a single character's love life and aspirations, Bridget Jones, a figure who also has connections with literature (Bridget begins her career working in publishing). Clive Bloom, in his study *Bestsellers: Popular Fiction since 1900* (2002), referred to the character of Bridget and her associates in their literary manifestation as 'an overweight and on-the-shelf, female, thirty-something, part-time feminist living in London with a group of equally unfocused friends drifting into middle age'.[32] Alexander Walker, in his review of *Bridget Jones's Diary* (2001), the film, was not much more complimentary, declaring that Bridget in his view lacked 'glamour, beauty, grace',[33] leading him to wonder how she attracted such handsome men as Daniel Cleaver and Mark Darcy. The three films released between 2001 and 2016 – *Bridget Jones's Diary* (Sharon Maguire, 2001), *Bridget Jones: The Edge of Reason* (Beeban Kidron, 2004) and *Bridget Jones's Baby* (Sharon Maguire, 2016) – show how Bridget's relationships with these two men (and later with a third) alter and develop over time. Bridget, by a series of indiscretions and indirections, tries to find direction, purpose and meaning in her romantic and sexual life. This chapter will explore how the narratives as a whole form a series of comedy-dramas which are distinctive, imaginative, fast moving and pertinent to the discussions of sex, love and dating undertaken in other chapters of the book. The movies, while undoubtedly approaching their subject material from a comic/ironic/parodic/self-referential perspective, engage with important issues around selfhood, sexual politics and what constitutes love and job satisfaction in a modern age. The impressive international success of the films suggests that British singleton Bridget's (mis)adventures (as enacted by Renée Zellweger, an American star) have made an emotional connection with audiences around the world, making them fascinating subjects for sustained critical analysis and exploration.

Chapter 4 will focus primarily on a number of British films from the 2000s which tended to concentrate on the life of the body rather than the mind, privileging the sexual over the cerebral and favouring explicitness over implicitness. These were films focusing on desire rather than love and favouring sexual activity over sublimation, raciness above repression, satisfaction over renunciation. Some of the films had unusual titles such as *I Want Candy* (2007) and *Animals* (Sophie Hyde, 2019), which possibly drew on some of the 'low comedy' traditions developed in the *Carry On* series of films, which, according to Fiona Sturges in the *Guardian*, 'reflected the collapse of the age of deference' and the 'working class in its heyday'.[34]

Such titles as *Sex Lives of the Potato Men* (Andy Humphries, 2004) and *Dogging – a Love Story* (2009) also reflect and gesture towards the era of the 1970s British sex comedy, when titles such as *No Sex Please, We're British* (Cliff Owen, 1973), *The Ups and Downs of a Handyman* (John Sealey, 1975) and *Intimate Games* (Tudor Gates, 1976) were not uncommon in British cinemas. The chapter will therefore include a short consideration of the significance and implications of this mode of film-making in British cinema as a means of establishing a critical context for discussion of the movies from the 2000s. Some of these more recent films were not well received critically, but are notable in terms of their attempts to extend earlier traditions of British cinema at its most salacious, farcical and irreverent, raising the question whether such 'comic' films about British sexuality continue to suggest that sex and dating practices in a British context might always be destined to appear at times slightly ridiculous, absurd and uneasy. In her 2004 study *Watching the English: The Hidden Rules of English Behaviour*, Kate Fox concludes that in other countries 'sex may be regarded as a sin, an art form, a healthy leisure activity ... or a problem ... In England, it is a joke.'[35]

Clarissa Smith, in an essay entitled 'British Sexual Cultures' in *The Cambridge Companion to Modern British Culture* (2010), also claims that 'traditionally, the British are characterised ... as rather sexually inept, in possession of a rather obsessive and puerile sexual humour and a lack of sophistication in their pursuit of the passions'.[36] Michael Winterbottom's *9 Songs* (2004) and *The Look of Love* (2013) appear to aim at demonstrating that such a statement may be both true and untrue. *9 Songs* eschews comedy and humour to take an unflinching look at an Anglo-American couple's sexual relationship, but Winterbottom's *The Look of Love* (2013) contains elements of comedy and irony in its study of an entrepreneur and impresario who amasses a personal fortune by challenging censorship restrictions in British culture from the 1950s onwards. The 'sexual revolution' of the 1960s and 1970s, of which Paul Raymond was a keen supporter and initiator, is shown as creating new possibilities and opportunities for men and women to experience sex outside any kind of permanent relationship; but this freedom and hedonism is depicted as inevitably making the concept of marriage and fatherhood more difficult to maintain, and the film subsequently moves towards a distinctly non-comic and disturbing conclusion.

'Never before in history has there been so much pornography to be had by so many in such numerous ways' wrote social commentator Ziauddin Sardar in 2005, referring to the infinite and ever-increasing number of sexual images available on the Internet in the 2000s.[37] Sardar consequently argued that people were now living in a 'masturbatory' and narcissistic 'society',[38] which he felt was psychologically unhealthy and spiritually rather empty. Sexual and pornographic images, by their very nature, do not identify with forces of restraint seeking to repress or constrain feelings of sexual desire. Nor is the concept of monogamous romantic love easily incorporated into a 'pornographic-type universe' constructed around unfettered sensual longings and unlimited sexual explorations, as *The Look of Love* graphically illustrates.

My study will therefore consider what kinds of perspectives on the life and career of Paul Raymond appear to be offered to audiences in *The Look of Love*. What, for instance, does the title of the film, given the narrative's emphasis on sex, nudity and drugs, appear to suggest or connote? Can Raymond be viewed as a kind of liberating and progressive figure in British culture, central to what a *New Statesman* 1971 editorial referred to as the 'democratisation of sexual pleasure'?[39] Or should he be more aptly seen as a symbol of what F.R. Leavis (1895–1978), responding to this particular editorial in 1972, claimed was the disastrous sectioning-off into sex, viewed purely as a 'field of potential physical pleasure or pornographically imaginative addiction', devoid of what Leavis described as the 'complexities and delicacies of love, and the crucial necessity of love to life'.[40] In the second edition of his seminal work *Sexual Dissidence* (2018), Jonathan Dollimore notes that 'increasing numbers' of people argued against 'unbridled liberation' because they felt it could lead 'ultimately to depression, narcissism ... and to social breakdown and ... drug addiction'.[41] The tragic story of Paul Raymond's daughter, Debbie, who dies from a drug overdose, leaving Raymond inconsolable in the narrative, implies that his hedonistic and materialistic philosophy of life may, if taken too far, lead to some of the undesirable outcomes listed by Dollimore.

Thus, a very different film to *9 Songs*, *On Chesil Beach* (Dominic Cooke, 2018), will also be considered in this chapter as contrasting with the former film's depiction of uninhibited and accomplished sexual interactions between male and female partners. This adaptation of an Ian McEwan novella illustrates that not all couples were or are comfortable with the concept or reality of sex (particularly in a pre-liberalised era, lacking in sexual representations and open discussions about sex). The ill-fated couple in *On Chesil Beach* experience difficulties in transforming a romantic friendship into a passionate and successful sexual encounter, a failure which leads to the couple dissolving their marriage after only a few hours. Such a film suggests that sexual innocence can come at a cost, adding to the difficulties of making definitive judgements about the kinds of changes Paul Raymond and his contemporaries and competitors brought about in British popular culture.

Chapter 5 will concentrate on how film-makers within British culture of the 2000s sought to depict the social and personal relationships and aspirations of characters in a series of contemporary settings and dramatic situations. The chapter will begin with a brief discussion of important examples of trends and traditions within British film production which have previously sought to explore connections between the personal, political and the sexual in British culture as it has evolved and developed since the 1960s, before proceeding to a detailed analysis of key films that explore such themes in new and probing ways during the 2000s.

In 2007, cultural commentator Mark Fisher wrote that the 'British landscape bristles with cinematic potential', but needed someone 'outside' what he termed the 'self-serving, self-pitying low gene pool' of British film-makers to realise 'this potential'.[42] During the 2000s, a number of non-British born directors came to Britain to make films exploring relationships within contemporary Britain. The dramas which emerged from directors such as Pawel Pawlikowski, Mike Nichols, Woody Allen and Lone Scherfig can be seen as continuing the work of previous visiting directors in British cinema during the 1960s (Michelangelo Antonioni, Stanley Donen, Roman Polanski, Jerzy Skolimowski and Joseph Losey), helping to make these portraits of modern relationships from creative, nuanced and somewhat distanced viewpoints as equally fascinating as their predecessors in the 1960s.

Pawel Pawlikowski's *Last Resort* (2000), for instance, allows audiences to see the kind of decaying seaside town (where citizens from other countries are held while their attempts to take up residence in Britain are processed) from new and startling perspectives. In the process, the film charts the 'unlikely' relationship which develops between a down-on-his-luck British man and a Russian woman whose hopes of forging a new life for herself in Britain with an ex-lover are thrown into disarray, when the ex-partner fails to put in an appearance and to welcome her into his world. *My Summer of Love* (2004) takes such scenarios unfolding in a state of flux and uncertainty even further. In this film, a public house is converted into a place of Christian worship; a born-again Christian is made to demonstrate that he can renounce his faith and become violent if pushed (or tempted) too far; and a loving relationship between two young women concludes with one woman trying to drown the other, after a supposedly dead sister has materialised back to life in a hallway.

Chapter 5 will include detailed studies of the following films made by directors and writers who approached relationships in a modern British context from something of an external perspective: Danish-born Lone Scherfig's *An Education* (2009) and *One Day* (2011), and American Mike Nichols's *Closer* (2004), a multi-character narrative about love, sex and desire, as experienced by educated, but restless and sometimes unfeeling individuals. Polish-born Pawel Pawlikowski's *My Summer of Love* (2004) and *Disobedience* (2017), directed by Chilean film-maker Sebastián Lelio, will be compared and contrasted for their treatments of female characters' love and sexual desire for each other, relationships which take place in opposition to religious forces represented by respectively, an unorthodox example of evangelical Christianity (in Yorkshire) and an Orthodox Jewish community (based in London).

Gay male relationships will be considered in two films with interesting and evocative titles. *God's Own Country* (2017) appears to reference a view of its Yorkshire setting as a place particularly blessed in its landscape and people. The film examines the potential for an antagonistic working relationship between a young and depressed British farm owner's son and a Romanian farm worker to develop into a sexual and emotional partnership, during what the film presents as a rather gloomy period in British life and culture. *Pride* (2014) also engages with homosexual alliances and relationships, but seeks to extend these relationships beyond studies of particular couples and to celebrate notions of political solidarity and camaraderie among different social classes and individuals of differing sexual orientations. To achieve this aim, *Pride* is based around an under-represented event in British cinema, the 1984–1985 miners' strike against proposed pit closures and focuses on what may have been seen as an 'unlikely' alliance between lesbians, gays and mining communities in different parts of the country. This film is particularly important for the ways in which it seeks to uncover and valorise a utopian sexual and communal moment within a time of crisis and extreme conflict.

Notes on a Scandal (2006), a drama about a woman teacher's damaging sexual behaviour outside the marital bedroom, will be analysed for its powerful investigation of the consequences of the woman's behaviour on her marriage, children, career and friendships. *Ae Fond Kiss...* (Ken Loach, 2004) falls into the category of narratives based around unlikely or unexpected alliances and romantic/sexual entanglements. Ken Loach and Paul Laverty's film offers an unpredictable and subtle study of a mixed-race relationship between a Glaswegian Muslim man (Casim) who works as a club DJ and an Irish Catholic woman (Roisin) who works as a music teacher in Glasgow. The two are brought together in a scene of violent disharmony within a music room, which possibly does not portend too well for their future together. The animosity shown to the couple by their contrasting religious communities raises – in an acute and urgent manner – the question of whether strong sexual desires and feelings of intense love will be enough for their relationship to sustain itself in the face of such opposition.

This book is aimed at showing that a focus on romance, courtship, representations of sexuality, likely/unlikely couples and contrasting communities in British film-making during the 2000s can also lead into a consideration of a wide range of topics and concerns, what W.H. Auden in his 1936 poem 'Letter to Lord Byron' referred to as discussing 'any subject' that he should 'choose/From natural scenery to men and women/Myself, the arts, [and] the European news'.[43] Thus, my study will seek to touch upon, where possible, such topics as the emotional and sensual connections between people and places; interactions between the rulers and the ruled; the perceived spiritual health of British modern society and the nation's relationships with American and European cultures; and the aesthetic and thematic accomplishments of British film-making during a time of transition, change and uncertainty.

W.H. Auden famously wrote that 'We must love one another or die' in his poem 'September 1, 1939', published as Britain declared war on Nazi Germany.[44] Later, Auden expressed some doubt about such a statement and claim, given that death cannot ultimately be avoided however we choose to spend or are able to live our lives.[45] However the statement is formulated, the phrase has a particular resonance in relation to the COVID-19 pandemic of 2020, which emerged during the final stages of the writing of this book. The 2011 film *Perfect Sense* (David Mackenzie) appears to have eerily anticipated such an unwelcome development in world history in its portrait of a virus that causes chaos and destruction. At its emotional centre, the film portrays a man (Ewan McGregor) and a woman (Eva Green) trying to forge an emotional and meaningful relationship, while humanity as we know it faces the prospect of gradual debilitation and possibly even extinction. It thus makes 'perfect sense' to include this film as something of an end point to the book's study of intimate and sensual relationships in modern British cinema and culture.

People can only hope that the threat posed by COVID-19 will be lifted or become significantly less oppressive and painful over time. While waiting for such an outcome, we may have to continue keeping a safe distance from our fellow human beings.[46] The decades covered in this book may consequently appear in comparison to the era of the virus as something of a 'golden age', when characters could (relatively) freely enter into romantic and sexual relationships with each other, without worrying if such encounters and engagements could lead to death or contamination from unseen external malign forces potentially hovering in the very air around them. Hopefully, happier and better times do lie ahead and the personal relationships examined in this book can be seen as offering up possibilities for an improved understanding and appreciation of how as film viewers, spectators and citizens of the world, we try to live out our desires and aspirations in relation to sexual matters and affairs of the heart, when circumstances, scenarios and situations allow.

Notes

1. The literary theorist Jonathan Culler has noted that to say 'I love you' will always be 'something of a quotation, as many lovers have attested'. Jonathan Culler, *On Deconstruction: Theory and Criticism after Structuralism* (London: Routledge & Kegan Paul, 1983), p. 120.
2. Terry Eagleton, *William Shakespeare* (Oxford: Basil Blackwell, 1986), p. 19. Eagleton also refers to what he describes as 'the whole tediously repetitive history of human sexual behaviour … with [its] strictly limited array of roles' (p. 19).
3. In the belated and little-known sequel to the original *Alfie* (Lewis Gilbert, 1966), *Alfie Darling* (Ken Hughes, 1975), Alfie, now played by Alan Price, does fall deeply in love with a woman (Jill Townsend) and asks her to marry him. In an unexpected plot twist, she dies in a plane crash and the film ends suddenly, with Alfie inconsolable at how his true love has been violently and cruelly taken away from him.
4. Sarah Bradford describes the Prince's reply to the question as 'disquieting' in *Elizabeth: A Biography of Her Majesty the Queen* (London: Heinemann, 1996), p. 438.
5. Iris Murdoch, 'The Fire and the Sun' (Romanes Lecture, 1976), *Existentialists and Mystics: Writings on Philosophy and Literature*, ed. Peter Conradi (London: Chatto & Windus, 1997), p. 417.
6. Laurie Penny, *Unspeakable Things: Sex, Lies and Revolution* (Bloomsbury: London and New York, 2014), p. 207.
7. Dolly Alderton, *Everything I Know about Love* (London: Fig Tree/Penguin, 2018), pp. 1–3.
8. *Ibid.*, p. 312.
9. Terry Eagleton, *After Theory* (London: Penguin, 2004 [2003]), pp. 168–9.
10. Raymond Williams, *Modern Tragedy* (London: Verso, 1979 [1966]), p. 137.
11. Thomas Wartenberg, *Unlikely Couples: Movie Romance as Social Criticism* (Boulder, CO: Avalon Publishing, 1999), p. 8.
12. Jasper Griffin, drawing upon Foucault's writings, defines sexuality as a term denoting 'the attitudes which men and woman have towards themselves as sexual agents, their ways of understanding the phenomena of sex'. Jasper Griffin, review of Michel Foucault, *The Care of the Self: History of Sexuality Volume IIII*, *Spectator*, 260:8344 (11 June 1988), p. 36.
13. Julian Wolfreys has noted that desire as a sexual and psychological force is based around notions of 'surplus or excess' and is resistant to those forms of thinking which seek to apply laws urging restraint or limits on satisfaction or fulfilment. Julian Wolfreys, *Critical Keywords in Literary and Cultural Theory* (Basingstoke: Palgrave Macmillan, 2004), p. 51.
14. An updated and revised edition of Raymond Williams's *Keywords* (1974) notes that society 'can be driven by self-interest, or by bonds of affection … Societies thus have values and feelings which unite and conflicts which divide.' Tony Bennett, Lawrence Grossberg and Meaghan Morris (eds), *New Keywords: A*

Revised Vocabulary of Culture and Society (Oxford: Blackwell Publishing, 2005), p. 328.
15 Penny, *Unspeakable Things*, p. 224.
16 Alan Franks, 'Too Much Too Young', *The Times Magazine* (25 January 2006), pp. 31–6: article on *Kidulthood*, consulted at the BFI Library, London.
17 David Sexton, 'The Posh are People too', *Evening Standard* (22 February 2010), pp. 32–3.
18 Dictionary.com defines Brexit as 'the probable withdrawal of the United Kingdom from membership in the European Union' and 'the nonbinding national referendum in 2016 that resulted in a vote for the United Kingdom to leave the European Union'. www.dictionary.com/browse/brexit?s=t (accessed 18 March 2020).
19 Robert Hanks, film review of *Closer*, *Independent* (14 January 2005), review section, pp. 6–7.
20 Tim Robey, film review of *Match Point*, *Daily Telegraph* (6 January 2006), p. 27.
21 The historian A.N. Wilson has suggested that during the years of Tony Blair's time as Prime Minister (1997 to 2006), he and Gordon Brown were locked in what he termed an 'abusive relationship', an 'implacable, relentless feud … between the increasingly mad-seeming Blair and the not-obviously-much-saner Brown'. This unhappy and unsettling situation may on a subconscious level have seeped into a number of the films discussed in this book, which focus on tempestuous or tormented relationships from which neither partner can easily escape. A.N. Wilson, *Our Times: The Age of Elizabeth II* (London: Arrow Books, 2009), pp. 409–10.
22 Tony Wood drew attention to the contentious nature of Tony Blair and Gordon Brown's time in office between 1997 and 2010 by writing an editorial in *New Left Review* which offered a damning verdict on their legacy: 'one murderous war after another; slavish devotion to finance; promotion of rampant inequality … Good riddance, this execrable government deserves to go.' Tony Wood, 'Good Riddance to New Labour', *New Left Review*, 62 (March/April 2010), pp. 22–8.
23 Raymond Durgnat, *A Mirror for England: British Movies from Austerity to Affluence* (London: Faber & Faber, 1970), pp. 163, 177 and 198, respectively. The subtitles of Chapters 4 and 5 in my book draw upon Anthony Trollope, *The Way We Live Now* (London: Chapman and Hall, 1875), a novel, and Julie Burchill, *Sex and Sensibility* (London: HarperCollins, 1992), which is a collection of essays.
24 Durgnat, *A Mirror for England*, p. 177. Durgnat claims that in late 1950s British cinema, film-makers tended to regard 'Eroticism' as 'something of a disease' and sickness which needed to be treated in the form of the social problem thriller (p. 194).
25 Durgnat notes that the introduction of the X certificate in British cinemas during the early 1950s (which meant that viewers of such classified films had to be aged sixteen or over) did enable 'a few British films' to 'study sexuality from more or

less the same stand-point which D.H. Lawrence had brought to *Sons and Lovers* in 1912'. *Ibid.*, p. 193.
26 Jim Leach, *British Film* (Cambridge: Cambridge University Press, 2004), title of chapter 7, p. 124.
27 James Leggott, *Contemporary British Cinema: From Heritage to Horror* (London: Wallflower Press, 2008), p. 84.
28 I.Q. Hunter, *Cult Film as a Guide to Life: Fandom, Adaptation and Identity* (London: Bloomsbury, 2016), p. 97.
29 D.H. Lawrence, 'The State of Funk' (1930), reprinted in A.A.H. Inglis, *D.H. Lawrence: A Selection from Phoenix* (London: Penguin Books, 1979 [1936]), p. 371.
30 D.H. Lawrence, 'A Propos of Lady Chatterley's Lover' (1930), reprinted in D.H. Lawrence, *A Propos of Lady Chatterley's Lover and Other Essays* (London: Penguin, 1961), p. 115.
31 In his updated study of *Britain on the Couch*, Oliver James reported that between the 1950s and the 1980s there was 'a fourfold increase in the divorce rate' in Britain, a rise which he felt could lead to 'anxious attachment and delinquency' among young people adversely affected by their parents' separations. Oliver James, *Britain on the Couch: How Keeping Up with the Joneses has Depressed us since 1950* (London: Vermillion, 2010 [1998]), p. 434.
32 Clive Bloom, *Bestsellers: Popular Fiction since 1900* (Basingstoke: Palgrave, 2002), p. 53.
33 Alexander Walker, 'Fantasy Made Flesh', review of *Bridget Jones's Diary* (2001), *Evening Standard* (12 April 2001), p. 35.
34 Fiona Sturges, 'Carry On films Celebrated the Working Class in its Heyday,' *Guardian* (4 July 2019), Opinion section, p. 4. Sturges compares the 1960s and 1970s context of the films favourably to the political and economic situation of 2019, which she sees as characterised by 'stagnating wages, rising homelessness … with a bunch of public schoolboys gambling with Britain's political future' (p. 4).
35 Kate Fox, *Watching the English: The Hidden Rules of English Behaviour* (London: Hodder, 2014 [2004]), p. 453. Fox sees the sex lives of modern English citizens as complicated by social awkwardness, 'hypocrisy' and 'class consciousness' (p. 482). Such factors, Fox argues, lead to the typical English person adopting a slightly ironic, humorous approach to sexual matters.
36 Clarissa Smith, 'British Sexual Cultures', in Michael Higgins, Clarissa Smith and John Storey (eds), *The Cambridge Companion to Modern British Culture* (Cambridge: Cambridge University Press, 2010), p. 245.
37 Ziauddin Sardar, '2005: The Decline of Sex – It's Just Mechanics', *New Statesman* (1 January 2005), p. 31. Sardar argues that one effect of the increased prevalence of pornography in modern societies is that 'No matter how dark your thoughts, how unethical your desires … everything [becomes normalised].' Writing at a time before pornography become so pervasive in capitalist societies in the same journal, Rosalind Coward argues that women 'dislike the idea that everywhere in our culture images of women's' bodies 'are available for men to

use in securing a release for a pressing functional need'. Coward concludes that 'women feel hostile to men's repeated use of tawdry sexual clichés to secure themselves physical relief'. Rosalind Coward, 'Porn: What's in it for Women?', *New Statesman*, 3:2881 (13 June 1986), p. 25. Toby Young, in a polemical essay written in favour of pornography, argues that 'the women in porn films are nearly always completely liberated beings', adding, 'the fact that the women are so unrepressed is what makes the films so exciting … the relationship between the man and the woman is scrupulously egalitarian, each taking a turn to pleasure the other'. Toby Young, 'Confessions of a Porn Addict', *Spectator*, 287:9040 (10 November 2001), p. 34.
38 Sardar, '2005: The Decline of Sex', p. 32.
39 Author not listed, Editorial, 'Full Frontal Hypocrisy', *New Statesman*, 81:2093 (30 April 1971), pp. 581–2. The editorial claims that 'Lord Longford and his supporters' were 'prepared to tolerate a society where pornography was available' to rich and affluent members of society, 'but kept discreetly hidden from the public gaze', thus, making its availability and accessibility, 'a class issue'.
40 F.R. Leavis, *Nor Shall My Sword: Discourses on Pluralism, Compassion and Social Hope* (London: Chatto & Windus, 1972), p. 33.
41 Jonathan Dollimore, *Sexual Dissidence*, 2nd edn (Oxford: Oxford University Press, 2018 [1991]), p. 7.
42 Mark Fisher, 'coffee bars and internment camps' (26 January 2007), republished in Darren Ambrose (ed.), *k-punk: The Collected and Unpublished Writings of Mark Fisher (2004–2016)* (London: Repeater Books, 2018), p. 179.
43 W.H. Auden, 'Letter to Lord Byron, Part 1' (1937), in W.H. Auden and Louis MacNeice, *Letters from Iceland* (London: Faber & Faber, 1985 [1937]) p. 19.
44 W.H. Auden, 'September 1, 1939', reprinted in *W. H. Auden Selected Poems*, ed. Edward Mendelson (London: Faber & Faber, 2009 [1979]), p. 97.
45 Arnold Kettle noted that Auden came to the conclusion that the claim 'We must love one another or die' was false and misleading 'because we will die anyway' in 'W.H. Auden: Poetry and Politics in the Thirties', in Carole Clark, John Heinemann, Margot Margolies and David Snee (eds), *Culture and Crisis in Britain in the 30s* (London: Lawrence and Wishart, 1979), p. 85.
46 D.H. Lawrence wrote in 1930 of how he believed modern life encouraged people to feel isolated and distanced from one another: 'as the feeling of oneness and community with our fellow-men declines', human beings tend towards viewing each other as 'a menace', he argued. With the onset of the COVID-19 pandemic, citizens of the world have been forced and encouraged to observe 'social distancing' in an attempt to stop the spread of the virus, something that can make people inevitably rather wary of each other. Lawrence, 'A Propos of Lady Chatterley's Lover', p. 122.

2

From *The Happy Prince* to 'Lady Lazarus' and *Iris: A Memoir*: Writers in British society and tales of their private lives and personal affairs

Patricia Beer, reviewing biographies of the writer Graham Greene, commented, 'In the 20th century ... what readers have come to demand from biography is not information but revelation, the favourite disclosures being in the field of sexual malpractice.'[1] A.N. Wilson, reflecting on changes in the ethics and practicalities of writing biographies of famous figures, observed, 'In the happier past, biographers felt it was their duty to *shield* their subjects from the gossipy curiosity of the public ... Nowadays, this would be viewed as a dereliction of the biographer's duty. If something is known it *must* be told, with all the details.'[2]

As if taking inspiration from such trends towards frankness in the writing of biographies, and perhaps sensing some business opportunities in the process, a number of film-makers in Britain turned their attentions during the 2000s to exploring the lives and personal relationships of certain seminal and innovative (and sometimes controversial) writers in British literary and cultural history – Jane Austen (1775–1817), John Keats (1795–1821), Charles Dickens (1812–1870), Oscar Wilde (1854–1900), Dylan Thomas (1914–1953), Sylvia Plath (1932–1963) and Iris Murdoch (1919–1999). The lives (and on occasions the deaths) of these authors were dramatised in *Becoming Jane* (Julian Jarrold, 2007), *Bright Star* (Jane Campion, 2009), *The Invisible Woman* (Ralph Fiennes, 2013), *The Happy Prince* (Rupert Everett, 2018), *The Edge of Love* (John Maybury, 2008), *Sylvia* (Christine Jeffs, 2010) and *Iris* (Richard Eyre, 2001).

This short cycle of films did not always meet with critical approval from British critics and reviewers. The title of Tanya Gold's (2009) article in the *Guardian*, 'One by one, [the cinema] is taking our great writers and ruining them for us', made its point clear even to those who did not go on to read its semi-humorous polemic against this kind of biographical picture. Gold, in particular, objected to the casting of American star actresses as eminent literary figures. Paltrow in *Sylvia* was too obviously 'an actress in a wig holding a copy of *The Bell Jar*', while 'If Austen had looked like [Anne Hathaway], she would never have written a word ... They have turned the patron saint of celibates into a hottie,' fumed Gold.[3] Kate Muir, writing for *The Times*, railed against what she saw as the cult of misery associated with Plath, a movement which she felt would be given a further boost by the release of this film of her life. Muir was also aghast at what she viewed as the 'gross disservice done to Iris Murdoch by the queasy, invasive and ever-growing memoirs of those who knew her and the egregious film', *Iris*.[4]

Becoming Jane aimed to discover why 'someone who had written six of the best romantic novels in history [had] not herself married'.[5] In the film, economic and social factors are depicted coming between a youthful Jane Austen (Anne Hathaway) and a possible partner-in-life for her, Tom Lefroy (James McAvoy), leaving their potential romance an essentially unrealised project. The film-makers suggest that this fuels Austen's desire to transmute and sublimate her emotional longings and latent desires into works of fiction instead.[6] *Becoming Jane* concludes with a much older Jane meeting an equally aged Lefroy at a formal occasion several decades after they parted ways. It emerges that he is now married with a daughter named Jane (Sophie Vavasseur), who is an avid admirer of Miss Austen's writings. At the close, these two are part of an audience listening raptly to Jane reading from one of her acclaimed novels about relationships and marriages between eligible men and desirable women. This ending implies that Austen has coped with the lack of romance and passion in her life by focusing on her writing, although Hathaway's slightly strained facial expressions and wistful demeanour during this sequence suggest that ideally she might have experienced both artistic and romantic success in her life.[7]

Bright Star presents the poetry of Keats (Ben Whishaw) as emanating from the poet's feeling that his time on earth will be short and that he will never be able to consummate and develop his relationship with Fanny Brawne (Abbie Cornish), the striking young woman who lives next door to him. Tragically, his fears prove to be well founded, and he dies abroad from tuberculosis, a long way away from Fanny and his friends and with no way of knowing that his poems and writings will live on for centuries after his death. Whishaw beautifully captures Keats's love of the natural world and beauty, alongside his concerns that he risks being distracted from his ambition to be a great writer by his love for Fanny Brawne. The film takes its title from what is reputedly the last poem written by Keats before his death, 'Bright Star'. This work suggests that life itself is a mixture of process and change – unlike the seemingly unchanging and eternal stars in the sky – and that the price we pay for living within this ever-altering matrix of unfolding events is ultimately death.[8] The narrative concludes with Fanny being given the terrible news that 'Mr Keats is dead.' As the credits unfold, we hear

Whishaw's voice reading 'Ode to a Nightingale' over mournful music on the soundtrack. Keats the author died far too young, but the film demonstrates (and commemorates) in this coda that his spirit, words and romantic yearnings live on and are capable of being embodied by a technological art form – the cinema – beyond his most fantastical imaginings.

Jane Campion's film gives almost equal weight to Fanny Brawne as it does to Keats, seeing her as a source of inspiration for many of his most famous poems about beauty, love and the transience of life. Ralph Fiennes's study of Charles Dickens's relationship with a much younger woman, Ellen Ternan (Felicity Jones), takes a similar approach. *The Invisible Woman* alluded to in the title is Ellen Ternan, a young woman who becomes the isolated and secluded mistress of Charles Dickens. The esteemed author leaves his wife and large family for Ternan, but her existence cannot be publicly acknowledged for fear of harming his reputation as a devoted family man. This makes their relationship a difficult and possibly unsatisfactory one for both partners, with Ternan occupying only a footnote in many biographies of Dickens, but in this 2013 film she is elevated to a prominent and important position in his life.

Dylan Thomas in *The Edge of Love* finds himself caught between two women; one his wife, the other a former lover in a London which is being devastated by German bombing raids during the Second World War. Thomas is meant to be helping to write the words to accompany film documentaries aimed at improving citizen morale, but his drinking and ambivalent attitude towards the war mean that his contributions to the war effort are sporadic. A retreat to Wales provides an escape from the horrors of the blitz, and fatherhood provides some possible hope for the future. But the awfulness of the conflict (as exemplified by the experiences of a captain in the British army who marries Thomas's former girlfriend) implies that the emotional disturbances caused by the Second World War will not be easily overcome, even by those (such as Thomas) who did not see active service. Thomas as depicted in the narrative appears committed to a life of fantasy and alcohol, which does not enhance his relationships with women or society. History, if not the film itself, tells us that he died in 1953, a long way from his Welsh roots and beginnings, while on a reading tour in America.

The following case studies will pay particular attention to a group of films which examined the lives and romantic and sexual experiences of three important and fascinating authors writing in Britain from between the late Victorian era up to the period of a 'New Labour' government in office during the 1990s – Oscar Wilde, Sylvia Plath and Iris Murdoch. Wilde had been the subject of three films before *The Happy Prince*, but Rupert Everett's 2018 film was the first to concentrate on the last years of his life when he was exiled from Britain and tried to make a new life for himself after being released from prison. The lives of Plath and Murdoch had not previously been explored by film-makers. Films about these particular authors are, I would argue, particularly worthy of serious critical attention given the extreme situations concerning love, togetherness, personal creativity, illness, sexual fidelity and sexual relationships in British social history which the film biographies explore and engage with in wide-ranging, dramatically stimulating and provocative ways. Sylvia Plath's complex story might seem as if it cannot be easily accommodated into a feature-length narrative, but I will seek to illustrate that Christine Jeff and John Brownlow's film *Sylvia* is a thoughtful and compelling account of two creative writers (Plath and the future Poet Laureate, Ted Hughes), torn apart by Hughes's infidelity and the passionate feelings of both love and resentment which they subsequently feel for each other. Mark Kermode writes that Plath is 'clinically embodied' by Gwyneth Paltrow,[9] which he does not mean as a compliment, but the phrase captures something of her icily precise depiction of Plath's changing moods and troubled responses to situations. Paltrow's performance creates a powerful and affecting version of Plath in a medium in which she has been under-represented, and presents a case for her ongoing importance as a figure around whom important questions about female subjectivity, creativity and experience continue to be posed. *Iris* presents a view of Iris Murdoch's life at a time when she, herself, cannot recall it, following the diagnosis that she is suffering from Alzheimer's disease. The film contrasts this disturbed present with her past as a liberated woman looking for a wide range of sexual and emotional experiences to draw upon in her desire to write a vast number of novels exploring the complexities of human relationships in post-Second World War Britain. The films of these writers' lives raise questions about the possibilities for sexual happiness and psychological well-being in British, American and European culture during the eras in which they lived. The films consider how the writers' desires for stability and security in their ongoing relationships were also sometimes at odds with their wishes to be free and unconfined so that their creative writing could best flourish. Plath and Murdoch's stories interrogate the nature and sustainability of heterosexual partnerships enshrined in marriage, while Oscar Wilde (without perhaps intending to do so) ended up questioning the whole basis of sexual relationships between various partners in late Victorian England.

Oscar Wilde (1854–1900)

W.H. Auden once declared in 1950, 'What a subject for a Big Feature Movie' Oscar Wilde's life would make. Auden claimed that the story had 'just about everything'; locations ranging from Dublin to Oxford, London to the 'Wild West' of America, and featuring the 'Old Bailey, Reading gaol' and 'Paris cafes' as key settings, amid a cast of unpredictable and uncompromising figures, particularly 'Bosey [sic] Douglas and his dotty choleric papa' and 'Carson the prosecutor who nearly became guilty of treason over Ulster'. 'Is there another life-story in history to compete with it?', he wondered.[10]

One of those figures who played a key part in Wilde's life (probably the key part in retrospect) was Lord Alfred Douglas (also known as Bosie). He wrote his own memoir, *Oscar Wilde and Myself* (1914), in which he argued that 'The biographies of persons who have done nothing are … unprofitable. Wilde made a stir in the world … It is right and proper that while the noise is still in the air we should endeavour to discover its true meaning.'[11] This section of the chapter will consider the implications and significance of Oscar Wilde's triumphs and tragedies, his romanticism and his bisexuality as depicted and dramatised in *The Happy Prince* (Rupert Everett, 2018), a fourth British film about the author's life and times.

In his 1891 essay, 'The Soul of Man Under Socialism', Oscar Wilde argued that in a socialistic society, 'marriage in its present form' would 'disappear', creating opportunities to 'make the love of man and woman more wonderful, more beautiful, and more ennobling'.[12] Wilde also wrote in this essay that he felt journalists in Britain at this time had too much power to provide the masses with information about the 'private lives of men and women', a situation he found deplorable and immoral ('English public opinion … compels the journalist to retail things that are ugly, or disgusting').[13] Wilde's distrust of and disdain for 'popular public opinion' in matters of sexuality and morality would only have been intensified by the coverage of his trials for indecent sexual conduct with other men and the legal judgment in his final trial that he be imprisoned for two years. This chapter will discuss and consider Wilde's rise and fall as depicted in *The Happy Prince* (2018), which concentrates on the writer's attempts to settle in Europe after he was released from prison. This part of his life has tended to be neglected in film biographies, and Everett seeks to prove that this is a fascinating and crucial part of his story, raising important questions about how he struggled to regain his creativity and talent in new non-British surroundings, while trying to reunite with Lord Alfred Douglas, the possible love of his life, but also one of the key protagonists in his ruination. Wilde's desire to live more openly as a gay man in France and Italy has to take place within situations where he is perilously short of money and aware that his terrible experiences have made him unable to write any more semi-comic plays about life in British high society. Everett's portrayal and film allows audiences an opportunity to assess how far Wilde could be said still to be suffering a kind of imprisonment for his sexual desires after he is officially released from jail.

In 1960, two films about Wilde were released and reviewed during the same week in May. The films were *Oscar Wilde* (Gregory Ratoff, 1960) and *The Trials of Oscar Wilde* (Ken Hughes, 1960). Leonard Mosley, writing in the *Daily Express*, claimed that the production and exhibition of these movies was in itself a sign of changing times in British society: 'Two years ago ... no film company in the English-speaking world would have dared to make a film about Oscar Wilde and tell the whole truth about him.'[14] The subject material of both films – the criminalisation of male homosexual relationships in British society and the attendant difficult and risk-taking lives led by gay men – was still a topical and contentious issue in 1960. In the week during which the two Wilde movies were released in London cinemas, the *Spectator* included a letter from the Homosexual Law Reform Society, observing that gay men who were being blackmailed, threatened and, in some cases, even 'robbed' and 'beaten' were often advised by the Society 'not to report the crime, since in many cases it is the victim who is prosecuted'.[15] Such correspondence indicated that Wilde's persecution and imprisonment because he acted on his sexual desires was by no means a singular and unique event in British society, and that in making films about the past sufferings of a famous homosexual in history, the film-makers were also producing narratives acutely relevant to an ongoing problematical social and sexual situation in Britain. David Thomson has claimed that 'In 1954, there were over a thousand men in prison in Britain for homosexual offenses.'[16]

What makes *Oscar Wilde* (1960) fascinating in comparison with Rupert Everett's 2018 movie is that the former concludes with a coda which attempts to convey what the final period of Wilde's life in Paris may have been like for a man who had, by now, lost his reputation, his savings and his ability to write. Wilde (Robert Morley) is pictured sitting on his own in a Parisian café, haggling with the waiter about settling his outstanding drinks bill ('I had hoped to live on in the patron's memory for not paying the bill', he wittily observes, conscious of his place in literary and cultural history). His loyal friend, Robert Ross (Dennis Price), stops by, but even he cannot bear to listen to Wilde's increasingly disoriented and confused musings about flowers and Jesus, and his admission that the terrible events of his life have finished him as a creative force. Stephen Bourne, in *Brief Encounters: Lesbian and Gays in British Cinema 1930–1971* (1996), notes that the film concludes with Wilde asking an accordionist to play 'something gay'. Wilde then roars 'like a madman with laughter', and the camera at this point tracks away from Wilde in the café to the tomb where he is buried in Paris. Bourne describes this as a 'grotesque, disturbing climax',[17] which in an economic and resonant fashion indicates how Wilde was unable to feel at peace with the world after his release from prison. The sequence implies that Wilde's exile abroad may have turned out to have been another kind of imprisonment for him, one which culminates in his entombment in a Paris churchyard. As the film has begun with Wilde's voice speaking to cinema audiences on the soundtrack over a view of his final resting place, as he invites spectators to learn how he ended up there, the disturbing and uncanny implication of the film as a whole is that even in death, Wilde has never achieved any final peace or release from his suffering.

The Trials of Oscar Wilde (1960), with a very different kind of actor and screen personality appearing as Wilde (Peter Finch), concludes with the author's departure from Britain to Dieppe on the day that he is released from prison. This film does not venture to indicate what his life may have been like after he arrived there and in contrast to the Morley/Ratoff film, *Trials* works towards a moderately hopeful and more open-ended conclusion. His wife, Constance Wilde (Yvonne Mitchell), is shown meeting Wilde in a carriage on the day he leaves prison, an event which historians are agreed did not actually take place. Wilde once had a character declare in 'The Critic as Artist' (1891) that 'The one duty we owe to history is to rewrite it,'[18] so he would not necessarily have objected to this particular fictionalising of events. Constance tells him the children send their love and that she has told them that he has been 'very ill', which is why he has been away from home (an observation which might be read as viewing homosexual desire as a kind of sick longing for which prison has possibly cured him). She promises to give him £150 a year, providing he does not meet his ex-lover, Bosie (John Fraser), ever again. As Constance bids Wilde farewell at the railway station, Bosie turns up, but Wilde does not acknowledge or greet him. Instead, he takes the train to a new life abroad, as a voice-over (spoken by Wilde) states that 'Each man kills the thing he loves', a famous line from Wilde's 'The Ballad of Reading Gaol' (1898). Married heterosexual love and illicit love and desire between two men are, thus, inextricably linked in this concluding segment, each existing separately from and in stark opposition to each other.

In his 1914 memoir *Oscar Wilde and Myself*, Lord Alfred Douglas was apt to blame Constance for what happened after Oscar was released from prison and she made her continued financial support for her ex-husband dependent on him cutting all ties and associations with himself. Douglas, never a person to let a possible slight to his character go unchallenged, declared ruefully that 'There have been many wives … who have stuck to their husbands through thick and thin … Mrs. Wilde, alas, was not one of them.'[19] This tale of a writer leading a kind of double life which catches up with him and leads to fatal consequences for the central protagonists in the story is thus clearly capable of generating a seemingly endless series of varied emotional responses and critical readings from male and female film spectators and readers; none of which can be eternally fixed, settled or simply consigned to a history which is deemed to be over.

Everett's *The Happy Prince* offers an account of what might previously have been seen as an anti-climactic period in Wilde's life, when the period of dramatic court cases, arrests and imprisonment was over, but so too largely was his career as a dramatist, writer and high-profile figure in cultured society. Everett, however, finds much localised drama and universal human interest in Wilde's attempts to forge some new kind of meaningful and fulfilling existence in Dieppe, Naples and Paris, amid a backdrop of financial impoverishment, increasing ill health and impending doom (in the film of *The Importance of Being Earnest* (Oliver Parker, 2002), Everett as Algy has a line, not in the original play, where he states, 'It could be worse. I could be dead in Paris'). Everett, as writer and director, presents plot and character developments in a fluid, colourful fashion, the intimate and fragmented nature of the camera angles and perspectives with which the story is conveyed reflecting Wilde's own idiosyncratic and at times desperate attempts to survive and make sense of this final period in his life ('It's a dream,' he declares at the beginning of the narrative).

The film opens with Wilde telling the eponymous story of the Prince to his two sons ('You tell me of marvellous things'), before the scene abruptly changes to Wilde as a solitary figure, looking tired and dishevelled, outside a café in Paris, as fiction transmutes into reality and attention moves from the writer's works to the current life of the author. The Happy Prince is now a 'broken man', cut off from his family, England and his former self, a lost soul, grateful for any loose change which an affluent passer-by might be persuaded to part with. 'I used to be quite famous,' he will later declare to a young French lover and friend, Jean (Benjamin Voisin), who understandably looks a bit sceptical about the likelihood of such a claim. Wilde will find some emotional solace in this man and his younger brother, Leon (Antonio Salamone), both of whom are orphans and who keep a photograph of their dead mother in their modest lodgings ('Family. So important,' declares Wilde on seeing the picture, which evokes memories of his own dead mother and wife, and the two sons from whom he is estranged). Wilde's ability to speak French fluently allows him to transcend English isolationism and separatism, and in these two young men, who have to live by their wits and imagination to acquire money, he can see a parallel with his own situation in Paris. Leon has absconded from an orphanage run by nuns. Jean aims to make money selling flowers, but is willing to have sex for money with Wilde. 'All well in the underworld?' he greets them when renewing their acquaintanceship. Nicholas Frankel, in his biography of the last years of Wilde's life, reports that 'Paris in 1898 possessed a thriving and extensive homosexual subculture', of whom 'some thirty percent active' in this world 'were aged between fourteen and twenty', young men who were prepared to offer companionship and sex to wealthier, older men for money or gifts',[20] and Jean is depicted as someone who is part of such a sub-culture. In his memoirs, Bosie wrote that Wilde's 'companionships and resorts' in this culminating part of his life 'were of the vilest and his self-respect was almost entirely gone'.[21] Douglas concluded from this that 'when Wilde is set up for a moralist, there is just a lunatic, anarchist end of morals', claiming that the overall message to be discerned from Wilde's writings and his life is to 'be as wicked and depraved as you like, provided that you are wicked and depraved in a graceful manner'.[22] Wilde's relationship with these two brothers, however, is not presented in such a light in Everett's film. His sexual relationship with Jean is one based on sexual favours undertaken for money in an establishment seemingly set up for such exchanges (we hear what Wilde refers to as 'adjacent copulation' taking place in the rented room above Wilde and Jean's). The film reveals only the aftermath of Oscar and Jean's sexual encounter in a room bathed in an orange light, where Wilde talks poetically of 'purple hours' paid for by 'green notes'. Jean kisses Wilde on the lips as he receives his payment, and the scene concludes with Leon gaining access to the room to hear a new instalment of *The Happy Prince*, suggesting that for Wilde, sexual activity and creative energy run parallel with each other. To those who condemned Wilde for resuming his sexual life as a gay man in Europe, his view (as stated to Robert Ross) was that 'To have altered my life would have been to have admitted that Uranian love is ignoble.'[23]

Nonetheless, the film demonstrates that England and those of his contemporaries who do not share his liberationist views cannot be completely left behind or forgotten, even in France. English men visiting France and playing cricket on the beach in the film are revealed as particularly threatening and insulting to Wilde in ways which recall his humiliation at Clapham Junction, while being transferred from one prison to another. Mrs Lydia Arbuthnott (Anna Chancellor) recognises Wilde in Paris from her attendance at his plays and, by claiming to have left her fan (!) behind in a café, takes the opportunity to speak to the famous (now infamous) author.[24] Wilde appreciates her kindness in speaking to him, while in a sign of how desperate his circumstances have become, asks her in begging fashion if she could lend him five pounds. Lydia gives Wilde money and indicates that she is sorry for his present plight. Her husband soon intervenes, though, and threatens to kill Wilde if he ever speaks to his wife again. The film then cuts to this same man enjoying one of Wilde's plays in the recent past, suggesting, perhaps, that some of the people for whom Wilde wrote his plays were unworthy of his efforts and talents.

'It is difficult to teach the English either pity or humanity',[25] Wilde wrote in a letter of May 1898, and the film suggests that he may ultimately have felt defeated by such experiences of English bigotry, cruelty and vindictiveness in the period 1895–1900. History has proved him to be someone who, even if he could not exactly escape his immediate tormentors and critics, at least succeeded in transcending them through his writings, which bestow upon him a certain kind of immortality (out of what was once seen as immorality). In a review of a biography of Wilde, Michael Bloch claims that one can 'see in his tragedy a microcosm of an eloquent and triumphant Europe heading gleefully for 1914'.[26] Thus, the ugly, aggressive and self-righteous attitudes of his oppressors might be seen in their own way as portending that breakdown of European civilisation known as the First World War (1914–1918), an event in which Wilde's own son Cyril was to lose his life in 1915.[27]

The Happy Prince doesn't wish to suggest, however, that Wilde's closing years were entirely marked by animosity, unpleasantness and disappointment. In a bar he meets up with his two young French friends and recognises Maurice (Tom Colley), a French legionnaire with whom he has been involved. Wilde is insulted once more by a member of the public, but in Maurice he has a strong defender (the French characters in the film are by and large supportive of Wilde). A subsequent brawl is broken up by the owner and, to make amends, Wilde stands on a table and performs the music hall song 'The boy I love is up in the gallery' to the patrons of the drinking establishment. This is the only moment in the film when Wilde once again has the attention of a mass audience (and significantly it does not involve him performing material which he has written). It is also something of a utopian moment in the film, celebrating the possibility that communities of people can come together in a positive fashion, something which elsewhere is in short supply. Even though Wilde is singing in English, the French citizens in the bar enthusiastically join in the chorus of the song and laugh at such English lines as 'If I were a duchess and had a lot of money'. The song contains the line, 'I haven't got a penny, so we'll live on love and kisses', a sentiment with some significance to Wilde's own situation with Bosie at this stage of his life. The sequence ends with an intoxicated Wilde crashing to the floor as his moment in the spotlight ends. He is next presented lying in bed with his head bandaged, with a doctor-in-attendance, warning of the need for an operation. Euphoric moments in Wilde's life during the late 1890s are apt to be short lived, therefore – and this moment of 'triumph' and mass appreciation may actually have taken place partly in Wilde's imagination given his alcohol consumption.

In the film, Wilde's incapacity leads him to think back to the beginning of his arrival in a new environment (Dieppe), where he was greeted by beautiful seaside scenery, his friends Robert Ross (Edwin Thomas) and Reggie Turner (Colin Firth), and what seemed like the possibility of making a fresh start after the horrors of England ('What high hopes we had'). Wilde is depicted as considering converting to Christianity after he claims to have been visited by Christ in prison ('What was she in for?' asks a sceptical and sacrilegious Turner.) The second possibility for a new way of life is (ironically) to seek a return to his old identity as a married man, a 'reconciliation' with Constance (Emily Watson) if she will have him. The film presents Constance, meanwhile, as suffering from her own exile in another country and, like her husband, living under a new name. Constance is pictured walking with great difficulty and only with the aid of sticks, her physical ailments seemingly linked to her psychical suffering. Any kind of reconciliation, however, is quickly ruled out by her insistence in a letter that if Wilde meets Bosie (Colin Morgan) again, she will withdraw any financial support offered to him. Although the film concentrates on Wilde's experiences during this valedictory time of his life, by cutting away to Constance while her character is alive the film suggests that her last few years were rather lonely and painful, and that she ultimately paid a very high price for becoming Mrs Oscar Wilde.

Wilde's third option for a fresh start – and the one he eventually chooses – also involves a return to a previously established way of living; namely, to resume his life as an actively homosexual man and to rekindle his relationship with Lord Alfred Douglas. Alex Dean, in a book review concerning Wilde's final years, has suggested that in *The Happy Prince*, Wilde is shown 'tragically' yearning for Bosie, 'who is, as usual, portrayed as a jealous monster'.[28] The film implies that their relationship, for better or worse, was possibly most passionate and intense before what Douglas referred to as 'the catastrophe' of Wilde being sent to prison,[29] and that what follows can only end up being something of an unhappy coda to their previous time spent together in England.

In his biography of Wilde's years in exile, Nicholas Frankel reports that in the 1890s homosexuality was not a 'crime in Italy' and 'little attempt' was made 'to ban homosexual behaviour',[30] with Naples, in particular, proving to be a popular destination for gay men of this time. *The Happy Prince* depicts Wilde and Bosie taking part in sensual all-male parties at a rented villa, with Bosie paying men for sex and Wilde, at one stage, seemingly acting out a moment from his (banned in England) play, *Salomé* (1891). As in this play, forces of sexual and sensual liberation are unleashed in the villa which go on to have disturbing consequences. In an ironic juxtaposition, one sequence parallels Constance's attempts to celebrate a traditional English Christmas, her children singing 'Good King Wenceslas', with Wilde and Douglas's all-male reveries and carnivalesque behaviour in Europe. By counterpointing these two ways of celebrating the festive season, Everett highlights the huge gulfs between a world of male camaraderie and interchangeable sexual partners, and a world of monogamous male–female partnerships based around the concepts of family, restraint and the concentration of sexual desire upon one specific individual in relationships sanctified by society, the state and the Church.

In the narrative, life in the villa and Naples gradually starts to pall, riven by tensions from within and without. Wilde stares out at a beautiful landscape of blue skies and men fishing in the sea, but is aware that although this is an idyllic setting in many respects, this freedom comes at a price. 'No more anxiety' in such a setting, he notes, but equally, 'No more ambition.' Even utopias may also depend on having adequate funds, and as Bosie's mother and Oscar's wife disapprove of their relationship and refuse to finance it, financial worries start to turn Wilde and Douglas into two individuals who have contempt for each other. Bosie accuses Wilde of being more concerned with style than substance and lacking sincerity ('For god's sake, stop acting'). Wilde retorts by declaring, 'I gave you my whole life' and 'Your family has destroyed me.' Thus, their hedonistic but somewhat fraught time together comes to a close ('Naples was a disaster', Wilde will later tell Robert Ross). Morgan's finely judged performance presents Bosie as handsome and desirable, but also as irrevocably self-centred and subject to disturbing mood shifts. Wilde's stay in Naples is finally terminated by the news (delivered via a telegram) that Constance is dead (dying off-stage, so to speak). Oscar inevitably feels a sense of responsibility for her death and is aware that his financial status is now destined to become even worse. The stage is set for the curtain to go up on the final act in Wilde's rise and fall.

Wilde's own health is shown to be in decline as his hopes for a better future start to recede. An operation undertaken in his hotel room to relieve a serious abscess is not a success, and soon he is in a terminal condition. As he approaches death, a decision is taken that a priest should be called for, and Wilde, though he is scarcely in a position to comprehend what is happening to him, is inducted into the Catholic Church on his deathbed by Father Cuthbert Dunne (Tom Wilkinson). In an ironic piece of imaginative casting, Wilkinson, who played his destroyer, the Marquis of Queensberry, in *Wilde* (Brian Gilbert, 1997), now appears as the figure blessing him and purportedly helping Wilde on his way to a better place.[31] The priest asks Wilde when he lost sight of 'our Lord', and Wilde thinks back to the time when he was mocked and spat at by a crowd of men and woman at Clapham Junction station while being transferred to another prison. By triggering such terrible memories, this religious ceremony does not necessarily bring relief to Wilde or the film's viewers; instead it leaves us thinking that it is the men and women tormenting Wilde who are featured in the flashback who should be asking for absolution and forgiveness for their sins. In 1940, Bosie writing as Lord Alfred felt that Wilde had been the victim of a British cultural belief at the time of his imprisonment that the 'vice' of homosexuality was 'far worse than murder'.[32]

Lord Alfred is not present at Wilde's deathbed, but he and Robert Ross clash violently at Wilde's funeral in the pouring rain; Everett does not stint from depicting how even Wilde's death cannot quell the strong and often divisive emotions he evokes among his admirers as well as his detractors. Bosie, the film suggests, is incapable of contrition or a regard for the unspoken codes about how to behave at a funeral. The film, however, appears to support Ross over Douglas as the positive force in Wilde's life (and afterlife) by stating in a caption that Robert Ross 'paid off Oscar's debts' and 'died in 1918. His ashes are buried with Oscar.' The mention afforded to Bosie states simply and starkly that he 'died penniless and alone in 1945'.[33] The years 1918 and 1945 are significantly when two terrible world wars finally came to an end, indicating that the century following Wilde's death inaugurated suffering, death and misery on a mass scale (the loathsome behaviour of the jeering crowd at Clapham station possibly offering a foretaste of what lay ahead for Britain and Europe). Everett does not, however, wish to end his film on an entirely bleak or negative note. A concluding caption informs the audience that 'Along with 75,000 other men convicted for homosexuality Oscar was pardoned in 2017', which might be seen as a positive attempt to try and rewrite history. However, one cannot but recall the ending to Auden's 1937 poem 'Spain', which declares that 'History to the defeated/May say Alas but cannot help or pardon.'[34]

As the credits roll, the film ends with a reprise of the moment Wilde captivated a French audience with his singing in a public bar; only this time Wilde is performing in French. The author is dead, the film seems to be saying, but refuses to lie down, his courageous spirit and lively attitude living on in an effort to create a European (rather than solely British) communal spirit that celebrates the sensual pleasures of life, appetites, longings and the need to feel that one 'belongs' somewhere.

The title of *The Happy Prince* for Everett's film finally emerges as both ironic and non-ironic. Wilde might appear at times to be like a figure in one of his plays, beset by anxiety and antagonistic forces which are just about held at bay, offstage in the wings. But he is also shown as someone who is able to improvise during the very real emotional and financial crises of his life, and not just appear as a character firing off witty remarks to an appreciative but somewhat fickle and possibly rather shallow London theatre audience of the 1890s. Wilde is depicted as striking up an alliance with some semi-destitute young people who are struggling to get by in Paris, and these individuals do not end up in a court of law testifying against him as was the case in England, but are present to mourn his passing in a French hotel room.

Everett's multifaceted performance as Wilde depicts him as a public performer who also maintains an ability to reflect privately and deeply on his experiences. Towards the end, Wilde imagines some of the figures at his deathbed appearing in a theatre production of *The Importance of Being Earnest*. Fact and fiction might be starting to blur in his mind at this stage, but the film's merging of his art and the stark reality of his passing points to how he succeeded in both writing dramas for the stage and creating endless dramas in his own life. These theatrical productions (and their attendant real-life situations) may begin as plays in a comic mode before turning into melodramas and possibly ending up as tragedies. *The Happy Prince* illustrates that the final years of Wilde's life contained a mixture of comedy and tragedy, joy and despair, but the film works hard to suggest that one of these moods and modes was never fully in the ascendant, and that Wilde remained his own man until the bitter end.

Sylvia Plath (1932–1963)

Philip Larkin once wryly described Sylvia Plath as a 'kind of Hammer Films poet'.[35] By this, he meant not that the legendary British film studio would have been keen to film her work, but that her poems dealt with dark subjects in an uncompromising, horrific and sometimes disturbing manner (without a saviour such as Van Helsing around to restore order and ward off evil).[36] Her 1962 poem 'Daddy', for instance, includes references to 'a love of the rack and the screw', 'The vampire who ... drank my blood for a year' and the stake placed in Daddy's 'fat black heart'.[37] Plath's suicide in 1963, following separation from husband and fellow poet Ted Hughes (1938–1998), has meant that she has consistently been the focus of critical attention and discussion. *Sylvia* (2010), a BBC films co-production (Plath worked with the BBC in the 1960s) explores her desire to find creative inspiration and sexual and emotional fulfilment through her relationship with Hughes. Critical acclaim for her poetry, the film will reveal, comes largely retrospectively; the marriage with Hughes is shown to be a dynamic one, but also a fraught and sometimes violent affair which implodes and self-destructs with tragic and terrible consequences. It was reported that Sylvia's daughter, Frieda, objected to these events being depicted in cinematic form.[38]

In *The Silent Woman: Sylvia Plath and Ted Hughes* (1993), Janet Malcolm suggests that the 'many voices' in which Sylvia Plath expressed herself, which included journals, letters, a novel, short stories and poetry, 'mocked the whole idea of biographical narrative',[39] thereby posing difficulties for prospective biographers. There have also been critical controversies about how best to categorise and evaluate the powerful and disturbing poems which emerged from her experiences of marriage, motherhood and life in British culture during the early 1960s. In his study of Plath's writing *Poetry and Existence* (1976), David Holbrook argues that the poems written when she was in a condition of despair and distress about the state of her life should not be valorised or privileged in her work because he felt 'the normal processes of finding a sense of identity and meaning in relationship[s] are rejected' in this stage of her writing. Holbrook equated 'Plath's attitude to sexuality' in some of these poems to what he termed a 'pornography explosion', believing them to partake of the nihilistic, 'schizoid and even psychotic' tendencies' that he associated with the phenomenon of pornography at large.[40]

However, Alan Sinfield, in a chapter on Plath in his study of *Literature, Politics and Culture in Postwar Britain* (1989), argued that she was essentially the victim of a pre-feminist age lacking in general support for women, and he interpreted her poems and death as 'partly [an act of] vengeance' on Ted Hughes and a violent and despairing response to the 'violence' she perceived in human interactions and the natural world.[41] This section of the chapter will consider how *Sylvia* engages with the challenges posed in portraying a writer described by *Empire* as a 'patron saint of teenage morbidity',[42] and the *New Statesman* as someone whose 'suicide did wonders to reconcile editors to her last poems'.[43] The study of the film will explore how marriage, sexuality, creativity and male–female relationships are presented in the narrative in relation to British (and American) culture and society in the early 1960s, and consider the ways in which the film-makers seek to find an appropriate style, tone and mood for exploring the many facets and aspects of Sylvia Plath and her tumultuous relationship with Ted Hughes.

The film begins with a close-up shot of Sylvia, motionless and lying face down with her eyes closed, as we hear her voice on the soundtrack actively contemplating her hopes for the future in terms of the branches of a tree (*Winter Trees* was the title of a posthumously published collection of her poems).[44] Each leaf signifies for her a poem, marriage, children and a successful career as a writer or academic, in what she terms the 'tree of life'. Suddenly, Sylvia opens her eyes and talks of the leaves turning brown and the tree becoming bare, suggesting that these hopes may not be realisable or possibly, in themselves, even that meaningful. This somewhat startling opening establishes that the film will be predominantly concerned with the emotional landscape of Plath's mind and the ways in which she is pulled between an active, hopeful, positive view of the world and a sense that all this striving for achievement and accomplishment may also be somewhat futile and without lasting value (given that we all die anyway).

The narrative proper begins with Sylvia (Gwyneth Paltrow) cycling frantically towards her university college over a screen caption which reads, 'Cambridge England 1956.' This places Sylvia in a specific time and place, something which the film will do throughout its narrative, emphasising that however abstract, timeless and metaphysical many of Sylvia's musings may be, they are seemingly formulated out of real places and periods in social history. This image of Sylvia in motion emphasises the ambitious, striving side of her nature. We see that she is so desperate to find out how a group of poems she has had printed in a student publication have been received that she doesn't even wait to see if her bike is properly stationary after arriving at the college. She subsequently learns that the poems have been reviewed (but not favourably) by a poetry group which includes one Edward Hughes (Daniel Craig), whom she then sets out to meet. This sets in motion a chain of events in which the pair will become both creative writers and critics, collaborators and competitors, friends and lovers, husband and wife, and finally a separated and somewhat embittered couple.

As the narrative unfolds, the film charts how both Sylvia and Ted embark on emotional and geographical journeys involving movements between continents, cities and rural communities in (ultimately failed) attempts to find the best place for their relationship and their writing to prosper. As dramatised in the film, Sylvia has initially moved from America to England on a temporary basis to study at Cambridge University. She and Ted subsequently move to London, get married and then travel to America to write and teach. They then return to London after American college life does not prove to be conducive to the well-being of their marriage or to the writing of poetry. London, however, does not turn out to be beneficial to the emotional and psychological state of their relationship either, so a move to rural Devon is undertaken. This, too, does not prove to be a success, and Ted subsequently leaves Sylvia and the children in Devon after falling in love with another woman and being told to 'get out' by Sylvia. She consequently finds the grey isolation and spiritual loneliness of the home in Devon too much to bear on her own, and she also returns to London. These ever more desperate moves end in Sylvia's conclusion that her journey should end within the confines of a gas oven, a place she defines in a voice-over on the film's soundtrack as offering no way out.

This varied series of locations and backdrops illustrates how for a woman of her time Sylvia was very socially and spatially mobile; but just as Oscar Wilde cannot find any real peace of mind in the places of his European exile, she does not appear to find happiness or a freedom from worry wherever she is based or located. This discontent with life is presented as having several sources, according to Sukhdev Sandhu in a *Daily Telegraph* review of *Sylvia*: being left by the man whom she adored and admired (Hughes), what she perceived as a lack of substantial attention and appreciation from the British 'literary establishment' and what can be viewed (perhaps more clearly now than it was at the time) as the stress and suffering she underwent as a woman experiencing everyday life within the ideological codes and practices of 'patriarchal society'.[45]

Early scenes in the film are more positive, demonstrating how writing poetry for Plath and for Hughes is a kind of religion and calling, an activity which celebrates the power of the human imagination, language and life itself. Hughes is good-looking, masculine and dedicated to poetry, making him for Plath an inspiring figure, a kind of ideal against whom all other men can be judged and found wanting. (The only other man in the film with whom she appears willing to have a sexual, emotional and collaborative relationship is literary critic Al Alvarez, played by Jared Harris.) Sylvia and Ted are shown having passionate sex soon after meeting, first with a naked Sylvia on top and then Ted (a possible index of the struggle for power and dominance which will come to symbolise their relationship). This sexual act takes place in a shadowy light, and is closely followed by talk of death as Sylvia admits to Ted (and the film audience) that she 'tried to kill herself three years ago' (referring to herself as 'Lady Lazarus', a title she will later use for one of her most famous poems). This ties in with the stylised opening of the film, rather than what we have witnessed of Sylvia's behaviour in Cambridge, so this sudden revelation comes as something of a shock. Kate Muir complained in a review of the film that 'Sylvia segues into suicide-speak after sex, every time',[46] but this is perhaps an indication that her character follows in the tradition of poets who make a deep connection between sex and death, desire and despair, ecstasy and emptiness and eternity and oblivion, connections which cannot be easily eradicated from her view of the world.

After leaving Cambridge University, the heady days of a small group of individuals in thrall to the possibilities offered by poetry fade away, leaving Plath and Hughes increasingly on their own and seemingly lacking a creative community outside themselves. America in the early 1960s (symbolised in the film by Sylvia, Ted and fellow cruise passengers looking in awe at the modern skyscrapers and landscape of New York City as their ship arrives in port there) is initially seen as offering the possibility of a new cultural and creative start. They both spend a summer in seemingly idyllic and timeless conditions, surrounded by endless sea and bright blue skies, as they live by the beach in the heart of the natural world; indeed, *Crossing the Water* is the title of a poetry collection by Plath published posthumously.[47] But even this idyll contains lurking dangers. Ted rows them too far out to sea, leaving him worried that they might drown; Sylvia uses this occasion to talk once more of death and not wanting to live after her father died. The scene concludes with the pair being rescued by a boat which tows them to safety, but we are not shown who undertook the rescue operation or how it came about. As the couple's relationship deteriorates and darkens, it becomes disturbingly clear that no one can subsequently come to their rescue, and help to keep their relationship and marriage afloat as it enters 'troubled waters' and uncharted territory.

When Sylvia takes up a teaching position at an American college, we see her teaching a class of rather dismayed female students that 'The American has got to destroy. It is his destiny,'[48] lines she is quoting from D.H. Lawrence's essay on Nathaniel Hawthorne's novel *The Scarlet Letter*, but which imply in the film that she is railing against what she sees as the conservative, imperialist tendencies of her native country. During this section of the narrative, Plath finds herself increasingly confined to the home, baking and marking student essays, while Ted is out socialising and networking. Sylvia starts to become convinced that Ted is having sex with one of his students and female admirers, someone he claims not to know very well ('Sheila? Sandra?'). The film leaves it open as to whether Ted is having sex with the character listed in the credits as 'Young American Girl Student' (although one might note that she is strikingly similar in appearance to the dark-haired woman for whom he will eventually leave Sylvia). During one bitter row, he tells Sylvia that he has indeed 'fucked' this student and that 'it was glorious'. It is unclear, though, as to whether he is admitting the truth or telling Sylvia (as he subsequently claims) what he believes she wants to hear (i.e. that her suspicions are justified).

The noted film academic Robin Wood believed that problems and tensions in long-term and married male–female relationships were often inevitable as partners would start to feel emotionally and socially stifled after spending so much time with one person, this feeling of oppressive containment being felt particularly in sexual terms. Wood argued that it was a mistake to make sexual exclusivity 'the defining factor' in maintaining relationships because this invariably led to feelings of 'jealousy and possessiveness' among partners and unhappiness and discontent.[49] However, Plath did believe in the concept of sexual fidelity within marriages, and in a 1962 letter to her psychiatrist, Dr Ruth Beuscher, she asked, 'Am I an idiot to think that there is some purpose in being bodily faithful to the person you love? In riding through infatuations without always indulging yourself, if you know it hurts someone?'[50] She was faced with the problem, though, that her husband did not believe in – or was unable to abide by – such mantras regarding the renouncing of sex with other partners outside wedlock. Robin Wood, however, claimed that 'sexually forsaking all others', is a 'profoundly foolish and repressive' stance.[51] Such a perspective would suggest that he might have viewed both

Plath and Hughes as caught up in an oppressive social arrangement (marriage) which made them both victims in a way, even if Plath – particularly once she had become a mother – suffered most from the breakdown of the marriage.

The film goes on to suggest that Sylvia tries to sublimate her rage at Ted for later unambiguously betraying her with a married woman, Assia (Amira Casar), by transmuting her anger into art; namely poems, which may draw upon incidents in their relationship but which through the elaborate workings of her mind are converted into a series of symbolic and resonant poetic images.[52] Her bursts of creative energy in this dark and disturbing time are in marked contrast to Wilde's experiences in *The Happy Prince*, where he finds that he cannot come up with new writings because he is too unhappy about how his relationships and life have turned out.

Sylvia implies there are two key turning points in Plath's life back in London which lead to her having no hopes for a better future. One involves being rebuffed sexually by literary critic and friend Al Alvarez after she intimates to him in a seductive manner that she is willing to have him as a 'lover'. He responds by looking uneasy, as if he does not welcome graduating from a supporting part in Sylvia's life to becoming one of the leading players. He tells her that he has also tried to commit suicide, which surprises but does not entirely comfort Sylvia, whose aloneness from this point starts to intensify. The second and decisive turning point comes after Sylvia initiates sex with Ted after he has left her and the children. We see these two characters, as personified by the attractive naked bodies of Paltrow and Craig, having sex on a couch before the two recline and lie together in a sensual embrace. This sexual reconnection appears to raise hopes that the two might get back together again; but these hopes are almost as immediately brutally shattered by Ted when he reveals that (in a situation common in the British 'new wave' films of this period) his partner is pregnant. Sylvia's tenuous hopes are destroyed in an instant, and the remaining parts of the film chart her movement towards death.

The freezing and snowbound conditions of London in the winter of 1962 and 1963 and a feeling of being alone in an alien country conspire to make Sylvia feel isolated, helpless and despondent. There are power cuts, and only a kindly downstairs neighbour, Professor Thomas (Michael Gambon), tries to offer any kind of help or comfort (although he appears baffled by Sylvia and her intense ways of explaining her unhappiness). 'You must think I'm some stupid American bitch', she informs him. 'Not at all. I assumed you were Canadian,' he replies dryly. 'Everything all right?' he enquires in their final encounter, only too aware that everything is not.[53] The film ends by showing that Sylvia seals up the kitchen with tape and places her head in the gas oven with the gas switched on. Her accompanying voice on the soundtrack as she kills herself speaks of a locked box with 'no windows', only a 'little grid' affording 'no exit'. It might seem as if these are words from a suicide note or a journal entry, but in fact they are lines taken from her 1962 poem, 'The Arrival of the Bee Box'.[54]

Britain in the 1960s is not presented as offering an answer to Plath's anxieties and concerns, but the publication of some letters by Plath which were unavailable when Christine Jeffs and John Brownlow produced their 2003 biographical picture has provided some further insight into how she viewed Britishness in comparison to America. In London, she could 'live on little' and receive 'free medical care'.[55] In a letter dated just days before her death, on 11 February 1963, she wrote 'There is nothing like the BBC in America—over there they do not publish my stuff my stuff as they do here, my poems & novel,'[56] leaving a tragic sense that these positives could not be built upon in her adopted country (the film only has her coming into contact with the BBC when she angrily rings the corporation to try and find information about Ted's whereabouts). Perhaps one of the saddest of Plath's remarks in this collection of letters is her observation that the breakdown of her marriage and relationship is, 'after all, what seems to happen to everybody'.[57] *Sylvia*, as its title suggests, is concerned overwhelmingly with the singular experiences of the American poet and writer who lived and died in Britain, but the film's depiction of her marriage can also be viewed as a warning that marriage is not a state to be entered into lightly. The film also suggests that a writer may formulate subject material out of the troubling experiences of his or her own life, but such a breakthrough in finding creative inspiration may come at the price of the writer feeling that there is then no escape from his or her problems and anxieties.

Iris Murdoch (1919–1999)

Iris (Richard Eyre, 2001) depicts the story of Iris Murdoch and her movement from being single to being married, and part of a couple sharing a common interest in literature, criticism and creativity. The film shows Murdoch becoming a popular and acclaimed novelist specialising in the study of relationships within British society. Moving between the past and present and featuring two different actors (Kate Winslet and Judi Dench) as Iris, the narrative draws particular attention to the torments and ravages inflicted by the onset and development of Alzheimer's disease. *Iris* explores what it is to love and care for someone who is radically changed from the person they were, and asks questions about the meaning of true love, the relationships between art and reality and the possibilities for romantic, sexual and artistic fulfilment within post-1945 British culture.

Despite her prolific output, Iris Murdoch's novels (with one exception) were not adapted into feature-length films. The exception was *A Severed Head* (Dick Clement, 1971), which was described by Christopher Hudson in the *Spectator* as 'a very dark comedy' about an upper-class London-based group of characters living a life of 'incest and promiscuity'.[58] After viewing *A Severed Head*, John Coleman of the *New Statesman* went so far as to hope there would be 'no more attempts to bring Miss Murdoch's work to the screen'.[59] The title, as Elizabeth Dipple points out in a study of Murdoch's novels, indicates 'the duality' of the book's concerns around the life of the mind in relation to the physical desires of the body.[60] The film adapts what appears to be a neutral and distanced perspective on the various permutations between the protagonists, but does not shy away from showing Georgie (played by Jennie Linden) attempting to commit suicide when the subterfuge involved in being a married man's mistress becomes too much.

Murdoch, herself, explained in a 1968 interview that her work partly stemmed from a sense that the power of religion to significantly influence people's behaviour was waning. One effect of this development was that individuals were possibly more aware of the complex and sometimes warring forces operating within the human psyche. Themes pertaining to sexuality, moral choices, desires and longings in a changing world were therefore of great interest and concern to Murdoch in her novels, which, as she explained, examined 'psychological forces working loose' in a 'society [in which one's confidence has] largely evaporated'.[61] The ramifications of love were important features of her novels, with a particular focus often being placed on the difficulties of remaining faithful to a married partner in an era which emphasised the importance of individual liberation.

In *The Sacred and Profane Love Machine* (1974), the narrator can wryly observe, 'At first ... the sheer force of love made them seem scarcely aware that Blaise was married and that he had to spend much of the week with his wife.'[62] Antonia declares to her unsuspecting husband in *A Severed Head* (1961) that she has fallen in love and had sex with her psychiatrist: 'This thing has overwhelmed me, Martin. I've simply had to give in to it ... We aren't getting anywhere. You know that as well as I do.'[63] In *Jackson's Dilemma* (1995), a male character states that 'Marriage is a mystery ... it can be a terrible mistake,' to which his female companion, Rosalind responds, 'Not if we love each other as *we* love each other. Love overcomes all.'[64] Such quotations demonstrate that relationships in Murdoch's novels are often in a state of flux, with characters conflicted between their urge to be morally good and their desire to be sexually and emotionally fulfilled. The sexual act is shown as capable of breaking up marriages and bringing unwanted or inconvenient children into the world, as well as being a source of incomparable joy: 'This was not just intense sexual bliss, it was absolute metaphysical justification.'[65]

In the *Daily Telegraph*, Iona McLaren notes that Iris Murdoch was 'so popular in her day that as soon as she died in 1999, a film – *Iris* ... was made about her life'.[66] This film was not based on her own writings or recollections, but was an adaptation of two memoirs by her husband, John Bayley, an esteemed Oxford University literary critic and academic. These books, *Iris: A Memoir of Iris Murdoch* (1998) and *Iris and the Friends: A Year of Memories* (1999), depicted in sometimes harrowing detail the anguish and pain suffered by Murdoch (and John Bayley as her carer) when the novelist was struck down by Alzheimer's disease during the last years of her life in the mid- to late 1990s.[67] These biographical writings proved to be popular with readers in both Britain and America, but Bayley's decision to make public his wife's condition and suffering while she was still alive was also questioned by her friends and admirers. One of these figures, A.N. Wilson, wrote his own memoir about Murdoch and her significance. Writing of the film directed by Richard Eyre, Wilson noted that 'Some of the critics ... spoke of it as the greatest love story ever told ... Here was a man [Bayley] so completely devoted ... he cared for her to the end.' Wilson, however, felt that what John Bayley 'wrote about her ... appeared to me a Pandora's box of which he quite clearly lost control', revealing, according to Wilson, 'resentments, envy, poisonously strong misogyny and outright hatred of his wife'.[68]

A film based on such contested writings always had the possibility of proving to be a controversial biographical picture, particularly as this female author's writings, life and work were being interpreted and scripted by male writers (the screenplay, based on Bayley's accounts, was written by Richard Eyre and Charles Wood). The following section will consider *Iris* in the light of issues about personal relationships raised by Murdoch's novels, her life as a writer rooted in British culture and the role played by John Bayley as her husband, carer and ultimately her biographer.

The film begins with images of water, evoking a sense of freedom and transcendence as a young Iris Murdoch (Kate Winslet) swims naked and feels at one with the natural world. We shortly see a close-up shot of a much older Iris (Judi Dench), writing (in pen) the opening sentences of what will turn out to be her final novel, *Jackson's Dilemma* (1995): 'Edward Lannion was sitting at his desk in his pleasant house in Notting Hill. The sun was shining. It was an early morning in June.'[69] The penultimate paragraph of the published novel will end in a very different kind of landscape and mood as the narrator ponders, 'Death, its closeness ... I have forgotten them and no one calls. Was I in prison once? I cannot remember. At the end of what is necessary, I have come to the place where there is no road.'[70] Caroline

Moore, in the *Spectator*, reviewed *Jackson's Dilemma* on its publication as 'pure Iris Murdoch ... the real McCoy ... a distilled quintessence of her art'.[71] Tragically, however, the film depicts Iris in her reduced state as oblivious to the novel when the finished copy is delivered by her publishers, Chatto & Windus. The author later tosses the book aside on a beach when asked to sign it by her friend and supporter, Janet Stone (Penelope Wilton). This valedictory novel, which she laboured so hard to complete, now appears without meaning or resonance to her, less interesting than a pebble on the beach.

Iris is structured around the past and present of Iris Murdoch and John Bayley, and by casting different actors to play the protagonists when young and old, the film emphasises continuities between past and present as well as divergences and severe ruptures. When one of Iris's early suitors, Maurice (Sam West), turns up late in the narrative, he is depicted returning her home after she is found in a confused state wandering around a supermarket. John Bayley (Jim Broadbent) does not recognise Maurice, as indeed audiences might not do, as the character in his 1990s incarnation is played by a different actor, Timothy West. Young Iris and John (Hugh Bonneville) are regularly interposed with ageing Iris and John, creating a contrast between how they appear hopeful, romantic and ambitious in the 1950s and troubled and traumatised in the 1990s: Martin Amis has summed up the film as being 'about the tragedy of time'.[72] Iris in middle age is depicted making speeches about the importance of language and the 'power of the imagination', while young Iris advises John to 'hang on' to her and to 'trust the body'. Young John's lack of sexual expertise is contrasted with Iris's diverse and more extensive sexual and emotional experiences with men and possibly women. Winslet's Iris takes the sexual lead with John – 'Perhaps it's time we made love' – and even has to inform him that the act is easier if he takes his trousers off. John, unlike Iris, is not presented as having any other lovers or admirers, leading reviewer Charlotte O'Sullivan to conclude that John Bayley 'seems such an inadequate lapdog ... Either Iris is settling for second best or there's something about Bayley we're not party to.'[73] Young John Bayley states that he has read you can 'use anyone in a novel just as long as you drop a hint somewhere that they're good in bed.' Iris Murdoch responds quickly by saying, 'Even though they might not be?' while looking directly at John.

Young Iris stands for the liberated and unconfined sexual life, seen as important for the aspiring novelist ('Is that all, roughly?' asks Bayley in a somewhat confounded and probing manner when Iris presents him with details of her previous lovers.) While Iris may be the subject of attention from lesbian women in her Oxford college, John's response to her question about whether he sleeps with homosexuals in his college is 'Lord, no.' And his response to the possibility of sex between him and Iris is to declare – in what might be seen as an example of a commonly held belief in 1950s Britain – that if they were 'married, we could do this all the time'. In his study *The Characters of Love: A Study in the Literature of Personality* (1960), Bayley suggests that the vagaries and practices of sex have 'something mechanical', determinist and 'predictable' about them, while feelings of love and desire (by contrast) are 'preoccupied with the uniqueness of the individual' whom one loves. Bayley believes that falling in love is a higher state of being than engaging in sex: 'We desire in obedience to the fixed patterns of our sexual imagination, but we fall in love because we are really seeing another person.'[74]

Iris's scenes set in the present, however, illustrate how married love ('Till death us do part') may be severely tested by circumstances beyond anyone's control. Medical tests indicate that Iris is suffering from Alzheimer's, a degenerative disease of the brain. She cannot remember that Tony Blair is the British Prime Minister during the late 1990s and is puzzled by his repetitive statement during a public speech shown on television, 'Education, Education, Education.' 'What does he mean?' she enquires, suggesting that Iris may not be the only one who is losing touch with reality. (Mark Fisher, writing in 2015, suggested that Tony Blair exhibited symptoms of 'self-deception, messianic delusion' and possibly a 'new kind of postmodern psychopathy'.)[75]

Language, for Murdoch the key element in understanding our experiences, becomes an enigma – she is puzzled by the word puzzled and confuses dog with god. The specialist calmly informs her that the disease is 'implacable' and 'inexorable', words which allow no negotiation or compromise. Science here has the last word over literature and the creative imagination ('The lights will go out', declares the doctor chillingly). Martin Amis has suggested, such is the harrowing nature of the film's depiction of the effects of dementia, that when 'the credits roll, you find you have developed a lively admiration for cancer'.[76] *Iris* does, however, dramatise some of the effects of that illness in its final stages as the Bayleys' close friend, Janet Stone, is shown to be suffering from terminal cancer – she will die a year before Iris – and the final image of Janet is of her white-faced and in pain as she sees Iris and John off from their visit. John is so caught up with Iris's condition that he doesn't really notice how ill his friend is, and at her funeral, asked to 'say a few words' in memory of Janet, this distinguished lecturer and literary critic fails to find the appropriate vocabulary, adding to the anguish of her family and the assembled mourners.

Iris is hysterical in the churchyard at Janet's funeral, her unease possibly heightened by a vague awareness that her own demise may be imminent. In the film, John Bayley oscillates between an awareness that 'Life will soon be over', while preparing (in words very similar to Macbeth's famous soliloquy) to get through 'Tomorrow and the next day and the next'. Iris's life indeed appears to be over after the funeral when she falls out of the car John is driving and lands in a nearby wood. He manages to find her, and she is able to hesitatingly state, 'I ... love ... you.' 'I know you do,' replies John, suggesting that even in this terrible and worrying situation, they still understand and gain sustenance from each other on a deep level.[77] This literal plunge into darkness does foreshadow the end, however.

Dr Gudgeon (Kris Marshall) tells John that the 'time has come' for Iris to enter a nursing home for terminally ill patients (one that, he ironically relates, is 'More difficult to get into than Eton'). A kindly taxi driver manages to prise Iris from her home for the journey to the hospice with the words, 'All right, my love?' (Barbara Ellen was somewhat sceptical about the 'astonishingly patient, saint-like people Iris encounters every step of the way'.)[78] Iris's death occurs not long after her move to the home. John Bayley is at her bedside at the end, as he has been for so long in her journey from lightness to darkness, hopefulness to suffering and from prolific creativity to a state of confusion, amnesia and distress.

Concluding observations

Wilde, Plath and Murdoch can all be viewed as meeting tragic and sad ends in the final years of their life. Wilde, at his close, is in exile from Britain, a former prisoner, low on funds and a largely ex-writer, shunned by his former public. Plath has conversely been very creatively productive in the last stages of her life, but this work will not be published until after her death, and she dies not knowing if anyone will ever read some of these late poems. Murdoch has published nearly a book a year for forty years, but the onset of Alzheimer's renders her seemingly incapable of recognising her achievements or indeed recognising her final novel on its publication. Wilde is surrounded on his deathbed by friends, old and new, and is even visited by a priest. Plath dies alone, by her own hand, with the risk that she will take others with her. Murdoch dies with her husband by her bedside, although she no longer appears to understand who he is or what an important role in her life he has played.

Wilde ends up being punished by a British society and culture which in his lifetime viewed homosexuality as a crime. Plath, arguably, suffered under a convention whereby people pledge undying allegiance and loyalty to each other in the form of marriage, but then find they can start to find each other's company intolerable, resulting in them questioning or reneging on those earlier commitments. *Sylvia* is notably not entitled *Sylvia and*

Ted, and the film presents Sylvia as suffering the most when Ted leaves her for another woman. However, through Daniel Craig's robust and solid performance, the movie does suggest that a man such as Ted Hughes (whose poems often focus on the inherent cruelty of the natural and animal world) is not easily confined to the family home. Paltrow's intelligent, perceptive (if self-absorbed) Sylvia harangues Ted for his absences, but the film suggests that this may only have succeeded in making him even more restless and determined to flee the 'family nest'. Beyond the singularity of their experiences as a couple, in *Sylvia* Plath and Hughes also point to the difficulties and pitfalls inherent in the concept of marriage and the demands it makes on participants to declare undying loyalty and endlessly think well of each other. If, as in the case of Sylvia and Ted, each partner is highly individualistic with a vivid and potentially limitless imagination, then the end result may be that the marriage is riddled with tensions as two powerful egos start to become at loggerheads with each other, and love and desire transmute into their opposites, resentment and ill-feeling.

Murdoch and Bayley do not suffer from this problem in *Iris*, which begins with them settling into a life of everyday routines for the elderly, revolving around shopping in supermarkets and drinking beer in slightly run-down English pubs. In their case, what affects their relationship is one partner being struck down by a terribly demeaning and unsettling illness. If *Iris* ends up being less depressing and disturbing than *Sylvia*, this may be because it presents the marriage as surviving the catastrophe which befalls the couple. John supports and looks after Iris to the best of his ability. Apart from one moment when he says that he hates her when she stops him from sleeping, he remains calm and comforting. And soon after this intemperate outburst, he corrects himself to make it clear that what he hates is the illness which has got inside Iris and left her in a state of torment, pain and irrationality. Since her death, Iris Murdoch has become better known for the illness that beset her last years than for her novels.[79] Plath's works remain in print, but a sceptical Kate Muir, writing in *The Times* of *Sylvia*, felt that if Plath had not committed suicide, she would have enjoyed a very different kind of reputation, 'as a good, quiet poet in her seventies with slim sales'.[80]

Wilde and Plath both died in exile from their native countries in different ways, and while Plath found some aspects of British life in the 1960s better than American culture, she was also capable of writing to her mother that in Britain 'they are lazy bastards. I work like a navvy ... & they sit & watch telly.'[81] Murdoch and Bayley appear to be well treated in 1990s Britain by everyone they come across, from supermarket check-out staff, medical personnel and taxi drivers, in stark contrast to Wilde's experiences of British culture and society in the 1890s and an improvement on Plath's experiences as depicted in *Sylvia* (the friendly neighbour aside). Murdoch and Bayley's marriage survives under much strain and discomfort, and becomes an example of the positive nature of the wedding vows when they are respected by both sides. Plath is let down and left distraught by Hughes, but he makes sure that her late poems see the light of the day. The ending of the film, as Hughes observes her dead body and finds the unpublished manuscript of poems, brings out the sense of loss he experiences at this stark, bleak moment, as outside the flat, Britain shivers in snowy wintry conditions.

The first-person narrator in Sylvia Plath's *The Bell Jar* (1963) at one stage comments, 'I didn't know whether it was the awful movie giving me a stomach-ache or all that caviar I had eaten,' as she depressingly realises that owing to the implicit production codes influencing and determining the outcome of the film she was watching, 'the nice girl was going to end up with the nice football hero and the sexy girl was going to end up with nobody'.[82] In his memoirs, John Bayley wrote more affectionately of the traditions of post-war Hollywood and British cinema, claiming that 'The old cinema dealt in public dreams, in some sense shared by everybody, and that gave them a kind of dignity, no matter how ridiculous they were.'[83] The films exploring the life and times of Wilde, Plath and Murdoch, I would argue, work fundamentally within the classical cinematic tradition outlined by Bayley, while deviating from the determinist and culturally ordained narrative and character developments disliked by Plath in the Hollywood movie which she was watching. *The Happy Prince* and *Iris* appear to be aimed at a relatively mass audience; the sex scenes in both films are discreetly filmed and short in duration; and both movies convey a sense that their protagonists' lives are filled with a mixture of the routine, the slightly absurd, the joyful and the truly terrible. In these respects, the films can be seen as operating within Bayley's concept of the cinema as a means of bringing people together in a shared emotional experience which draws upon and stimulates people's hopes, fears and desires. While all three films offer fictionalised and speculative versions of the writers' lives, they do not seek to rewrite history by concluding with happier endings than appear to have occurred in the central protagonists' 'actual' lives.

Sylvia features two star actors and a sometimes heavy orchestral score on the soundtrack to convey a feeling of the characters' emotions and moods, but it also ventures into the kind of territory explored in Ingmar Bergman's films, showing how men and women can inspire passion and desire but also deep resentments in each other. If a couple can be viewed as an island, offering a refuge from a sometimes inhospitable world, *Sylvia* also conveys how this notion of an exclusive couple can become oppressive and limiting to personal development. Possibly for legal reasons, the two children in *Sylvia* do not speak a single word in the film, but the narrative makes clear that they, like their mother, are in the front line of suffering when Ted Hughes leaves home, and that divorces and separations leave no one emotionally unscarred.

In *The Happy Prince*, Everett plays Wilde as a man who, although past his professional best, is nevertheless capable of being the centre of attention and of turning his life (not always through choice) into a work of art. Deploying different actors to play Iris and John when young and old implies that the difference between these characters in these varying times is more marked than in the case of Wilde, where Everett plays him in both past and present sequences. Sylvia and Ted do not noticeably age in *Sylvia*, but this also indicates that Plath will die young. *Sylvia* includes two sensuous sex scenes between Sylvia and Ted, bookended as heralding the beginning and ending of their relationship. The film presents Ted as drawn to the mysterious Assia, but does not dwell on their sexual relationship as it develops. Tragically, Sylvia, Ted and Assia are all caught up in a sexual triangle which brings about two deaths and unassailable anguish. The ageing Iris and John are comfortable in each other's company at the beginning of *Iris*, but Iris's sexual allure and magnetism that is prevalent in the scenes featuring Winslet as young Iris are absent, as if she has become another person altogether (the onset of Alzheimer's will enact another change in her character very soon). Wilde also suffers from ill health in *The Happy Prince*, but he is rejuvenated to a certain extent by the company of young men who are glad to encounter such an individualistic and idiosyncratic figure in Paris at the end of the nineteenth century.

Oscar Wilde finds that after leaving prison his ability and desire to write witty and ironic plays about the charms and hidden secrets of Victorian upper-class English society have (understandably) vanished completely. Iris Murdoch's illness means that she cannot remember any of the novels she has composed, including the most recent. Sylvia Plath finds creative inspiration for her poetry in the darkest hours of her life, but this is not enough for her to feel that her life is ultimately bearable or worth continuing. Art cannot compensate for the loss of her relationship with Ted Hughes.

Wilde, Plath and Murdoch all die in the final scenes of the movies which have explored (sometimes quite harrowingly) the final years of their lives. One of the values and achievements of the film biographies is that they demonstrate that even though the characters at the heart of these narratives are exceptional, creative people, they are also shown as experiencing many of the traumas concerning relationships, marriage, sexuality, spiritual and physical health which many of those watching the films will go on to experience in one form or another. These films treat the writers' lives with integrity, good humour and compassion. Wilde, Plath and Murdoch suffer a great deal, but they are each shown striving to hang onto their sense of personal identity and worth before the 'death of the author' intervenes in an all too real and literal sense, bringing to a close the respective narratives exploring their lives and loves.

Notes

1 Patricia Beer, 'Full of Teeth', reviews of several biographies of Graham Greene, *London Review of Books*, 17:4 (20 July 1995), p. 21.
2 A.N. Wilson, 'Biographical Snoopers', *Literary Review*, 69 (March 1984), p. 21.
3 Tanya Gold, 'One by one, Hollywood is taking our great writers and ruining them for us', *Guardian* (10 November 2009), G2 section, p. 5.
4 Kate Muir, 'Fright to the End of the Plath,' film review of *Sylvia*, *The Times* (10 January 2004), review section, pp. 8–9.
5 Sally Williams, 'Not so Plain Jane', *Daily Telegraph Magazine* (17 February 2007), p. 31.
6 Liz Beardsworth, reviewing *Becoming Jane*, argued that the film dramatises Jane Austen having 'to pit love against duty' and finding that 'real life is revealed to be far messier, agonising even, than any work of fiction'. Writing novels, Beardsworth concludes, offered Austen the possibility of 'happy endings that reality ... could not'. Liz Beardsworth, '*Becoming Jane*', *Empire*, 214 (April 2007), p. 56.
7 It should be noted that Jack Malvern quoted Helen Lefroy, the vice-chairman of the Jane Austen Society at the time of the film's release, as dismissing the premise of *Becoming Jane* as 'fanciful'. Malvern also cited a letter written by Austen in 1796 in which she claims not to 'care sixpence' about Tom Lefroy. Jack Malvern, 'Austen Movie "a Fanciful Affair,"' *The Times* (18 March 2006), p. 42.
8 George Thomson claims that Keats 'composed' the poem 'Bright Star' on his troubled journey by ship to Italy. 'Four months later he died in Italy of consumption.' The message of the poem, according to Thomson, is that there can be 'no love without death' as life itself is based around movement, cycles and developments. George Thomson, *Marxism and Poetry* (New York: International Publishers, 1946), pp. 15–16.
9 Mark Kermode, film review of *Sylvia*, *New Statesman* (2 February 2004), p. 46.
10 W.H. Auden, 'A Playboy of the Western World: St Oscar, the Hominterm Martyr', review of *The Paradox of Oscar Wilde* by George Woodcock, first published in the *Partisan Review* (April 1950), reprinted in *W.H. Auden: Prose, Volume 3, 1949–1955* edited by Edward Mendelson (Princeton, NJ: Princeton University Press, 2008), p. 184.
11 Lord Alfred Douglas, *Oscar Wilde and Myself* (London: John Long Limited, 1914), p. 245.
12 Oscar Wilde, 'The Soul of Man Under Socialism' (1891), reprinted in the *Complete Works of Oscar Wilde* with an introduction by Vyvyan Holland (London and Glasgow: Collins, 1988 [1948]), p. 1086.
13 *Ibid.*, p. 1095.

14 Leonard Mosley, film review of *Oscar Wilde* (1960), *Daily Express* (20 May 1960), page number not listed, consulted at the BFI Library, London.
15 Letter, 'Homosexual Prosecutions', signed The Homosexual Law Reform Society, *Spectator*, 204: 6883 (27 May 1960), p. 765.
16 David Thomson, *Sleeping with Strangers: How the Movies Shaped Desire* (New York: Alfred A. Knopf, 2019), p. 201.
17 Stephen Bourne, *Brief Encounters: Lesbians and Gays in British Cinema 1930–1971* (London: Cassell, 1996), p. 142.
18 Oscar Wilde, 'The Critic as Artist' (1891), reprinted in *The Artist As Critic: Critical Writings of Oscar Wilde*, ed. Richard Ellmann (London: W.H. Allen, 1970), p. 359.
19 Douglas, *Oscar Wilde and Myself*, p. 87.
20 Nicholas Frankel, *Oscar Wilde: The Unrepentant Years* (Cambridge, MA, and London: Harvard University Press, 2017), pp. 206–7.
21 Douglas, *Oscar Wilde and Myself*, p. 149.
22 *Ibid.*, pp. 243–4.
23 Letter to Robert Ross (18 February 1898), published in Rupert Hart-Davis (ed.), *The Letters of Oscar Wilde* (London: Rupert Hart-Davis, 1962), p. 705.
24 The name Arbuthnot is used in Wilde's *A Woman of No Importance* (1893) for a female character who has a guilty secret. The credits circulated for Everett's film spell the name Arbuthnott.
25 Letter to Georgina Weldon (31 May 1898), published in Rupert Hart-Davis (editor), *The Letters of Oscar Wilde* (1962), p. 751.
26 Michael Bloch, 'Portrait of the Artist', review of *Oscar Wilde* by Richard Ellman, *Literary Review* (October 1987), p. 10.
27 Lord Alfred Douglas in *Oscar Wilde: A Summing Up* (London: Icon Books, 1962 [1940]) reports that Wilde's 'elder boy Cyril was killed in the Great War of 1914–18', p. 85.
28 Alex Dean, 'When *Love* Dared to Speak', book review of Nicholas Frankel, *Oscar Wilde: The Unrepentant Years* (2017), *Prospect*, 269 (August 2018), p. 71. Dean describes *The Happy Prince* (2018) as a 'moving and unsettling' film, portraying Wilde moving 'from one humiliation to the next', living a 'half life' (p. 70).
29 Douglas, *Oscar Wilde and Myself*, p. 87.
30 Frankel, *Oscar Wilde*, p. 129.
31 In the film *Wilde* (1997), the Marquis of Queensberry as played by Tom Wilkinson has a discussion with Wilde on matters pertaining to death and religious customs, and states that he has no time for the 'tomfoolery' of 'Christians'.
32 Douglas, *A Summing Up*, p. 22. Douglas claimed that Wilde's incarceration led to the 'almost complete paralysis of his creative brain-power.' He looked forward to a time (not yet reached in 1940) when British law would view homosexuality as a 'sin of the flesh … no worse than adultery' and not a matter for criminal prosecution (p. 22).
33 In 1963, Julian Symons expressed a different view to that offered by the concluding captions in Everett's film, describing Ross as a 'lickspittle toady' and

Bosie as 'direct, honest and naïve'. Julian Symons, 'Horns of Selfland', book review of *Bosie* by Rupert Broft-Cooke and *Oscar Wilde: The Aftermath* by H. Montgomery-Hyde, *Spectator*, 7039 (24 May 1963), p. 674.

34 W.H. Auden, 'Spain' (1937) reprinted in W.H. Auden, *The English Auden*, ed. Edward Mendelson (London: Faber, 1986 [1977]), p. 212.

35 Anthony Thwaite (ed.), *Selected Letters of Philip Larkin 1940–1985* (London: Faber & Faber, 1992), letter to Andrew Motion (1981), p. 660.

36 In a review of Plath's collected poems, Philip Larkin summed up her 'subject-matter' as 'neurosis, insanity, disease, death, horror, terror'. Philip Larkin, 'Horror Poet' (1982), reprinted in Philip Larkin, *Required Writing: Miscellaneous Pieces 1955–1982* (London: Faber & Faber, 1983), p. 279.

37 Sylvia Plath, 'Daddy' (1962), reprinted in Sylvia Plath, *Collected Poems*, ed. Ted Hughes (London: Faber & Faber, 1989 [1981]), p. 224.

38 Muir, 'Fright to the End of the Plath', quotes Frieda Hughes as being 'sick of' what she calls the 'Sylvia Suicide Doll' phenomenon.

39 Janet Malcolm, *The Silent Woman: Sylvia Plath and Ted Hughes* (London: Picador, 1994 [1993]), p. 17.

40 David Holbrook, *Sylvia Plath: Poetry and Existence* (London: Athlone Press, 1976), p. 265.

41 Alan Sinfield, *Literature, Politics and Culture in Postwar Britain* (Oxford: Basil Blackwell, 1989), p. 225.

42 Damon Wise, 'Poetry in Emotion', *Empire*, 176 (February 2004), p. 84. In this interview with Gwyneth Paltrow, the writer reports that Paltrow's father died 'two weeks before *Sylvia* went into production', leading her to wonder if she would be able to 'do the film'. Wise believed that Paltrow's 'performance', which possibly draws upon the actor's personal grief and sadness, 'might be her best ever' (p. 84).

43 Eric Homberger, 'The Uncollected Plath', *New Statesman*, 84:2166 (22 September 1972), p. 404. The author argued in this article that since her death in 1963 and the subsequent lack of a collected works of Plath's poems, the poet was 'big business.' Homberger claimed, however, that in her lifetime 'there was no market' for some of her more 'Highly personal, bitter' poems (p. 404).

44 Sylvia Plath, *Winter Trees* (London: Faber & Faber, 1971).

45 Sukhdev Sandhu, review of *Sylvia*, *Daily Telegraph* (30 January 2004), p. 21.

46 Muir, 'Fright to the end of the Plath'.

47 Sylvia Plath, *Crossing the Water* (London: Faber & Faber, 1971).

48 D.H. Lawrence, 'Nathaniel Hawthorne and *The Scarlet Letter*' (1924), reprinted in D.H. Lawrence, *Selected Literary Criticism*, ed. Anthony Beal (London: William Heinemann Ltd, 1955), p. 347.

49 Robin Wood, 'The New Queer Cinema and Gay Culture: Notes from an Outsider', *CineAction*, 35 (August 1994), p. 8.

50 Peter K. Steinberg and Karen V. Kukil (eds), *The Letters of Sylvia Plath Volume II: 1956–1963* (London: Faber & Faber, 2018), letter to Dr Ruth Beuscher, 30 July 1962, p. 804.

51 Wood, 'The New Queer Cinema'.

52 For instance, the lines in the poem 'Daddy', 'The black telephone's off at the root/The voices just can't get through' would seem to correspond with the moment in the film in which Sylvia pulls the telephone cord out of the wall in the belief that Assia, Ted's lover ('I know who you are') is phoning him. The poem 'Daddy' was first published in *Encounter*, 21:10 (October 1963), p. 52.
53 David Holbrook has suggested that in choosing such a way to die she was dangerously risking the life of the neighbour who had been kind to her (as well as that of her own children, despite the precautions which she took in sealing up the kitchen area). Holbrook, *Sylvia Plath*, p. 277.
54 Sylvia Plath, 'The Arrival of the Bee Box' (1962), reprinted in Plath, *Collected Poems*, p. 213. The poem ends with the speaker promising to set the bees 'free' the following day, their containment being 'only temporary'. *Sylvia* concludes with the sight from above of her body being carried out in the box-like form of a coffin. Earlier, Alvarez has tried to dissuade Sylvia from adopting a view of death as a place of liberating freedom, insisting that it is just a state of nothingness, 'fuck all'.
55 Steinberg and Kukil, *The Letters of Sylvia Plath Volume II*, letter to Warren Plath (18 October 1962), p. 871.
56 *Ibid.*, letter to Aurelia Plath (4 February 1963), p. 963.
57 *Ibid.*, letter to Ruth Beuscher (11 July 1962), p. 792.
58 Christopher Hudson, 'Love Stories', film review of *A Severed Head*, *Spectator*, 226:7440 (30 January 1971), p. 167.
59 John Coleman, 'Iris Out', film review of *A Severed Head*, *New Statesman*, 81:2079 (22 January 1971), p. 121.
60 Elizabeth Dipple, *Iris Murdoch: Work for the Spirit* (London: Methuen & Co., 1982), p. 149. Dipple concludes that 'far from being an advocate of the sophisticated society' depicted in *A Severed Head*, Iris Murdoch had 'more than a touch of the judging puritan in her' (p. 150).
61 Ronald Bryden, 'Talking to Iris Murdoch', *Listener*, 79:2036 (4 April 1968), p. 434.
62 Iris Murdoch, *The Sacred and Profane Love Machine* (London: Chatto & Windus, 1974), p. 61.
63 Iris Murdoch, *A Severed Head* (St Albans: Triad/Granada, 1981 [1961], p. 26.
64 Iris Murdoch, *Jackson's Dilemma* (London: Chatto & Windus, 1995), p. 182.
65 Murdoch, *Sacred and Profane Love Machine*, p. 60.
66 Iona McLaren, 'Isn't it Time We Embraced Iris Murdoch Again?', *Daily Telegraph* (13 June 2019), p. 21.
67 The two books were subsequently published in a single volume: John Bayley, *Iris: A memoir of Iris Murdoch* and *Iris and the friends: A year of memories* (London: Duckworth, 2002). In *Iris and the Friends*, Bayley explains that the illness is named after the doctor who 'wrote a treatise in 1907 on the disease or condition'. Bayley notes that the doctor found 'no cases of remission or recovery' (p. 160).
68 A.N. Wilson, *Iris Murdoch as I Knew Her* (London: Arrow Books, 2004 [2003]), pp. 6–9.

69 Murdoch, *Jackson's Dilemma*, p. 1.
70 *Ibid.*, p. 249.
71 Caroline Moore, 'A Fine Romance', book review of *Jackson's Dilemma* by Iris Murdoch, *Spectator*, 275:8725 (7 October 1995), p. 41. While *Iris* will celebrate water and swimming as therapeutic, *Jackson's Dilemma* contains a 'description of the death by drowning' of a leading character in the novel, an example of how, Moore notes, 'Violent death, despair and fear are never far away in her writing', p. 42.
72 Martin Amis, *The Rub of Time: Bellow, Nabokov, Hitchens, Travolta, Trump: Essays and Reportage: 1994–2016* (London: Jonathan Cape, 2017), p. 75.
73 Charlotte O'Sullivan, film review of *Iris*, *Sight and Sound*, 12:2 (February 2002), p. 47.
74 John Bayley, *The Characters of Love: A Study in the Literature of Personality* (London: Chatto & Windus, 1968 [1960]), pp. 4–5. In the opening chapter, Bayley claims that sex is 'always and inescapably ridiculous. Love is not' (pp. 4–5). In *The Book and the Brotherhood* (London: Chatto & Windus, 1987), Iris Murdoch has a female character declare, 'What does sex matter anyway, it's a mere technicality. Love is what matters' (p. 332).
75 Mark Fisher, 'anti-therapy' (2015) in Darren Ambrose (editor), *k-punk: The Collected and Unpublished Writings of Mark Fisher (2004–2016)* (London: Repeater Books, 2018), p. 590.
76 Amis, *The Rub of Time*, p. 73.
77 In her film review, Barbara Ellen felt that Iris Murdoch 'gets to experience moments of lucidity that one rather doubts real-Iris enjoyed', concluding that 'this must be an example of Hollywood Alzheimer's where the reality of the illness ... is never allowed to get in the way of the script'. Barbara Ellen, 'Agony in Slow Fade-Out', film review of *Iris*, *The Times* (17 January 2002), section 2, pp. 10–11.
78 *Ibid.*, pp. 10–11.
79 Iona McLaren (writing in 2019) claimed that Iris Murdoch 'has fallen out of fashion – but no one has ever written better about tangled love lives'. McLaren, 'Isn't it Time?', p. 21.
80 Muir, 'Fright to the End of the Plath'.
81 Steinberg and Kukil, *The Letters of Sylvia Plath Volume II*, letter to Aurelia Plath (22 November 1962), p. 919.
82 Sylvia Plath, *The Bell Jar* (London: Faber & Faber, 1996 [1963]), p. 39. The narrator describes the audience with whom she is watching the film as 'a lot of stupid moon-brains' (p. 39).
83 Bayley, *Iris and the Friends*, pp. 288–9.

3

'Diary of a somebody': Bridget Jones's journey from the 'edge of reason' to marriage and motherhood

In April, 2001, *Screen International* reported that *Bridget Jones's Diary* (Sharon Maguire, 2001) had 'scored the biggest opening of any British film ever at the UK box office' on its opening weekend.[1] A few weeks after the sequel, *Bridget Jones: The Edge of Reason* (Beeban Kidron, 2004), opened in cinemas during late November, 2004, Working Title Films paid for a full-colour one-page *Screen International* advertisement announcing in bold capitals that 'BRIDGET'S BACK AND BIGGER THAN EVER!' This promotional page reported that the film was the number one box-office attraction in sixteen countries and 'Universal's biggest opening ever in eight countries'.[2] *Empire* magazine reported that within six months of its release, *Bridget Jones's Baby* (Sharon Maguire, 2016), the third film in the series, had made 'over $200 million' in cinemas worldwide (it was notable that *Empire* chose to report this news in dollars, rather than pounds).[3] Such high-achieving figures, alongside the worldwide popularity of the novels by Helen Fielding,[4] demonstrate that dramatisations of Bridget's attempts to find happiness and romantic and sexual fulfilment have made a connection with audiences all around the world.

The character of Bridget Jones has become an iconic figure associated with forever worrying about whether she will find love with Mark Darcy or Daniel Cleaver, or possibly end up alone in the world. In a *Guardian* article about being happy with one's own company ('self-partnering'), Lizzie Cernik joked that 'No one wants to end up like Bridget Jones, that vodka-slurping poster child for miserable spinsters.'[5] Bridget in the novels and film versions also became known as someone who worried regularly about her sexual attractiveness, particularly in relation to her weight. When American star Renée Zellweger was cast as Bridget, there was a lot of press and media speculation as to how she would cope with the weight increase needed to look the part: Alexander Walker claimed that Bridget weighed 136 pounds in this first film of the series.[6] In her review of *Bridget Jones's Diary* (2001), 'Feeling single, seeing double', Barbara Ellen argued that although it was evident 'that Zellweger did pile on some pounds' for the role, this did not make her performance equal in terms of dedication and artistic integrity to that of Robert De Niro's in *Raging Bull* (Martin Scorsese, 1980). 'There has to be more to method acting than a few bags of doughnuts', concluded Ellen wryly, while at the same time stating that she did not 'agree with all the Little Englander sniping about the casting of an American actress for Bridget'.[7] Zellweger's performances in the films (which portray Bridget at the particular ages of thirty-two, thirty-three and forty-three) are clearly key elements in the commercial and overall critical success of the movies, even if some might say there is an inescapable irony in the fact that an American actor was chosen to portray a character whom Zellweger herself has described as 'quintessentially British'.[8]

What kinds of reasons have been put forward to explain the popularity of Bridget Jones in novel and film form? Might Bridget symbolise particular aspects of female lived experience in the 1990s and 2000s, which make the character's exploits and adventures especially resonant, meaningful and appealing for women readers and film-goers? Clive Bloom, in a study of best-selling fiction since 1900, felt that Bridget Jones 'seemed to sum up the dilemma of the successful woman of the late twentieth century, a woman who had gained everything her grandmothers had fought for ... and yet who was left with little of value'.[9] In a review of *Bridget Jones's Diary* (2001) entitled 'Fantasy made flesh', *Evening Standard* film critic Alexander Walker, somewhat unchivalrously, and in the kind of language and vocabulary which probably would not be deemed acceptable by readers today, speculated that for female viewers especially, the main attractions of Bridget's character lay solidly in the realms of escapist melodrama and wishing-it-were-so, with Bridget's story as presented on screen demonstrating that 'you can be a domestic slut, a social embarrassment, a professional no-hoper and fat too, and still have two handsome hunks fighting over you'.[10]

Angela McRobbie, writing in 2005 about the conceptualisation of Bridget's character and her defining features, suggested that Bridget may have been perceived by author Helen Fielding 'as a counter to feminism', given that Bridget is more 'interested in calories' than 'politics', does not base her life around a 'career' and 'craves the security of a well-qualified husband'.[11] Bryony Gordon, in an article for the *Daily Telegraph*, claimed, however, that the main contribution of the character to popular culture was that she 'made it OK' for women to 'be imperfect'. Gordon, in particular, admired the resilience of Bridget: here was someone in the 'public consciousness who was brave enough to fall down and get back up',[12] making Bridget a comic, implacably hopeful and romantic character, rather than a forlorn figure who becomes disenchanted with the world when things do not work out.

In the first-person narration style adopted in the novels, Bridget is aware, though, that her diary entries can appear both amusing and, on occasion, sad and wistful. In *Bridget Jones: Mad about the Boy* (Helen Fielding, 2013), Bridget fears that her modernised screenplay of Ibsen's *Hedda Gabler* entitled *The Leaves in his Hair* is being treated by prospective film producers solely as if it were a comedy, rather than a drama about a woman's frustration with her life, leaving her to wonder if 'the tragedy' in her writing had 'somehow inadvertently come out as comic?'.[13] When Bridget is alarmed by events in the films' narratives (sexual and emotional betrayal by a boyfriend; being incarcerated in jail for a crime she did not commit; losing her job just after learning she is pregnant), we might also wonder about the emotional effects on female *and* male audiences created by such a combination of comedy and pathos, failure and success and triumph and disaster in the Bridget Jones films.[14]

This chapter will explore a series of issues for debate and discussion arising from the three films' depiction of Bridget's loves, hopes and desires as a single young woman living in contemporary Britain. How, for instance, might we respond to possible criticisms that Bridget's concern to find 'Mr Right' (a partner for life) is essentially a conservative and somewhat regressive ambition? How are relationships, parents and friends portrayed in the films? What kinds of comedic and dramatic effects are generated out of Bridget's experiences as depicted in the workplace and the bedroom? What are we to make of the eclectic range of cultural allusions in the films to William Shakespeare, D.H. Lawrence, George Orwell, Adolf Hitler, Saddam Hussein and Ed Sheeran? What are the implications of the filmmakers declining, when producing *Bridget Jones's Baby* (2016), to follow the tragic and sad narrative developments of the third Bridget Jones novel, *Mad about the Boy* (Helen Fielding, 2013), in which Darcy and Bridget's father have died?

Claire Mortimer, in her study *Romantic Comedy* (2010), describes Bridget in somewhat less than positive terms as 'a character who yearns for security and love, yet who struggles to maintain control, both of her insecurities and of her life',[15] while noting that throughout the series her character can be viewed as that of 'a needy, neurotic woman who seemingly can only find happiness and fulfilment through a man, marriage and family'.[16] This leads to the question of whether the cinematic and narrative style of the films encourages viewers to perceive Bridget as a unique individual whose personal experiences are not explored in relation to wider social, sexual and political concerns within a modern-day patriarchal capitalist society. Novelist Fay Weldon, for example, claimed in a review of the 2004 film in the series that Bridget 'worries about her sex life and her social life and not the state of the nation or social justice'.[17] In connection with this, one can ask to what extent the films engage with issues around class and race, as well as those of gender. Is sex in the films depicted as an act existing uneasily (or uncertainly) with notions of love, affection and lasting relationships? How do the films compare with earlier depictions of 'women in London' movies, such as *Darling* (John Schlesinger, 1965) and *Georgy Girl* (Silvio Narizzano, 1966)?

And what are we to make of the male characters upon whom Bridget's happiness appears to rest? Bridget is continually drawn to *both* Daniel Cleaver (Hugh Grant) and Mark Darcy (Colin Firth). These two characters are presented as representing very different values and being complete opposites in terms of personality and behaviour. Cleaver is sexual, charming and witty, but also intrinsically unfaithful and non-committal, while Darcy is intelligent and dedicated to his praiseworthy work, but also emotionally rather cold, socially uneasy and not always fun to be with.[18] (Bridget's diary, which Mark finds and reads at the end of the first film, describes him at a low point in their relationship as 'rude' and 'unpleasant', adding for good measure that it is 'no wonder his clever wife left him'.) Andrew Spicer, in his essay 'The Reluctance to Commit: Hugh Grant and the New Romantic Comedy' (2004), argues that Grant as the 'Byronic' Cleaver demonstrates the point that non-virtuous and hedonistic charm is more attractive to women 'than tedious virtue'.[19] Cleaver, as the title of Spicer's essay might suggest, stands for a certain kind of hedonist viewpoint which emphasises personal pleasure and individual fulfilment over being part of an exclusive couple eschewing all other possible sexual partners, opportunities and possibilities.[20]

The introduction of a new character, Jack Quant (Patrick Dempsey), in *Bridget Jones's Baby* extends the options available to Bridget, but essentially the films' narratives revolve around Bridget having to choose between these two very different kinds of men and the values and beliefs they embody.[21] Her best male friend, Tom (James Callis), is described by Bridget as a 'total poof', making him unavailable for the kinds of sexual and romantic experiences desired by Bridget. Notably, Tom's own sexual desires and experiences are not featured or explored in the films.[22] Whether Bridget can and will settle down for life with either Cleaver or Darcy (what one might term 'cleaving to Cleaver' or engaging in 'dalliances with Darcy') becomes the essential story arc around which the narratives revolve (Daniel is supposedly dead in the third film, but it is true to say that his spirit lives on).

Therefore, in what kinds of ways do the films – and the accompanying novels – contribute to our deeper understanding of such concepts as love and desire and the efforts involved in creating and sustaining romantic and sexual relationships? Do the narratives always appear to work towards an ultimate affirmation of marriage as an institution (in particular) and the exclusive male–female partnership (in general) as a continuing and desirable basis for civilised societies in the modern world? Do the tales of Bridget's life suggest that as a modern woman she can succeed in 'having it all'?

My examination of these questions will be based around a consideration of each film individually in terms of its areas of interest and for the way in which each movie in the cycle contributes distinctively to the furtherance and deepening of Bridget's story (for a long time it appeared that *Bridget Jones: The Edge of Reason* would be the final movie in the series). Unusually, for high-profile mainstream cinema releases, all three films were directed by women film-makers. In Britain, the two films directed by Sharon Maguire were generally viewed in favourable terms by film critics, although some alleged aesthetic and narrative deficiencies were noted. Barbara Ellen, in *The Times*, concluded jovially in 2001 that 'Bridget Jones the Movie' was 'just like its heroine: lovable, funny and lumpy in places'.[23] Alexander Walker argued in the *Evening Standard* that the first movie offered what he termed an 'enthronement' of Bridget's character following her earlier appearances in print form. The narrative, as a whole, he felt resembled 'an extended sitcom', drawing upon elements of British stage farces, such as those performed by Brian Rix (1924–2016).[24] In his *New Statesman* review, Philip Kerr also referenced television comedic traditions, while claiming unflatteringly that the movie had 'the air of a cheesy BBC film for Christmas Day back in 1996'.[25] The involvement of three different writers in the screenplay (Helen Fielding, Richard Curtis and Andrew Davies) could also be seen by sceptical observers as evidence of the challenges involved in constructing a coherent and free-flowing romantic comedy-drama adapted from a first-person novel told in the form of diary entries.

Bridget Jones's Baby was similarly the product of three writers working on the screenplay (Helen Fielding, Dan Mazer and Emma Thompson) and was the first of the films not to be based around a pre-existing novel. Peter Bradshaw, in the *Guardian*, summed up director Sharon Maguire's return to the series with this film as a product of 'Love and labour', but added that this was 'not quite the mother of all comebacks' (his review concluded by stating that the film resembled 'a likeable, good-natured one-off TV holiday special').[26] Olly Richards, writing in *Empire*, however, declared that Sharon Maguire had 'rescued' the 'franchise' and was 'key to the big-screen success of Bridget Jones'.[27]

Richards's praise for Maguire was also a means of suggesting that Beeban Kidron had not succeeded in creating a successful film featuring the eponymous heroine. *Bridget Jones: The Edge of Reason*, while commercially very successful around the world, did not receive overly positive reviews in Britain. Mark Kermode went so far as to claim in the *New Statesman* that Kidron 'could not direct traffic, let alone a romantic comedy'.[28] Novelist

Will Self, writing in the *Evening Standard*, attacked the film for deploying what he termed 'three middle-aged men' (Andrew Davies, Richard Curtis and Adam Brooks), working alongside Helen Fielding, to write a 'script for a rom-com about a thirtysomething young woman'. This, in his view, led to a lack of authenticity and emotional sincerity, failings which he believed were exacerbated by the style, look and pacing of the film: 'The producers must have selected Beeban Kidron ... on the basis that anything she shot didn't look remotely filmic.'[29] Some reviewers perceived the film to be both lacking in content and style, and constituting more of a remake than a sequel, with Jessica Winter, in *Sight and Sound*, going so far as to argue that the film contained a 'void' at its 'centre'.[30]

Such critical claims will be kept in mind during the explorations to follow. The Bridget Jones film trilogy as a whole offers a comically complex portrait of one modern woman's ongoing search for fulfilment in her private life and a degree of success in her career choices (working in publishing and television). The films deal in both the everyday and the exaggerated, the outrageous and the recognisable, leading us to possibly ponder by the end of the series if it is not just Bridget – but we as spectators, too – who have been transported to the 'edge of reason' by her adventures and aspirations on screen. This chapter will explore Bridget's story as 'Her story' and possibly the story of lots of other people, too.

Bridget Jones's Diary (Sharon Maguire, 2001)

This first and defining film begins with images of Bridget walking towards her parents' house in a landscape covered in snow, conjuring up a sense that this is a scene of an idyllic Christmas in Britain. In fact, it turns out that Christmas is over – it is New Year's Day – and the opening conversation between Bridget and her mother (Gemma Jones) about the possibility of Bridget dating Mark Darcy features Mrs Jones making some strikingly unseasonal observations. From the very beginning of the series, there is, therefore, something of a disjunction between how situations and settings appear to be and what they may actually be like in reality. Such discrepancies will be the source of all the films' moments of high farce and ongoing drama. Pamela Jones refers to the 'Japanese' as a cruel race' (Mark's ex-wife was apparently Japanese),[31] and Bridget is told that she is unlikely to acquire a boyfriend if she looks as though she has just 'wandered out of Auschwitz'. Such remarks coming at the very beginning of the film imply a potential lack of sentimentality and 'political correctness' in what is to follow. Shortly afterwards, Uncle Geoffrey (James Faulkner) – who according to Bridget's voice-over is not really her uncle – is shown groping her bottom as she enters the room, while enquiring about her love life and warning that time may be running out for 'career girls' who put off having children for too long. Bridget subsequently overhears Mark Darcy comparing her to a spinster, a fish and her mother (the latter comparison is not meant as a compliment), indicating that this is a world which beneath its polite manners, middle-class setting and seemingly tranquil surface can be quite a ruthless and demanding place for a young woman such as Bridget.

These opening moments set up a number of the paradigms and dramatic challenges which Bridget will go on to face and explore in the future. She will have to deal with men who may be attracted to her, but who feel a need to point out what they see as her personal shortcomings and possible failure to conform to 'society's conventional expectations' of a 'woman's life'. In particular, Geoffrey's reference to Bridget as a 'career girl' opens up possibilities for the films to explore Bridget's experiences in the workplace (Bridget begins working in publishing before moving into television presenting).

In this 2001 film, it is noticeable that both Mark Darcy and Daniel Cleaver have a significantly higher professional status in the world of work than Bridget herself possesses. In the novel *Bridget Jones's Diary* (Helen Fielding, 1996), Bridget describes work as 'an annoying nuisance', which later becomes 'an agonizing torture' after she becomes sexually and emotionally involved with Daniel Cleaver.[32] Any study of the Bridget Jones films would have to acknowledge that distinctions between the worlds of work and play in the narratives are somewhat arbitrary, as the two spheres consistently interact and intermingle with each other. To a certain extent, as befits the genre of romantic comedy, work is presented as a 'form of play', while the 'play' element sometimes has a laborious quality to it as Bridget struggles to create something more lasting and meaningful in her private life. (Laurie Penny, in *Unspeakable Things: Sex, Lies and Revolution* (2014), writes of how 'Love can also be work. Love is … difficult and challenging as well as rewarding.')[33] Bridget is shown experiencing what we would now clearly identify as unacceptable sexist behaviour in her place of work – Cleaver, for instance, emails Bridget with the message that he likes her 'tits in that top'. Bridget, however, is depicted as essentially resilient in the face of such experiences, treating such happenings as instances to be transcended and overcome, rather than as experiences to be depressed or oppressed by.[34] In September 2018, Helen Fielding published a contemporary diary entry from Bridget in the *Sunday Times Style* magazine, which acknowledged that what was presented as amusing in this first film might no longer be viewed in the same light. In this 2018 extract from her journal, Bridget reflects, 'I just accepted that part and parcel of having a job was that my boss would stare freely at my breasts' and 'not know my name … None of that could happen now ... [such employers] would lose their jobs, no question.'[35] Conversely, Bridget's boss (Neil Pearson) at the TV station where she finds work wryly declares that at '*Sit-Up Britain*, no one ever gets sacked for shagging the boss' as a 'matter of principle', and Bridget is hired seemingly on the basis she admits to having had sexual relations with her previous employer.

Bridget's expertise and competence in the world of work is questioned early on in the movie when she is caught taking a personal phone call from her friend Jude (Shirley Henderson) during publishing office hours. As her boss, Daniel Cleaver, hovers over her with a sceptical look in his eyes, she gives the impression that she is speaking to 'Professor Leavis' about Kafka. Cleaver asks her if she has been speaking to '*the* F.R. Leavis, the author of *Mass Civilisation and Minority Culture*'.[36] 'Yes,' replies Bridget. 'The same F.R. Leavis who died in 1978?' asks Daniel, exposing Bridget as someone who has heard of F.R. Leavis, but is not familiar enough with this academic author to know that he is (a) dead and (b) championed those whom he saw as the great authors working within the traditions of English literature, rather than Eastern European modernist writers such as Kafka, and was notoriously not made a professor by his employers at Cambridge University (Dr Leavis being the professional title by which he was known).[37]

For contemporary audiences, this might seem an obscure and esoteric reference for a mainstream film to make; however, when Bridget subsequently asks for advice from her friends as to the best way to deal with her literary/professional mistake, Shazzer (Sally Phillips) offers the following advice: 'Fuck them. Tell them they can stick fucking Leavis up their fucking arses,' language a long way from Leavis's concept of a 'Great Tradition' in English literature and British culture.

Why this eminent (and historically important) cultural and literary critic deserves such abuse within the film remains something of a mystery – the presence of ex-academic Andrew Davies as one of the film's writers may offer some explanation – but Shazzer's outburst also reveals how far English discourses of the 2000s have moved away from the kinds of ways in which men and women verbally communicated with each other in the novels of Jane Austen, for example. (Austen was one of F.R. Leavis's literary touchstones in the 'Great Tradition', although he tended to leave studies of Austen to his wife, Q.D. Leavis, while he wrote about D.H. Lawrence, an author who believed in the importance of an earthy and uninhibited vocabulary when depicting sexual and emotional relationships between men and women.)[38]

While the worlds of publishing and television news in the film are largely portrayed as enjoyable places for characters to interact socially with each other, these places are not presented as possessing much gravitas or depth in this modern era of late/high capitalism. Writers as different as Salman Rushdie and Jeffrey Archer appear as versions of themselves at a book launch in *Bridget Jones's Diary*,[39] but Rushdie's main role appears to be as someone who is expected by guests to know where the toilets are located, while Archer is damned by faint praise from Bridget (his books 'aren't bad', she announces in a phrase and judgement which would scandalise F.R. Leavis if he were alive). Rushdie might be said to represent a certain form of post-colonial literary high culture, while Archer is associated with more popular and accessible styles of writing and narratives. Both writers have faced and survived some turbulent experiences in their lifetimes, a fact which may prove inspiring to Bridget, who is a kind of writer in that she keeps a diary, which appears sporadically in the films.

As regards the role of work in a modern society, Laurie Penny suggests that job flexibility and its accompanying uncertainty are now everyday facts of life: 'Your job is now [like] your boyfriend: neither of them can be trusted to stick around', she claims, adding that 'You have to be passionate about your work, even if your work is lining up packets of pasta shapes on a shelf.'[40] Bridget's employment opportunities are more exciting than working in a supermarket and stacking shelves, but the roles offered to her in the workplace are not depicted as being particularly satisfying, meaningful or intellectually challenging, and (as if to prove Penny's point) neither her relationship with Daniel Cleaver or her job in publishing turn out to be permanent in the end.

Bridget's problems with her love life and career are the central topics of conversation with the support group of Shazzer, Jude and Tom. Bridget's friendship with these characters is extremely important to her, but one would have to note that this friendship appears to be almost entirely one sided. The group has to act as a kind of 'Greek chorus' or assembled group of counsellors/psychologists/advisers to whatever updates Bridget offers them about her personal or professional life, voicing enthusiasm, scepticism and concern (as is deemed appropriate) about Bridget's latest news, while she appears to have very little – if any – interest in how happy they are with their own lives.

What the films are really concerned about is the state of Bridget's love life at any particular moment in time, and as her relationships appears to be in a constant state of flux and change, such uncertainties are used to propel the narrative forward. As Bridget travels towards the country hotel which Daniel has selected for their weekend break together, the wind from the journey in his open-top car literally makes her hair stand on end, but this change in her appearance can also be seen as a sign of how excited she is by the possibility of the weekend excursion that heralds the start of an ongoing and developing relationship with Daniel Cleaver.

This potentially happy state of affairs between the two of them culminates in what Mark Steyn described as a scene which 'will earn a small footnote in history as the first heterosexual romance with post-anal [sex]-coital banter'.[41] The scene in question opens with Bridget lying in bed with her back to Daniel, telling him 'that thing you just did' is illegal in several countries; to which Cleaver replies, 'That is the major reason I'm so thrilled to be living in Britain today.' This is followed by a close-up shot of Bridget asking Daniel, 'Do you love me?', shifting the topic of conversation from sex to love. Daniel's reply is 'Shut up or I'll do it again.' She asks him again if he is in love with her, and Daniel remarks, 'Right. You asked for it.' What happens next in the bedroom is not shown, as the film moves away from their hotel room and comes to rest on a just married couple dancing outside on the lawn (the woman is still wearing her wedding dress). The scene can be read as suggesting that a certain kind of man (personified by Daniel) will always be pursuing sexual experimentation, diversity and intensity, while a certain kind of woman (personified by Bridget) will always be looking for some form of emotional attachment alongside a sexual experience with a partner. Sex and love in Bridget's world will sometimes turn out to be uncomfortable bed partners. At the same time, humour, irony and misunderstandings are never far away from her experiences of sex and desire. When she answers the phone while in bed with Cleaver and talks of having 'a very bad man between my thighs', identifying herself as a 'wanton sex goddess' in the process, it will turn out to be her mother on the other end of the phone.

The idyllic situation of Bridget's weekend break with Daniel is soon disrupted by some bad news for Bridget (this sets a pattern of how her romantic and sexual encounters with Cleaver and Darcy will work out in the narratives – ecstatic happiness will soon be followed by disappointing turns of events). Daniel, sitting by (but significantly not in) Bridget's bed, informs her as she wakes up that he has to return to London to 'work on some figures' as the 'Americans are flying in' and thinking about closing the publishing company down. This appears only too plausible and possible in the difficult and challenging economic environment and changing cultural climate of the early 2000s. Daniel's claims appear to be untrue, however, as the American 'flying in' turns out to be an attractive woman, Lara (Lisa Barbuscia), who works in publishing, but appears to be in Britain largely for a romantic and sexual assignation with Daniel himself. (Her first appearance in the film, sitting naked in Daniel Cleaver's bathroom, would seem to confirm this hypothesis.) In her 2014 study *Unspeakable Things: Sex, Lies and Revolution*, Laurie Penny writes, 'Under late capitalism, love has become ... an object to be attained, a commodity to be hoarded until it loses value or can be traded up for a better bargain.'[42]

This scenario could be interpreted as reflecting how modern-day dating is echoing the practices and principles of contemporary capitalism in its belief that no one is irreplaceable or inviolable. Here, Lara, in Daniel's eyes, appears to be a more attractive and potentially career helpful partner than Bridget. 'I thought you said she was thin' is Lara's cutting response to seeing Bridget in the flesh, another example of Bridget being the subject of harsh and unpleasant comments during the course of the narrative.

The fact that Lara is similar in appearance and looks to Natasha (Embeth Davidtz), the woman whom Bridget will go on to suspect is more than just a law partner to Mark, suggests that Bridget may always fear being passed over in favour of someone deemed to be more desirable and successful than herself. Daniel tries to explain that his dalliance with a New York female publisher has come about partly because, in his view, Americans tend to have more social confidence and self-belief than British people (an exchange which takes on an extra layer of meaning and irony once one remembers that this scene involves Grant addressing these lines to an American actor, Zellweger, playing a British character).

The film proceeds to show Bridget falling into a state of apathy and listlessness after her relationship with Daniel declines and seemingly dies, culminating in her experiencing a nightmarish vision of dying alone, with her dead body being 'found three weeks' after her death, 'eaten by Alsatians'.[43] Her fears of not being romantically attached to someone reaches a kind of apotheosis at a dinner party for 'smug couples' which she attends. In a cleverly cinematic piece of exposition, each upper-class couple in turn – 'Magda and Jeremy, Hugo and Jane, Cosmo and Sweeney, Alistair and Henrietta' – is introduced to the audience in an exaggerated close-up, which emphasises that these are characters living in a self-contained world in which one's partner is one's 'other half'. Cosmo asks Bridget why are there so many single women in their thirties who can't seem to find a partner with whom to settle down. Bridget, at a loss to explain this phenomenon, puts it down to the women in question having 'disgusting scales' all over their bodies. This certainly shocks the dinner guests into silence, and appears to put the diners off their lavish meal, but her unexpected response does little to counter the arrogance and insensitivity of Cosmo in asking the question in the first place.

Bridget's mother's relationship with her husband (Jim Broadbent) is depicted in this initial film as falling apart, with Pamela Jones expressing a deeply felt dissatisfaction with the quality of her sex life, the endless time she spends looking after her husband and her lack of a career. Clive Bloom, in his study *Bestsellers: Popular Fiction since 1900*, somewhat bizarrely describes Bridget's mother as 'living the feminist ideal life', adding that her character in the first novel is 'nothing less than a perpetual embarrassment'.[44] Both mother and daughter, one married, the other single, therefore find themselves deeply unhappy about the state of their lives as the narrative unfolds. (Mrs Jones will even embark on an affair as a result of what she sees as the atrophied state of her marriage.)

Melancholy is not allowed to gain too strong a hold over Ms and Mrs Jones for long, however. Bridget eventually revives herself by going to the gym and replacing self-help guides on her bookshelves – with such plausible, but presumably parodic titles as *How to Make Men Want What They Don't Think They Want* – with others bearing such titles as *Women Who Love Men are Mad*. Pamela Jones returns to her husband after her relationship with a shopping channel TV presenter comes to an end, with her husband welcoming her back with the decidedly non-romantic, but pragmatic message, 'You daft cow, I don't work without you.'[45]

Bridget resigns from her job in publishing and tells Daniel that given the choice of working for him or spending time 'wiping Saddam Hussein's arse', she would choose the latter. This unexpected allusion to a ruthless dictator, coming as it does in 2001, pre-dates Hussein's fall from power two years later as a result of an Anglo-American invasion of Iraq. Daniel Cleaver has his faults, but he is clearly not as bad a person as Saddam Hussein (1937–2006), and Bridget knows this too, underneath her hyperbolic language; but this moment signals a move away from Daniel, who is only interested in foreign affairs if they involve attractive foreign women, to Mark, who works selflessly to fight injustice, cruelty and intolerance in the field of international relationships and politics.

This change in the narrative is heralded by Bridget finding a job in television news as the 'new face of British current affairs' for *Sit-Up Britain*. Mark also appears to be moving towards a new career and life with Natasha in New York, but he is presented as having a sudden change of heart, and he returns to Britain to be with Bridget at the close of the narrative. Significantly, after reading Bridget's unflattering observations about him, he goes out to buy her a new diary, so that a fresh and hopefully promising new start to their life together can be made. In an attempt to appease Mark, and to erase such diary entries as 'I hate him! HATE HIM!' from his memory,[46] Bridget rewrites history as fiction by declaring that she 'didn't mean' what she 'meant' in the diary, implying that the diary has not in fact revealed the whole 'truth' about Bridget Jones. Mark, in turn, at the close of the film, adopts the kind of language which Mellors in *Lady Chatterley's Lover* (1928) would appreciate, by declaring that 'posh boys' do indeed 'fucking' kiss in a passionate and uninhibited manner ...

Bridget Jones: The Edge of Reason (Beeban Kidron, 2004)

Despite being released three years after *Bridget Jones's Diary*, this sequel takes place shortly after events have concluded in the first movie and describes what happens next for Bridget, Mark and Daniel. This second film – which has the most interesting and resonant title of the series – does, however, transport Bridget to a world and universe beyond her parents' 'picture postcard' English village home and the more 'knowable communities' of the London publishing house and television station featured in the first film (Switzerland and Thailand feature in the film, while Dubai, Saudi Arabia and Bangkok are mentioned).[47] In *The Edge of Reason*, one mournful sequence has Bridget fantasising (Scrooge-like) about being led to a tombstone in a church graveyard bearing her name. The inscription on the tombstone simply reads, 'Bridget Jones Spinster: 1972 – 2050', implying that she lived a long but uneventful and unfulfilled life. This film as a whole seeks to illustrate that Bridget's life is, in fact, far from dull and that her 'reason', resolve and fortitude are all severely tested as events unfold.

Bridget's relationship with Mark is shown as suffering because she is depicted regularly making ill-judged interruptions while he is conducting what appear to be grave meetings on matters of world importance with foreign ambassadors. Bridget is keen to ascertain how things stand between them and to be reassured that Mark still loves her. These embarrassing interventions may indicate that Bridget is essentially a self-centred character, concerned only with her own private affairs and not the wider world, thus comically parodying stereotypes of how women may be 'traditionally expected to behave', according to Natasha Walter in *The New Feminism* (1999): 'fixated on the domestic, on sexual matters, on their bodies, on their romantic relationships'.[48] Bridget's interventions into Mark's world of international diplomacy, however, do serve to deflate some of his pomposity, propensity for name-dropping and generally humourless manner. Mark may also be immersing himself in international concerns at the cost of developing, valuing and nurturing his own personal relationships with individuals outside work. From this perspective, Bridget could be seen as gradually humanising Mark.

Mark's professional expertise, concern for justice and contacts with members of the British establishment ('two cabinet members and half of MI5') prove to be invaluable, though, when Bridget faces the prospect of ten to fifteen years' imprisonment at a Thailand Women's Correction Centre for allegedly attempting to smuggle a large amount of cocaine out of the country. Bridget has earlier (and unwittingly) taken hallucinatory drugs on a Thailand beach, Daniel Cleaver, untypically, coming to her rescue. Shazzer's lover (Paul Nicholls in a wordless role) is really responsible for the cocaine smuggling operation, but Bridget, through helping Shazzer by carrying some of her extra luggage, is found by the Thai authorities in possession of the illegal substance. (Interestingly, Bridget and Shazzer are never shown as being such close friends again in the remainder of this narrative and the third film.)

In these prison sequences, Bridget's angry feelings about how Mark has treated her in an aloof manner back home are depicted as minor, parochial and rather inconsequential concerns, compared with the very painful experiences of the Thailand women with whom she is imprisoned. Bridget (whose name a Thai inmate mispronounces as 'Be shit' at first), complains to the women around her that her 'bad boyfriend' did not 'stick up for her at the lawyers' supper', before realising how incredibly lame and insular a problem this sounds in relation to the tales of woe and real suffering touched upon by the women inmates. Consequently, Bridget elaborates that Mark also hit her, made her take drugs and was involved in 'stealing' all 'her stuff', none of which, of course, is true.

David Harvey, in *The Enigma of Capital and the Crises of Capitalism* (2010), writes of the paradoxes and stark contrasts of contemporary capitalism in its first, second and third world dimensions – 'spiralling poverty among burgeoning populations ... alienations and social exclusions galore and the anxieties of insecurity, violence and unfulfilled desires' in comparison with areas of the world in which 'standards of material living and well-being have never been higher, where travel and communications have been revolutionised'.[49] These scenes set in the Thailand women's jail allude to such stark contrasts, as we are invited to compare Bridget's 'first world' dilemmas with the everyday problems experienced by these incarcerated women. The Thai women's prison sequences were not well regarded by some critics (Anthony Quinn, writing in the *Independent*, condemned them as 'offensive' and 'tasteless'),[50] but Sukhdev Sandhu, in the *Daily Telegraph*, felt they served to demonstrate that Bridget is 'able to raise a stiff upper lip when life goes bad', and noted that she succeeds in charming and disarming what he describes (a bit unfeelingly) as 'her prostitute crammed cell'.[51]

It is indeed notable that we do not learn what becomes of the mistreated, but kind and friendly women imprisoned in the Thailand prison – no Darcy-like figure comes along to rescue them and Bridget does not highlight their plight when back in Britain – but they are presented in a warm and affectionate light, and we, arguably, do not entirely forget them once they no longer feature in the narrative. Bridget's leaving gifts to the women – copies of a 'self-help' book about male–female relationships invoking the distant planets of Mars and Venus, 'wonder bras' and some Galaxy chocolate bars – may appear jokily irrelevant to their dire situation – but they do imply a possible international sisterhood for women of different races, cultures and situations around the world.

Mark and Bridget's relationship (like the negative result of a pregnancy test she takes in the narrative) still contains a sense of mutual disappointment about it, as if Mark can never quite grow to tolerate Bridget's bumbling behaviour or find value in her relationships with either her friends or her former lover, Daniel Cleaver. Bridget and film viewers are also led in this second instalment of the series to suspect that Mark is having an affair with Rebecca (Jacinda Barrett), a beautiful lawyer who has replaced Natasha as his partner-in-law. An unexpected and ironic development in the film, however, occurs when Rebecca declares to Bridget that she is really in love with her and not Mark.[52]

At this point, the film wittily and intriguingly flashes back to those moments when we have witnessed Rebecca seemingly gazing with affection and admiration at Mark, only to realise that Bridget was the object of her romantic yearnings. This instance of what we might term 'Love, Actually' means that the name of Rebecca can be added to Bridget's small but dedicated band of admirers. The film, though, shows Bridget politely and awkwardly (but firmly) rebuffing Rebecca's advances after a short intimate kiss, informing her that it is still 'men in general' and 'Darcy in particular' as far as she is concerned. Bridget does add, however, that if she ever changes her sexual persuasion and inclination, Rebecca would be the only one for her. A radical move for some spectators at this point would have been to depict Bridget enthusiastically reciprocating and welcoming Rebecca's declarations of love and longing, with the film swerving away from its emphasis on (and obsession with?) heterosexual relationships, but this might put the two films' seeming emotional investment in Bridget settling down with Darcy at risk. This comic/dramatic twist is therefore not the end of the story, and Rebecca (like Natasha, Mark's previous partner-in-law) disappears from the Bridget Jones story. Rebecca's declaration and the subsequent kiss between her and Bridget are nonetheless fascinating moments in the film which open up – even if they are immediately closed down again – other sexual and emotional possibilities for Bridget to pursue in her quest for personal fulfilment and happiness.[53] (At the very least, like the scenes involving Bridget's encounters with the Thai women, the liaison with Rebecca serves to deepen and strengthen Bridget's relationships with other women characters in the film.)

Rebecca's 'coming out' intervention also works as a moment which appears to liberate the film from its broadly (sometimes very broadly) semi-realist manner of relating the story in a chronological fashion. We now see Bridget taking advice several times from a London taxi driver as to which dress suits her best for an attempt at a reconciliation with Mark

Darcy, and subsequently asking to replay a romantic declaration scene when her attempt at reconnecting with Mark goes awry. These playful and self-reflexive moments conjure up something of the spirit (if not the more serious tone and intent) of some of Jean-Luc Godard's films of the 1960s when Anna Karina acted as his muse (and are an example of Kidron's skilful and, I think, under-rated direction). Significantly, Bridget at this stage of proceedings does seem to be treated with greater kindness and consideration than has been evident in the previous film ('How can we help you young lady?' asks a member of Darcy's Peruvian delegation, who will shortly be astonished that Mark's 'girlfriend is actually a lesbian'). This playful and joyful chain of events (Bridget pledges undying love to an ageing employee of the law society by mistake when she enters the wrong room) carries through right until the end of the film, when we are led to believe that Bridget and Mark are getting married, only to learn that it is her parents who are renewing their wedding vows at the close. Despite appearing to end Bridget's story with her *nearly* marrying Mark, this was not to be how the story of Bridget Jones finally concluded.

Bridget Jones's Baby (Sharon Maguire, 2016)

Laurie Penny, in *Unspeakable Things: Sex, Lies and Revolution* (2014), writes that 'Love is meant to be the overwhelming object of a woman's early life; her story ends when she finds it, or fails to find it.'[54] At the conclusion of the second film, Bridget may have found love with Mark, but she is not married to him, and the tempestuous nature of their relationship does not necessarily bode well for their future together. Hence, after a twelve-year gap, a third film appeared, continuing the story of Bridget Jones's troubled love life. Sharon Maguire returned as director, and admitted in an *Empire* article on the making of the movie that the script for this second sequel had been in a process of development for over eleven years, suggesting a lack of creative agreement as to where the story should go next. In the same article, Maguire claimed that for all the comic misunderstandings in *Bridget Jones's Baby*, this film was dealing with serious subjects concerning 'women ... in their thirties, [who] not having settled for marriage and children ... are thinking, Okay, what do we do now? We're still looking for the meaning of life.'[55]

Such a search for deeper meanings in this 2016 film is evident at the beginning, when friends and lovers of Daniel Cleaver are gathered together to attend his funeral (in Helen Fielding's novel *Bridget Jones: Mad about the Boy* (2013), it is, by way of a complete contrast, Mark Darcy who has died, while working abroad).[56] Evoking memories of *Four Weddings and a Funeral*

(Mike Newell, 1994) and including lines that the *Carry On* movies might have rejected as too risqué, we are informed that Cleaver 'died going down in the bush' (i.e. during a plane crash in Africa) and that he 'touched many' of those attending his funeral (the service is shown to be attended by many attractive female 'supermodels'). Mark Darcy, it appears, has finally married one of those mysterious women who seem to be constantly at his side, although, it will turn out that he is actually in the process of getting divorced, suggesting that he may not, in fact, be the perfect answer to a woman's dreams. Shazzer and Jude are now married with children, while Tom announces that he is on the verge of adopting a baby with his male partner. Bridget is, subsequently, less close to this old group of friends now, as she is still single and they are married mothers. Shazzer and Jude have familial responsibilities and cannot act in the carefree manner adopted in the previous films. The key development of *Bridget Jones's Baby* (as the title suggests) is that Bridget will join them in becoming a mother (in her case at the age of forty-three and without being sure whether the father is Mark or Jack). In modern medical terminology, she is defined as a 'geriatric mother' who has to proceed carefully to make sure that nothing goes wrong.

Both Bridget and Mark are presented as older and seemingly slightly worn down by life in this film. Mark's second marriage has failed and Bridget's life doesn't seem to have changed much in the years since the previous film (she still lives in the same flat). Mark, in particular, seems more joyless than ever (though he does touchingly greet the news that Bridget is pregnant – and that he is presumably the father – as 'wonderful news'). With Cleaver out of the way, he is disappointed (perhaps understandably) to learn that Bridget's American lover, Jack Quant, a millionaire seeking to make dating into a more scientific and precise art, may turn out to be the father of her unborn child instead of himself. This narrative conundrum, both farcical and serious by turns, tends to make a mockery of Quant's professed desire to make dating a more mathematical and rational proposition (Quant presumably stands for quantify), and to illustrate that Bridget is not someone who can be rationalised or classified in the ways his dating system might try to suggest.

The film, prior to this development, has sought to revitalise Bridget by setting her among some new women characters who are not (as Bridget puts it) 'obsessed with marriage and children'. Miranda (Sarah Solemani) is a witty and lively work colleague, willing to make risqué observations about her sex life off air in between announcing the TV station's news headlines (one example of this flair for split-second comic timing has Miranda appearing to claim that she had a 'threesome with ... Prince Andrew [who] has just written his first children's book'). Miranda is confident about modern dating practices on Tinder and has a striking on-screen presence and aura on television (she thanks Jack Quant, when he is a guest on her programme, for 'coming on my sofa'). She is also importantly a good friend to Bridget, keen to end Bridget's sexual abstinence at a colourful pop festival, the atmosphere and mood of which she compares to 'Sodom and Gomorrah'. Miranda will also be the person who is by Bridget's side when she learns that she is pregnant in the prosaic setting of the workplace toilets.

If Miranda helps to rejuvenate Bridget, Alice Peabody (Kate O'Flynn), a hip television executive from the north of England who becomes Bridget's new boss, will act as someone who does not wish to become one of Bridget's admirers or supporters and fires her for 'gross incompetence' from her job as a news producer for a cable TV channel. Alice's 'northern realist' pragmatism will clash with Bridget's southern English vowels and more laid-back way of operating. As the workforce appears to be getting younger, Bridget cannot help but be conscious that she is noticeably older than those around her (one of her forty-third birthday cards includes the term RIP). Just as Dexter's TV career in the ephemeral world of youth television in *One Day* (2011) comes to a sudden end, so does Bridget's involvement in populist TV news broadcasting, suggesting that she is possibly not in touch with significant trends and movements in British popular culture during the 2000s. (Bridget's dismissal from her job comes as she learns that she is expecting a child and, like Dexter, she is subsequently plunged into something of a crisis.)

If Bridget's knowledge of the literary critic F.R. Leavis fell short of realising that he was dead in the first film, here (as a point of contrast and a sign of changing cultural reference points), Bridget and Miranda appear to be unaware of the fame enjoyed by Ed Sheeran (1991–), an extremely popular singer and performer of the 2000s. The sound of Ed Sheeran playing live to a small audience at the festival she attends is juxtaposed with images of Bridget's lovemaking with Jack, though, implying that that his success and appeal is not confined to young audiences (Bridget's sexual encounter with Jack is accompanied by Ed singing the line, 'Take me in your loving arms'). In the 2001 movie, Bridget contemplated the prospect of working for Saddam Hussein rather than Daniel Cleaver. In this 2016 film, Bridget's voice-over (in a more serious tone) makes a brief and rather bizarre reference to the American–British invasion/liberation of Iraq in 2003. A fleeting image of a statue of Saddam is shown being toppled on screen as Bridget comments that 'It's surely weird you can do something as complicated and important as having a baby and invading Iraq without any instruction at all.' Zellweger appears to have been instructed to read the line in this sequence very quickly indeed – as if this allusion should not be unduly dwelt upon – but it arguably serves as a positive testimony to the films' anti-dictatorial and totalitarian sentiments throughout (in a previous film, Bridget has declared that everyone deserves a 'second chance except Hitler'). This almost subliminal reference to Iraq touches lightly upon the debates raised about the legitimacy of the invasion and the adequacy of George Bush and Tony Blair's plans for how Iraq would be governed after Saddam Hussein was captured, tried and executed, topics that dominated British politics in the years following his removal from power.[57]

Through the character of Pamela Jones, the film also obliquely explores the problems women (and men) may face in finding meaning, purpose and variety in their lives after retiring from work. Although dissatisfied with the moribund state of her marriage and sex life in the first movie (emphasising her discontent, with a rather unflattering and inaccurate reference to 'Germaine sodding Geer'), she ends up renewing her marriage vows at the conclusion of *The Edge of Reason*. Here, she stands for election to her local parish council on the bold and frank platform of saving 'our society from rack and ruin' (how such a situation might be best brought about has been a pressing concern for British politicians since the release of *Bridget Jones's Baby* in September 2016). Pamela's subsequent triumph in the election campaign coincides with the birth of Bridget's baby, and in a witty reference – which may be lost on younger or international audiences – she evokes the spirit and regal air of Margaret Thatcher (1925–2013), when Prime Minister, by publicly declaring, 'We are about to become a grandmother.'[58] Her final utterance in the film declares that women 'don't need any more rights' (a reference to the protest march undertaken by women which delays Bridget's perilous journey to the maternity hospital), implying that her politics are of a conservative rather than a liberal nature. It should be noted, however, that she remains a lively woman to the close with an active imagination (she wonders if Bridget not knowing who the baby's father is might be the result of her having a 'threesome'). Pamela's husband looks on somewhat lethargically throughout, seemingly bewildered by his wife's restless ambitions and desire to keep on reinventing her identity and intervening in public life.[59]

While dramatising births and rebirths, this third film (as noted earlier) has a very different kind of narrative end point in mind for the character of Daniel Cleaver, who is reported as presumed dead at the start. In retrospect, one can see that his character's removal from the scenario was necessary for Bridget to break out of a pattern of behaviour which was repetitive, unsatisfactory and damaging to her well-being. Jack Quant is probably the most likeable, pleasant (and wealthy) of Bridget's three lovers, but when he asks Bridget if she is in love with him, her reply is that she 'could be one day', but seemingly is not at present. Jack's desire to make dating a more methodical and structured affair cannot make his own romantic and emotional wishes come true, and this adds to the elegiac and slightly melancholy tone of those parts of the narrative which engage with the romantic hopes and aspirations of those characters in the film who are middle aged and single.

Jack is imbued with an optimistic and enthusiastic nature, however, and he sees the fatherhood situation with Bridget as something which 'could be a great adventure'. Mark makes a point of declaring that he lives in Ealing, not among the shared parenting tribes of Peru (a country referenced in *The Edge of Reason*), and he is notably less conciliatory and hopeful about the future. A positive development in this third film, though, is to finally present the two possible fathers for Bridget's baby boy not just as rivals for her affection and attention, but as two men who can potentially *both* play a part in nurturing the child's development and upbringing. Such a development avoids the amusing, but also rather ugly and petulant, fights between Mark and Daniel which have occurred previously. Darcy refers to 'My son' at his wedding to Bridget, but Quant is happy to be revealed 'holding the baby' as Bridget enters the church to eventually marry Mark, a year after giving birth to a boy. Here, the artificial-looking snow scenes featured in the conclusions to *Baby's* predecessors have been replaced by luscious green lawns in scenes shot in realistic-looking locations, indicating that this is now spring (a time associated with comedy and renewal by literary theorist Northrop Frye),[60] rather than the winter of the previous movies' endings.

Justine King, in an essay on women in British cinema, praises such 1980s British films as *Educating Rita* (Lewis Gilbert, 1983) and *Letter to Brezhnev* (Chris Bernard, 1985) for avoiding what she describes as a 'final five minutes of the narrative when suddenly but inevitably, the female protagonist would be forced to concede to the ... heterosexual coupling so characteristic of the classical woman's film genre'.[61] David Lodge, however, has argued that a narrative ending in a marriage for the central protagonists of a narrative can be used to convey an impression 'that the nice and the good are one and shall inherit the earth'.[62] Certainly for Bridget, this 'official confirmation' of her relationship with Mark ('I now pronounce you, finally, husband and wife' announces the presiding clergyman) is presented as a desirable and pleasing conclusion to events for Bridget and the film's viewers – 'the normal response of the audience to a happy ending' (according to Frye) is that 'this should be'.[63] In the film's final images, as Bridget's wedding veil blows into the wind, we are encouraged to visualise her finally letting go of the past and being able to look forward to a more hopeful future. The presence of a new piece of music on the soundtrack, specially commissioned for the film at the close – *Still Falling for You* performed by Ellie Goulding – adds to the feeling of a new beginning as the series seemingly comes to an end.[64]

However, these closing images and sounds denoting a happy and content Bridget are not quite the end of the story. In an unexpected development, evoking the redemptive optimism behind the conclusions of some of William Shakespeare's late comic/romance plays,[65] particularly *The Winter's Tale* (1623), a closing shot of the *Guardian* on a bench reveals that Daniel Cleaver (described as a 'publishing playboy') has been 'discovered alive one year after plane goes down in bush'. Whether a 'serious' newspaper such as the *Guardian* would feel that this was front-page news is unlikely, but this non-realist conclusion is in keeping with Northrop Frye's belief that 'in any well-constructed comedy there ought to be a character or two who remains isolated from the action, spectators of it, and identifiable with the spectator aspect of ourselves'.[66] It is notable, therefore, that the final image in the film before the credits appear is not one of the eponymous Bridget, but of a photograph of Daniel Cleaver, seemingly back from the dead as the song *Still Falling for You* plays on the soundtrack ...

Conclusion

F.R. Leavis, the notable literary critic and cultural commentator referenced in the first film, wrote of D.H. Lawrence's 'intense conviction that the relations between men and women are profoundly important; that they are central and crucial; so that if they have gone wrong there is something desperately wrong with life and civilisation'.[67] Relationships between male and female characters in the Bridget Jones films are presented as existing in a rather troubled and uncertain condition, but these relationships are depicted as ultimately rather farcical and non-tragic in their nature, and thus capable of being resolved in a comic and optimistic manner in the third film. This state of affairs is very different to Bridget's world as depicted in the third (2013) novel, where Darcy is dead, Cleaver is a depressed figure given to heavy drinking and Bridget is having to bring up two children as a single mother.[68] The novels and films therefore go in different directions at this historical juncture (a process which became somewhat confusing when Helen Fielding resurrected Mark and wrote Jack out of the fourth Bridget novel, *Bridget Jones's Baby: The Diaries*, published in 2016).

Darcy, in a moment of heightened self-awareness as Bridget is giving birth, praises the ways in which she has survived 'repressed men and cheating boyfriends', and the films as a whole are wary of those who – in the words of the Foreign Secretary (Patrick Malahide) when interviewed in *Bridget Jones's Baby* – fall on the 'wrong side of history'.[69] Exclusive coupledom (as exemplified by the gathering of self-satisfied couples in the first film) can be viewed as smug, oppressive and suffocating in the narratives. However, when Bridget laments her aloneness during a sad moment in *The Edge of Reason*, the camera moves out of her apartment to reveal a world of happy couples all around her, as if to demonstrate how such a feeling of being excluded from having a loving partner may feel to those in that position. Bridget, in the end, wants to be in the partnered position of Magda and Jeremy, Hugo and Jane, Cosmo and Sweeney, Alistair and Henrietta, but without adopting their constrained and rather self-adoring upper-middle-class view of the world (Bridget is adamant that she does not want a son of hers to be sent away to boarding school).

Clive James, reviewing and responding to a seminal work by Germaine Greer, stated that Greer's call for women (and men) to aim for a radically changed way of living in *The Female Eunuch* (1970) did not – in his view – take account of the fact that most people ultimately settle 'for a quiet, unadventurous life'. He did, however, acknowledge that her book could convince future generations of women who faced a possible 'life of frustrations and cheap dreams' to 'walk away from it, and hang loose'. James concluded from Greer's study that it might be sensible for people to get 'married later' in life, 'rather than sooner'.[70]

This is precisely what Bridget does in the third film, with her wedding following a year after the birth of her son. This could not be said to be the result of a carefully worked-out life-plan on Bridget's part; it is more an example of how she achieves her goals somewhat inadvertently out of a series of unplanned adventures. Bridget is made redundant shortly after learning that she is pregnant, so her good fortune could not be said to be unlimited. In fact at one stage, middle-class Bridget is faced with the prospect of becoming a single mother who cannot identity her child's father for certain. Angela McRobbie has noted how in modern British culture, women who fall into such categories are often deemed to be 'feckless' and accused of 'depriving a child of his or her "human right" to a father'.[71] At (literally) one of her lowest moments, Bridget is revealed to be pregnant, jobless, bereft of flat keys and bank cards and reduced to lying in the street. Mark's unexpected but welcome arrival at this point does allow Bridget to gain access to her apartment, thus begetting a series of events which will lead to the maternity hospital and marriage with Mark, and away from what briefly appears to be a narrative strand veering in the direction of a Ken Loach movie about the 'condition of England'. This chain of events could be read as Bridget depending on a 'Prince-like' figure to rescue and save her when things go badly and disturbingly wrong, but this scenario also exemplifies how male and female relationships and partnerships at their best can be positive, helpful, supportive, enriching and life-sustaining, especially when children are involved. Bridget does appear to value marriage to the right man above all else in her life, but she does not rush into marriage or treat the concept of a permanent union lightly.

The relationship between Mark and Bridget is singular and idiosyncratic enough to limit its possible representativeness as an example of modern-day relationships in British culture, but Mark in cinematic terms can be seen as following in the footsteps of figures such as Leslie Howard and Kenneth More who personified a certain kind of English-based integrity, who actively resisted 'ungentlemanly' behaviour both at home and abroad. Indeed, some of the key characters with their attendant world views can be read as emanating from 1940s and 1950s British film culture. Hugh Grant plays the kind of cad portrayed by Rex Harrison in *The Rake's Progress* (Sidney Gilliat, 1945), although he lacks a war in which to redeem his character. Bridget's mother, judging from the remarks which introduce her character, appears to recall the Second World War as a quite recent event, leading to what philosopher Simon Critchley has described as a form of humour which 'is powerfully connected to ... outdated, national styles and national differences'.[72]

Annette Kuhn has praised genres such as the melodrama and the women's film for offering 'the possibility of female desire and female point-of-view' in their narratives,[73] and the Bridget Jones films could be said to work within such traditions and to evoke memories of some earlier seminal women-in-London films. Bridget's adventures as a young woman living in London, for instance, echo some of the experiences of Diana Scott (the 'happiness girl'), played by Julie Christie in *Darling* (1965). Diana's lovers include Miles Brand (Laurence Harvey), a playboy-type character dedicated to mass sensual experiences, alongside the more reserved and staid Robert Gold (Dirk Bogarde), figures who can be read as corresponding to the traits and tendencies of Bridget's principal male partners, Daniel and Mark. (Diana, like Bridget, also has a gay male best friend.) However, in this more serious and stylistically diverse treatment of the story of a 'woman's life' and loves in 'Swinging London', Diana Scott is not rewarded with happiness at the close, being left in a state of exile in Italy. Bridget is a very different sort of character to Diana, more rooted in family and place and committed to the idea of settling down with one person.

Georgy Girl (Silvio Narizzano, 1966), another seminal 1960s London-based film, has the eponymous Georgy (Lynn Redgrave) also involved with two contrasting male suitors, James Leamington (James Mason), a father-figure, alongside her flatmate's boyfriend, the rootless and unreliable Jos Jones (Alan Bates). Georgy is witty, but presented as ungainly, not showing a great concern over her appearance and consequently being something of a worry to her parents. The narrative concludes with Georgy marrying her ageing admirer because he can provide financial security for Jos's child, whom she wishes to gain custody of and bring up as her own. As the popular 1960s title song plays over the credits, this ending is presented as a bittersweet one, with Georgy seemingly shunning Leamington in the wedding car and the camera finally focusing in on Georgy and her 'baby' to the exclusion of her new husband. The ending of *Bridget Jones's Baby* is clearly a much happier one than this 1960s film, but the film-makers here decide to end proceedings with an image of Bridget and her baby, rather than Bridget, her baby and Mark, making an interesting parallel with the earlier movie.

The first two Bridget Jones films could be retitled *Bridget, Mark and Daniel Too* but that would their only connection to Alan Clarke and Andrea Dunbar's raucous and ribald *Rita, Sue and Bob Too* (1987). The involvement of Richard Curtis and Hugh Grant in the first two Jones movies suggests that the films may have developed logically out of the three Curtis and Grant movies produced over a nine-year period: *Four Weddings and a Funeral* (Mike Newell, 1994), *Notting Hill* (Roger Michell, 1999) and *Love Actually* (Richard Curtis, 2003). Sarah Crompton, in a witty and perceptive article, claims that these films have several things in common, such as 'extreme but picturesque' weather conditions; a 'hero or heroine' who is surrounded by 'a group of eccentric but loyal friends'; the inclusion of 'at least one scene' in the narrative where 'someone has to drive a car very fast'; and a finale with love emerging triumphant at the close.[74] All these features could be said to apply to the cinematic world of Bridget Jones as well (where Helen Fielding is clearly a major authorial presence), but the absence of Curtis and Grant from *Bridget Jones's Baby* may be one factor behind the different aesthetic look and narrative structure of this film, alongside its distance from the period of 'New Labour' in office (1997–2010), an era which witnessed the release of two of Curtis's hugely popular British comedy-dramas.

In *Bridget Jones's Baby*, Mark Darcy, while defending a group of (apparently) Russian women who have dared to protest against oppressive features of their nation, praises Britain as a land of democracy and freedom which will always be ready to 'protect and defend brave young women' in their quest for the right to free speech. Darcy refers to Shakespeare, Orwell and D.H. Lawrence to illustrate his point, although, notably, he does not refer to any women writers when making this claim and plays down the fact that Orwell and Lawrence were critical of many aspects of British social and political life. Lawrence, in particular, ended his days in exile from Britain, while his final novel and paintings were banned and confiscated by the British authorities in the late 1920s. (Lawrence's chief literary supporter in British literary criticism, F.R. Leavis, wearily declared that in 1955 'the country that in its time produced Shakespeare, George Eliot and Lawrence ... has become, irretrievably, the country of the Welfare State, the Football Pools, and the literary culture of the *New Statesman*'.[75] Given

Leavis's pessimistic view of how British cultural life was developing, he would not be surprised that Bridget is unaware of whether he is alive or dead in the first film.)

One other link that might be made between the Bridget Jones films and *Four Weddings* and *Notting Hill* is that they do not engage with issues of race and cultural diversity in modern Britain. *Bridget Jones's Diary* briefly features one black character, but his role is simply to ask Tom if he really is a former pop singer with one hit single before he disappears from the narrative. Angela McRobbie therefore describes *Bridget Jones's Diary* as evoking 'a landscape of whiteness with barely a gesture towards London as a multicultural city'.[76] The films consistently censure and ridicule oppressive dictatorships abroad, but Bridget doesn't return from Thailand with a view to petitioning the British Foreign Office to pressure the Thai authorities into adopting more humane responses to the plight of the women detained in its correction centres. In the novel *The Edge of Reason*, Bridget refers to the election of a Labour government in 1997 as an optimistic and hopeful development in British political history and to the early death and unhappy marriage of Princess Diana as a tragic event ('if someone so beautiful and gorgeous could … feel unloved and lonely' writes Bridget, wistfully),[77] but such external references and observations are notably not included in the corresponding film.

The following chapter will focus on British cinema's more direct treatment of sex and sexuality, but before that one can note that sex scenes featuring Bridget in bed with a lover are certainly discreetly presented in the third film (and largely absent from the second movie, where Bridget declines to join Daniel in a 'threesome' sexual encounter with a Thai escort). This may be part of the romantic comedic traditions in which film-makers are reluctant to stage explicit scenes of sexual coupling for fear of gaining an 18 certificate or of diluting the romantic and comedic aspect of these narratives by emphasising the sexual side of the relationships. Given that the films hark back in some ways to earlier decades of British cinema, there may also be something of the reticence and discreetness associated with post-war British film-making in the presentation of events. Bridget also appears to feel that her sex life is over in *Bridget Jones's Baby*, and it is only through Miranda's efforts and encouragement that she finds herself in a setting where she does end up sleeping with someone whom she has just met.

As for Bridget's successors in British cinema, two characters portrayed by Emilia Clarke appear to evoke Bridget Jones's way of behaving and perceiving the world, but in a more selfless manner, perhaps, than Bridget herself. In *Me Before You* (Thea Sharrock, 2016), Clarke plays Louisa Clark, a happy-go-lucky, optimistic, but unambitious woman, who finds work caring for a young man, Will Traynor (Sam Claflin). Will has been left almost completely paralysed following a road accident and has come to feel that his life is no longer worth living, particularly as his former girlfriend has married a former work partner of his. Clark's warm and loving nature and her colourful way of dressing brings Will out of his depression to some extent.[78] But in a sad narrative development (which has more in common with tragic events in the third Bridget Jones novel than with any of the Bridget films), she fails in trying to deter him from ending his life and accompanies him to an assisted suicide clinic in Switzerland, where he dies. Prior to his death, Louisa had expressed a desire for them to be together as a couple, despite his condition. Will believed, however, that this would limit her life far too much for him to contemplate the possibility of such a union. In one sense, Will ends his life so that Lou can live, having bequeathed her a significant sum of money in his will. This offers her the possibility of building a new and potentially better life for herself, and the final scene in the film reveals Lou residing in Paris, seemingly mulling over her options for the future.

In *Last Christmas* (Paul Feig, 2018), Emilia Clarke plays Kate (or Katerina, as her mother prefers to call her), a young Yugoslavian woman who makes a living working in an all-year-round Christmas shop in London's Covent Garden. Kate claims that performing in musical theatre is what she really wishes to do – 'I'm not a career elf', she stresses – but success in this field proves to be elusive in what she admits are 'dark times'. Kate, like Scrooge in Charles Dickens's *A Christmas Carol* (1843), is encouraged to become a better, more caring person by a mysterious spirit (in Kate's case by the ghost of the dead man who had agreed to let his heart be donated to someone in need after his death, and therefore ends up saving Kate's life when she needs a new heart). Kate subsequently becomes a focus for helping the homeless and manages to build bridges with her estranged sister, Marta (Lydia Leonard), whom she has 'outed' as a lesbian to her surprised family. Through Clarke's witty, self-reflexive, effervescent performance, her character becomes less self-centred and pleasure-seeking (the earlier part of the narrative presents Kate sleeping with men whom she has just met, although the film does not include any actual sex scenes). The film concludes with a joyful charity concert for the homeless which brings disparate communities of people together, the occasion acting as a metaphor for the film-makers' suggestion that such transnational and communal fellow-feeling was the path which Britain's citizens (in a time of 'Brexit means Brexit') should pursue, if the country was to become, once again, a worthy, welcoming, self-respecting nation with 'love in its heart' for all humanity.

The real successor to Bridget Jones as an iconic female figure has undoubtedly been Phoebe Waller-Bridge's creation of *Fleabag*, broadcast on BBC television between 2016 and 2019. Cosmo Landesman, writing in the *Sunday Times*, recalled a date with a woman he had been on where he was asked, 'Would you rather go out ... with Bridget Jones or with Fleabag?' His reply was 'neither. Bridget is too sweet, Fleabag too crazy,' although he claimed to have learned 'from experience' not 'to express any reservations, however minor, about Fleabag'.[79] Certainly, the series and the one-woman play from which it stemmed became a cultural phenomenon (viewers of the 2015 British romantic comedy *Man Up* (Ben Palmer, 2015) will be surprised that Phoebe Waller-Bridge appears only in an early scene before disappearing from view).

The third and possibly final Bridget movie focuses on Bridget as an older woman (quite different to the much younger and more outspoken character of Fleabag) and shows how she tries to cope with the challenges of having a baby in her forties and losing her job. Despite setbacks, she aims to demonstrate that people should not give up their hopes for a potentially better future to come. When Miranda interviews George Wilkins (Patrick Malahide), the British Foreign Secretary, about the possibility of the 'spirit of democracy' being allowed to grow in a part of West Africa now free of a ruthless dictatorship, he replies, 'Let's hope so.' 'I'll take that,' replies Miranda enthusiastically, and this exchange (even though it does not involve Bridget herself) might stand ultimately for all the positive emotions and feelings underlying the films' consistently entertaining mission to tell us nothing less than the 'whole truth' about Bridget Jones and her desires, hopes and experiences in modern-day British culture and society.

Notes

1 Box-office figure cited in Nick Hunt, 'Close Up: Sharon Maguire', *Screen International*, 1305 (20–26 April 2001), p. 15.
2 Box-office claim made in 'Advertisement: Working Title Films would like to thank UIP and Universal very much for this outstanding result', *Screen International*, 1478 (26 November–2 December 2004), p. 38.
3 Box-office figure cited in Olly Richards, 'Saving Bridget Jones: How Director Sharon Maguire Delivered *Bridget Jones's Baby* and Rescued a Franchise', *Empire*, 333 (March 2017), p. 139.
4 *Screen International* reported that up to autumn 2003, the novels written by Helen Fielding, *Bridget Jones's Diary* (London: Picador, 1997 [1996]) and *Bridget Jones: The Edge of Reason* (London: Picador, 2000 [1999]), had achieved worldwide sales of 10.5 million and 5.5 million respectively. Author not identified, *Screen International*, 1474 (29 October–4 November 2004), p. 31.
5 Lizzie Cernik, 'Consciously Uncoupled!', *Guardian* (6 November 2019), G2, p. 9.

6 Alexander Walker, 'Fantasy Made Flesh', review of *Bridget Jones's Diary* (2001), *Evening Standard* (12 April 2001), p. 35.
7 Barbara Ellen, 'Feeling Single, Seeing Double', review of *Bridget Jones's Diary* (2001), *The Times* (12 April 2001), p. 14.
8 Renée Zellweger quoted in Terri White, 'How a Baby Is Made', *Empire*, 327 (September 2016), p. 97.
9 Clive Bloom, *Bestsellers: Popular Fiction since 1900* (Basingstoke: Palgrave, 2002), p. 53. Bloom sees Bridget as symbolising what he describes as a 'lost "post"-feminist generation of women' who are 'avid readers of both self-help manuals and neurotic comedy novels that satirise them' (p. 53).
10 Walker, 'Fantasy Made Flesh', p. 35. Annette Kuhn described Bridget in only slightly more flattering language as a 'less than beautiful, socially inept woman proving irresistible to suave, handsome – if slightly long-in-the-tooth men'. Annette Kuhn, 'Beeban Kidron', in Robert Murphy, Geoff Brown and Alan Burton (eds), *Directors in British and Irish Cinema* (London: British Film Institute, 2006), p. 343.
11 Angela McRobbie, *The Uses of Cultural Studies: A Textbook* (London: Sage Publications, 2005), p. 193. McRobbie notes that Bridget's character can be read as symbolising a certain kind of 'white Englishness', which is focused on 'tradition' and an 'ironic celebration of marriage … as the solution to the fears and anxieties of being a single girl' (p. 193).
12 Journalist Bryony Gordon's article celebrates the inclusion of Bridget Jones in a BBC *Woman's Hour* 2016 Power List of women 'who have made the most impact on female lives in the past seven decades'. Gordon praises the conception of the character, stating that Bridget 'took all the terrible bits of being single and made' audiences 'laugh about them. That ability to turn a negative into a positive is a wonderful quality to possess.' Bryony Gordon, 'Bridget Jones Made it OK to just Be Ourselves', *Daily Telegraph* (15 December 2016), p. 27.
13 Helen Fielding, *Bridget Jones: Mad about the Boy* (London: Vintage, 2014 [2013]), p. 212.
14 In the novel, *Bridget Jones: The Edge of Reason*, Bridget reads Rudyard Kipling's 1910 poem 'If' about the importance of treating 'Triumph and Disaster' in a similar fashion, while incarcerated in a Thailand women's correction prison. Bridget declares that the poem is 'Very good, almost like self-help book', although she is disturbed by the line about people losing their heads. In the film of *Bridget Jones's Baby* (2016), Mark congratulates Bridget on her ability to convert 'disasters into triumphs'. Fielding, *The Edge of Reason*, p. 308.
15 Claire Mortimer, *Romantic Comedy* (London: Routledge, 2010), p. 126.
16 *Ibid.*, p. 120.
17 Fay Weldon, 'Let's Hear it for Big Knickers', review of *Bridget Jones: The Edge of Reason*, *The Times* (6 November 2004), p. 4.
18 Mark Kermode, in his review of *Bridget Jones: The Edge of Reason*, touched upon what he saw as the essentialist binary opposition nature of the two characters by referring to them simply as 'nice Mark Darcy and nasty Daniel Cleaver'. In her review of *Bridget Jones's Diary* (2001), Barbara Ellen described them as

'dull Mark' and 'dashing bounder Daniel'. Mark Kermode, 'Big Girls' Pants', *New Statesman* (15 November 2004), p. 45 and Ellen, 'Feeling Single, Seeing Double', p. 14.
19 Andrew Spicer, 'The Reluctance to Commit: Hugh Grant and the New British Romantic Comedy', in Phil Powrie, Ann Davies and Bruce Babington (eds), *The Trouble with Men: Masculinities in European and Hollywood Cinema* (London: Wallflower Press, 2004), p. 84.
20 In a 2002 interview, Hugh Grant expressed similar views to Daniel Cleaver about how even the best relationships may only be fleeting as he felt that attempts at monogamy and marriage are possibly not viable over a long period of time. He commented philosophically: 'I know people who are serial boyfriends and I'm not like that. I want to say: "Why not have some fun for a few months?" ... I worry that I've made the wrong choice being unmarried and without a family. Although I take satisfaction from the hugely prevalent failures of my friends' marriages.' Ed Halliwell, 'Comic Genius, 41, Seeks Steady Relationship, Or Failing That, Sex', interview with Hugh Grant, *Empire*, 155 (May 2002), p. 66.
21 One might wonder at the circumscribed nature of the opportunities available to Bridget in terms of love and sex in the three films. Geoffrey Macnab, reviewing the 2004 film, concluded that 'Paradoxically, Bridget is a prim and naïve figure' who 'despite talking endlessly of "shagging", does little of it'. Geoffrey Macnab, review of *Bridget Jones: The Edge of Reason*, *Screen International*, 1474 (29 October 2004), p. 31.
22 Tom's sex life as a gay man is not quite so invisible in the novels. Bridget in one diary entry states (in relation to Tom's sexual activities) that she 'Felt familiar flash of envy at ease of gay sex, where people seem to shag each other immediately just because they both feel like it and nobody worries about having three dates first or how long to leave it before phoning afterwards.' Fielding, *The Edge of Reason*, p. 83.
23 Ellen, 'Feeling Single, Seeing Double, p. 13.
24 Walker, 'Fantasy Made Flesh', p. 35.
25 Philip Kerr, 'A Bridget too Far', review of *Bridget Jones's Diary* (2001), *New Statesman* (23 April 2001), p. 44.
26 Peter Bradshaw, review of *Bridget Jones's Baby*, *Guardian* (6 September 2016), p. 7.
27 Richards, 'Saving Bridget Jones', p. 138.
28 Kermode, 'Big Girls' Pants'.
29 Will Self, 'It's Downhill all the Way for Bridget and her Diary', review of *Bridget Jones: The Edge of Reason*, *Evening Standard* (11 November 2004), p. 29.
30 Jessica Winter, film review of *Bridget Jones: The Edge of Reason*, *Sight and Sound*, 14:12 (December 2004), p. 41.
31 In his seminal essay on British comic strips in the 1930s, George Orwell noted that they all seemed to exist in a world which appeared unchanged since around 1910 – 'foreigners are exactly the same figures of fun that they always were ... and no one has heard of slumps, booms, unemployment'. One might say that Bridget's mother appears to have acquired a view of the world outside Britain

which contains many similar traits. George Orwell, 'Boys' Weeklies' (1940), reprinted in Orwell, *Inside the Whale and Other Essays* (Middlesex: Penguin, 1978), pp. 196–7.

32 Fielding, *Bridget Jones's Diary*, p. 7.

33 Laurie Penny, *Unspeakable Things: Sex, Lies and Revolution* (London: Bloomsbury, 2015 [2014]), p. 225.

34 Regarding representations of sexual banter in the workplace, what is deemed permissible in comic terms may also change over time. In the first movie, Daniel Cleaver, described by Bridget as the 'office scoundrel', promises to avoid 'non-PC overtones in future' in his email correspondence with Bridget. This declaration is, however, immediately followed by his statement that he likes her 'tits in that top'. The directness and lack of wit in this rather crude remark to a co-worker may appear less funny and acceptable to a modern-day audience than it possibly did at the time of the film's release (in *The Edge of Reason* film, Bridget does tell Cleaver to 'Back off or I'll report you to a sexual harassment tribunal').

35 Rosamund Unwin, 'Bridget's #MeToo Moment at Hands of Mr Tits Pervert: Helen Fielding's beloved Character Reassesses her Past in a New Work', *Sunday Times* (30 September 2018), p. 3.

36 The Bridget Jones novels would almost certainly not have been highly regarded by Dr Leavis had he been able to witness their publication, and the film adaptations most definitely would not have been, as Leavis saw the cinema as having a wholly pernicious and regrettable cultural impact on its audiences. His 1930 *Mass Civilisation and Minority Culture* (the publication referred to by Cleaver) expresses particular concerns about the effects of the motion picture industry on passive audiences, writing that 'films … involve surrender, under conditions of hypnotic receptivity, to the cheapest emotional appeals, appeals the more insidious because they are associated with a compellingly vivid illusion of actual life'. F.R. Leavis, *Mass Civilisation and Minority Culture* (place of publication not identified: the Folcroft Press, 1969 edition; first published Cambridge: Minority Press, 1930), pp. 9–11.

37 In the novel *Bridget Jones: Mad about the Boy*, Bridget reveals that she got a 'Third in English Literature at Bangor University', which, perhaps, explains why her knowledge about F.R. Leavis proves to be rather shaky. Fielding, *Mad about the Boy*, p. 16. Ian Mackillop, in *F.R. Leavis: A Life in Criticism* (London: Allen Lane: The Penguin Press, 1995), records that F.R. Leavis 'did not become [a] professor and in the years after 1939 became increasingly bitter about his position in Cambridge' (p. 225). In his introduction to *English Literature In Our Time and the University* (London: Chatto & Windus, 1969), Leavis himself recorded in a spirited manner that he was only made a Reader in his 'sixty-fifth year', while 'charlatans' and 'dull mediocrities' were appointed to the Cambridge English faculty (pp. 22–3). This short imaginary exchange between Bridget and the late Dr Leavis therefore touches upon a number of complex issues about the class system, culture, English literature and the importance of value judgements in British culture, past and present.

38 For all his admiration of D.H. Lawrence, F.R. Leavis did not approve of the use of four letter words such as 'fucking' to describe the series of sexual acts which take place in *Lady Chatterley's Lover* (1928), declaring, 'To me, I must report, a great deal in them has always been strongly distasteful … perhaps … that only shows how little I have been able to submit myself to the beneficent potency of which I am still in need.' F.R. Leavis, 'The Orthodoxy of Enlightenment', *Anna Karenina and Other Essays* (London: Chatto & Windus, 1973), p. 237. Novelist Will Self imagines Richard Curtis in conversation with Bridget's creator, Helen Fielding, during his review of the second film as to whether Bridget would refer to sexual intercourse as shagging or fucking: 'Bridget would never use the F-word to describe having sex. She's not that sort of girl, is she Helen?' Self has Fielding replying that 'Shags' is the desired terminology for the film. Self, 'It's Downhill all the Way', p. 29.

39 Alwyn W. Turner in *Rejoice! Rejoice! Britain in the 1980s* (London: Aurum Press, 2013 [2010]) records that following the publication of his novel *The Satanic Verses* in 1988, Salman Rushdie had to go into hiding and enter a police protection programme in 1989 after the Ayatollah Khomeini called on 'Muslims to murder the writer and his publishers in revenge for alleged blasphemies' (p. 344). The presence of Rushdie in the film can be seen as a sign of how his situation had changed by 2001, and a positive statement by the film-makers in favour of artistic freedom of expression for writers.

40 Penny, *Unspeakable Things*, pp. 230–1.

41 Mark Steyn, 'The Cad v. the Stiff', *Spectator*, 286:9011 (21 April 2001), p. 50. Steyn informs his readers that 'there's no sodomy in the book', and concludes 'we must [therefore] be grateful for innovation where we find it'.

42 Penny, *Unspeakable Things*, p. 224.

43 Catherine Townsend's witty memoir of her romantic and sexual experiences as an American woman living in London in the 2000s possibly has a negative view of Bridget Jones's way of thinking in mind when she writes, 'Personally, I was sick of the assumption that a girl who was passionate about her job was condemning herself to a future of watching *Trisha* in a tracksuit while dozens of mewling cats weaved their way through her front room … maybe instead of moaning about their partners' success, men should raise their own game.' Catherine Townsend, *Sleeping Around: Secrets of a Sexual Adventuress* (London: John Murray, 2007), p. 244.

44 Bloom, *Bestsellers*, p. 53.

45 This attempt to say just what his wife means to him evokes memories of a scene from *Flame in the Streets* (Roy Ward Baker, 1961) in which John Mills's character states to his similarly dissatisfied and disappointed wife (as a way of reassuring her that their marriage has been worthwhile), 'People like me are always going to need people like you.'

46 Mark Steyn describes these diary entries glimpsed towards the end of the film as 'bog-standard schoolgirl effusions', lacking in the 'thirtysomething girls' confessional style that struck a chord with those millions of singletons' in the diary entries featured in the novels. Steyn, 'The Cad v. the Stiff'.

47 The phrase 'knowable communities' is taken from Raymond Williams's writings on the impersonality of the typical city in contrast to life in the country. Bridget works and lives in London, but her parents appear to live in the country. The change in setting when Bridget travels to Thailand serves to broaden the scope of the films' representations of modern life. Raymond Williams, *The Country and the City* (London: Chatto & Windus, 1973), p. 165.
48 Natasha Walter, *The New Feminism* (London: Virago, 2013 [1999]), p. 64.
49 David Harvey, *The Enigma of Capital and the Crises of Capitalism* (London: Profile Books, 2010), p. 120.
50 Anthony Quinn, 'Bridget Hits Rock Bottom', review of *Bridget Jones: The Edge of Reason, Independent* (12 November 2004), pp. 6–7.
51 Sukhdev Sandhu, review of *Bridget Jones: The Edge of Reason*, Daily Telegraph (12 November 2004), p. 19.
52 Novelist Fay Weldon felt that the decision to reveal Rebecca as a lesbian was something of a cynical move on the part of the production company, Working Title, to create a new kind of talking point for the film: 'One can almost hear them in the conference room creasing up ... we can have a girl-on-girl kiss. The press will have a field day. What a hoot.' Weldon, 'Let's Hear it for Big Knickers'.
53 Shere Hite, in *The Hite Report: A Nationwide Study on Female Sexuality* (London: Talmy Franklin Ltd, 1977 [1976]), argued that 'It is important for women to recognise their own potential for having sexual feelings for other women' (p. 276). Hite's view as applied to Bridget and Rebecca would seem to suggest that Bridget is ill advised to reject Rebecca's offer of love and affection as quickly as she does in the film.
54 Penny, *Unspeakable Things*, p. 215.
55 Sharon Maguire quoted in White, 'How a Baby Is Made', p. 97.
56 In *Bridget Jones: Mad about the Boy*, readers are informed in a terse sentence that Darcy dies in the 'Darfur region of Sudan' after he secures the release of 'British aid workers, who had been hostages of the rebel regime' in the area. Fielding, *Mad about the Boy*, pp. 122–3.
57 In his autobiography, Blair defended his controversial decision to assist the American military in bringing about regime change, claiming that he 'did what [he] thought was right. I stood by America when it needed standing by. Together we rid the world of a tyrant. Together we fought to uphold the Iraqis' right to a democratic government.' Blair acknowledged, however, that 'The cost in money and blood has been enormous', leading many to ponder this question – 'Had we foreseen what Iraq was going to be like following the removal of Saddam ... Should we have still done it?' Tony Blair, *Tony Blair: A Journey* (London: Hutchinson, 2010), p. 479.
58 Historian Alwyn W. Turner claimed that when Margaret Thatcher stated in 'March 1989, on the birth of a child to her son, Mark, that "We have become a grandmother", the use of the royal "we" did little to reassure those of her supporters who worried that she was becoming hopelessly out of touch.' Turner, *Rejoice! Rejoice!*, p. 349.

59 Fay Weldon describes Bridget's father as 'melancholy' in her article 'Let's Hear it for Big Knickers'. In the third novel in the series, Bridget's father is dead – 'The lung cancer took him in six months from diagnosis to funeral', records Bridget. Fielding, *Mad about the Boy*, p. 69.
60 Northrop Frye, *Anatomy of Criticism: Four Essays* (Princeton, NJ: Princeton University Press, 1973 [1957]), pp. 163–86. In the chapter entitled 'The Mythos of Spring: Comedy', Frye writes that 'The green world charges the comedies with the symbolism of the victory of summer over winter', while noting that 'In the rituals and myths the earth that produces the rebirth is generally a female figure' (p. 183).
61 Justine King, 'Crossing Thresholds: The Contemporary British Woman's Film', in Andrew Higson (ed.), *Dissolving Views: Key Writings on British Cinema* (London: Cassell, 1996), p. 231.
62 David Lodge, *Working with Structuralism: Essays and Reviews on Nineteenth- and Twentieth-Century Literature* (London: Routledge & Kegan Paul, 1981), p. 149. Lodge also notes that an author's 'refusal to tie the marriage knot' between leading characters may be deployed to express 'a bleaker and more pessimistic view that life rarely conforms to our desires, or our notions of justice' (p. 149).
63 Frye, *Anatomy of Criticism*, p. 167.
64 Eithne O'Neill in a *Positif* (October 2016) review of *Bridget Jones's Baby* claims that 'A fourth film seems promised for the fans' ('Pour les fans, un quatrième film est promis'), p. 48. The ending of the film can be seen as offering a formally satisfying conclusion to events, although enthusiasts of the movies might naturally be interested in what happens next, particularly as plot developments in the third novel are quite different and much darker.
65 Northrop Frye, in *A Natural Perspective: The Development of Shakespearean Comedy and Romance* (New York and London: Columbia University Press, 1965), associates comedic endings in Shakespeare with a move from 'death to rebirth, decadence to renewal, winter to spring, darkness to a new dawn' (p. 121). Germaine Greer has claimed that 'One of the most significant apologists of marriage as a way of life and a road to salvation was Shakespeare', while acknowledging that Shakespeare 'recognised it as a difficult state of life, requiring discipline, sexual energy, mutual respect and great forbearance', knowing that 'there were no easy answers to marital problems'. Germaine Greer, *The Female Eunuch* (London: Fourth Estate, 2012 [1970]), pp. 232–5.
66 Frye, *A Natural Perspective*, p. 92.
67 F.R. Leavis, 'D.H. Lawrence – the Novelist', *Listener*, 42:1079 (29 September 1949), p. 544.
68 In the novel, *Bridget Jones: Mad about the Boy*, the relationships between Mark, Daniel and Bridget are presented as ultimately tragic, rather than farcical, with Daniel having become a rather pathetic, faded drunk who no longer appeals to Bridget, and Mark (as noted earlier) having been killed while working abroad and trying to save the lives of others. Fielding, *Mad about the Boy*.
69 Among those who 'fall on the wrong side of history' in the films are Adolf Hitler (1889–1945) and Saddam Hussein (1937–2006). Bridget does refer to

Hitler twice in the films – declaring in *The Edge of Reason* that everyone in life deserves a second chance except him – and she also alludes to Saddam Hussein twice. These unexpected and somewhat surreal references testify to her ability to prove that she can laugh at such dictators and show that she is not afraid of what they represent.

70 Clive James, 'Getting Married Later', review of *The Female Eunuch* by Germaine Greer, *Listener*, 84:2169 (22 October 1970), p. 553.
71 Angela McRobbie, *The Aftermath of Feminism: Gender, Culture and Social Change* (London: Sage, 2009), pp. 85–6.
72 Simon Critchley, *On Humour* (London: Routledge, 2002), pp. 70–1.
73 Annette Kuhn, 'Women's Genres', *Screen*, 25:1 (January/February 1984), pp. 27–8.
74 Sarah Crompton, 'Curtis Land in 10 Steps', *Daily Telegraph* (7 April 2001), Arts and Books section, p. 9.
75 F.R. Leavis, 'In Defence of *Scrutiny*', letter to the *London Magazine* (March 1955), reprinted in John Tasker (ed.), *Letters in Criticism by F.R. Leavis* (London: Chatto & Windus, 1974), p. 51.
76 McRobbie, *The Aftermath of Feminism*, p. 71.
77 Fielding, *The Edge of Reason*, p. 326. In this novel, Bridget declares that 'Labour stands for the principle of sharing, kindness, gays' and 'single mothers' (p. 58).
78 Anna Smith described Emilia Clarke's character in *Me Before You* (2016) as 'a caricatured Bridget Jones pretender whose pratfalling sits oddly with the story's mawkish tone'. Anna Smith, film review, *Empire*, 325 (July 2016), p. 57.
79 Cosmo Landesman, 'Don't be Frightened of Fleabag, Chaps. She's really One of the Lads', *Sunday Times* (3 March 2019), p. 27.

1 Bosie (Colin Morgan) and Oscar (Rupert Everett) reunite on foreign shores in *The Happy Prince* (2018).

2 'Till Death Do Us Part': Ted (Daniel Craig) and Sylvia (Gwyneth Paltrow) get married in *Sylvia* (2003).

3 Iris Murdoch (Judi Dench) and John Bayley (Jim Broadbent) face the future together in *Iris* (2001).

4 Professional colleagues or potential partners in love? Rebecca (Jacinda Barrett) and Mark (Colin Firth) enjoy each other's company in *Bridget Jones: The Edge of Reason* (2004).

5 'Was every look I ever gave you a lie?': Bridget (Renée Zellweger), Rebecca and the 'female gaze' in *Bridget Jones: The Edge of Reason* (2004).

6 'He really didn't stick up for me at the lawyers' supper': Bridget compares tales of woe with her fellow inmates in *Bridget Jones: The Edge of Reason* (2004).

7 'I need someone to please help me': Candy Fiveways (Carmen Electra) seeks release from her chains in *I Want Candy* (2007).

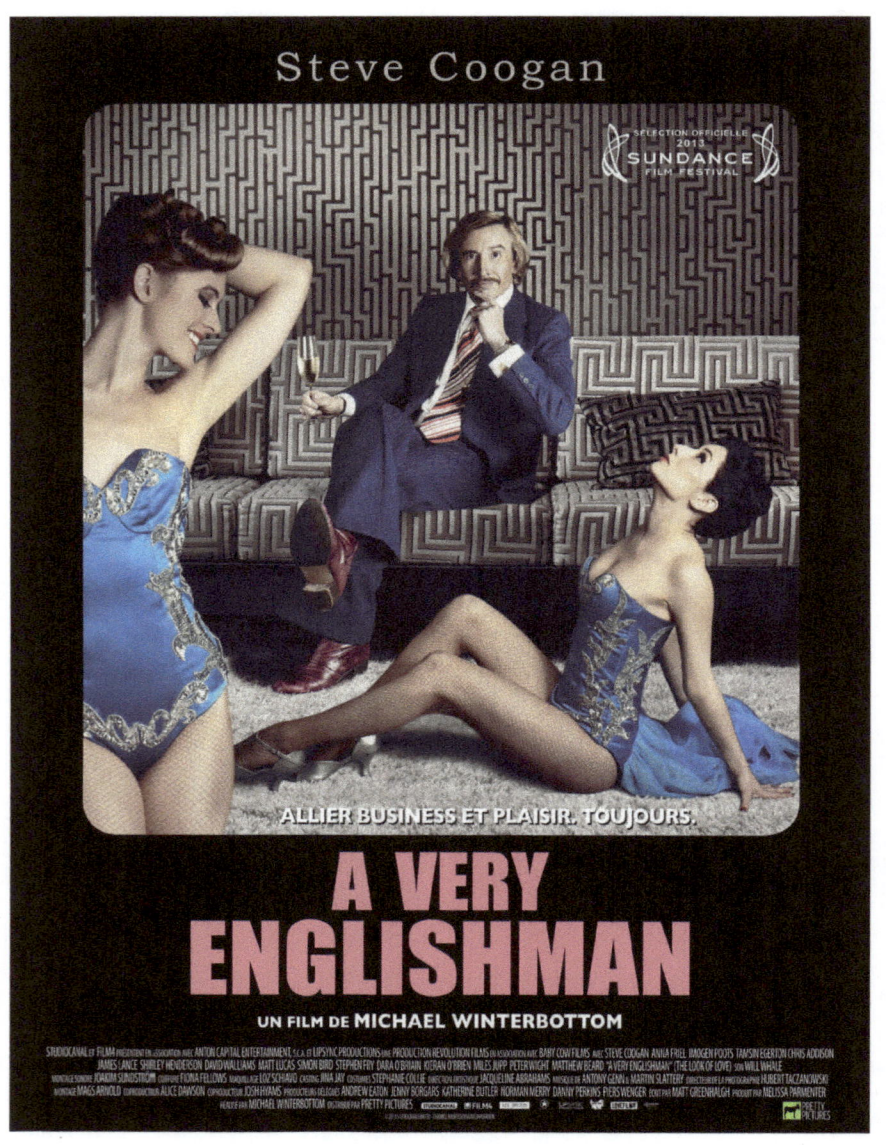

8 Paul Raymond (Steve Coogan) discovers the power of the 'male gaze' in *The Look of Love* (2013).

9 Florence (Saoirse Ronan) and Edward (Billy Howle) part company forever in *On Chesil Beach* (2017).

10 'Isn't marriage part of the whole system we've been railing against all these years?': Laura (Holliday Grainger) and Tyler (Alia Shawkat) discuss the concept of the 'modern wedding' in *Animals* (2019).

11 Emma (Anne Hathaway) and Dexter (Jim Sturgess) share an idyllic moment on holiday in *One Day* (2011).

12 'It's about making a bond with someone': Anna (Kathryn Worth) and Oakley (Tom Hiddleston) discuss sex, marriage and having children in *Unrelated* (2007).

13 Pupil and teacher interaction: Steven (Andrew Simpson) and Miss Hart (Cate Blanchett), his art teacher, in *Notes on a Scandal* (2006).

14 Barbara (Judi Dench) gets the inside story on Sheba's shocking behaviour in *Notes on a Scandal* (2006).

15 'I've been here before': Dan (Jude Law) and Alice (Natalie Portman) revisit the past in *Closer* (2004).

16 'It's not a war': Alice and Larry (Clive Owen) discuss sexual politics in the 'Paradise Suite' in *Closer* (2004).

17 'That's my dad': Ronit (Rachel Weisz) and the Jewish community pay their respects in *Disobedience* (2017).

18 Mutual disdain hiding mutual desire? Johnny (Josh O'Connor) and Gheorghe (Alec Secareanu) in *God's Own Country* (2017).

19 The teenage group about to tear itself apart in *Kidulthood* (2006).

20 Sam (Noel Clarke) and Lexi (Scarlett Alice Johnson) wonder whether they can trust each other in *Adulthood* (2008).

21 Members of 'Lesbians and Gays Support the Miners' commemorate the end of the strike in *Pride* (2014).

22 Intimate encounters in a virus-ridden world: Michael (Ewan McGregor) and Susan (Eva Green) in *Perfect Sense* (2011).

4

'No sex, please – we're British?': Sex, sensibility and British cinema

In a *Monthly Film Bulletin* review of *Carry On Loving* (Gerald Thomas, 1970), the anonymous reviewer noted that 'The subject is sex, but needless to say it remains a subject, since the characters shy away ... from any practical manifestation of their ceaseless preoccupation with copulation.'[1] *Carry On Emmannuelle* (Gerald Thomas, 1978), however, aimed to show that the franchise could engage with sexual acts in a more upfront fashion, in this case by placing a woman, the eponymous Emmannuelle (Suzanne Danielle), at the centre of events. French-born Emmannuelle is revealed to be unabashed at enjoying having sex with as many different men as possible. She refuses to express any regrets about her behaviour on national television ('This is, how you say, bullshit', she declares forcefully), much to the amusement of the characters played by such *Carry On* stalwarts as Joan Sims, Kenneth Connor and Peter Butterworth. Emmannuelle's sexual activities are not directly shown to audiences, but her behaviour is seen as shocking by the British media and newspapers (she admits to sleeping with both the Prime Minister and the Leader of the Opposition). Emmannuelle, who arrives in Britain on Concorde, is in effect, though, ultimately 'grounded' in her searches for sexual satisfaction when her ambassador husband (Kenneth Williams) replaces her contraceptive pills with fertility pills, and she subsequently gives birth to six children. Having more openly acknowledged the power of female sexual desire than was the case in previous *Carry On* narratives, alongside presenting Williams's character as a prolific father and successful lover of women ('That was wonderful, darling'), the writers and directors of the long-running series perhaps felt they could go no further in their comic-based explorations of changing sexual mores and times. It was therefore left to other film-makers and film franchises to examine issues around everyday British erotic behaviour and individuals' fantasies of sexual fulfilment and contentment.

Activist and writer Richard Neville (1941–2016) proclaims in his polemical study *Power Play* (published in 1970, the year of *Carry On Loving*) that a new youthful generation had done away with such courtship conventions as a 'Table for two ... saying it with flowers, cementing it with diamonds'. According to Neville, such traditional courtship rituals were as 'dated as Terry Thomas in a smoking jacket ... If a couple like each other, they make love.'[2] Such a claim, suggesting that satisfying sexual desires now took precedence over the cultivation of romantic feelings or dogged adherence to conventional dating practices appears to be confirmed by such 1970s British films as *Au Pair Girls* (Val Guest, 1972), *Eskimo Nell* (Martin Campbell, 1975), *Confessions of a Window Cleaner* (Val Guest, 1974), *Percy's Progress* (Ralph Thomas, 1974) and *The Ups and Downs of a Handyman* (John Sealey, 1976), films offering a fundamentally carnivalesque, celebratory and sometimes ironic perspective on sex in modern British society. By way of a contrast, films such as *Cool It, Carol!* (Peter Walker, 1970), *Permissive* (Lindsay Shonteff, 1970), *Escort Girls* (Donovan Winter, 1974) and *Intimate Games* (Tudor Gates, 1976) were 1970s British films which presented a more probing and, at times, disturbing view of sexual relationships, attitudes and pairings during this particular decade (the latter film ends with a psychology lecturer (George Baker) having a nervous breakdown after listening to details of his students' varied sexual fantasies).

This chapter will explore how British cinema during the 2000s witnessed the production and release of a number of films which harked back to these 1970s treatments of sex as a subject for both humorous and dramatic exploration. *Sex Lives of the Potato Men* (Andy Humphries, 2004), *Dogging – a Love Story* (Simon Ellis, 2009) and *I Want Candy* (Stephen Surjik, 2007) were all films which might be placed essentially within the comic mode of exploring sex in modern British culture. *Sex Lives of the Potato Men*, with its rather prosaic and matter-of-fact title, appears to evoke (in particular) 1970s sex comedy films featuring an occupation such as window cleaner, salesman or handyman in the title. *Dogging – a Love Story*, with its seemingly contradictory title, explores the world of men and women who wish to have sex in public places and do not mind being watched (or possibly even recorded) by groups of voyeuristic and enthusiastic spectators. The title raises the question of how romance might fit into what appears on the surface to be a form of sexual behaviour which privileges non-exclusive, non-sentimental and monogamous relationships. *I Want Candy*, drawing upon the plot of a self-referential 1970s sex comedy, *Eskimo Nell* (1975), depicts the chaotic and farcical situations which arise when a group of film production students embark on making a low budget pornographic movie in the British suburban home of one of the film-making group's parents.

Animals (Sophie Hyde, 2019) probes the inherent physicality of human beings and the desires felt by individuals (in this case, two women friends living in Dublin) to experience the exciting sensations created by drugs, drink and sexual encounters. *9 Songs* (Michael Winterbottom, 2004), with its single-minded focus on the sexual behaviour of a particular couple (a British man and an American woman), arguably seeks to question the whole concept of pornography itself as a helpful term. The film also seems to ask why most mainstream film-makers have shied away from depicting and exploring the sexual interactions and behaviour of couples on screen in unmediated and uncensored forms, instead often presenting lovers as pursuing their passions under bedclothes, a convenient method, perhaps, for shielding their naked bodies and inflamed desires. *The Look of Love* (2013), also directed by Michael Winterbottom, was a biographical picture which sought to explore the life and times of Paul Raymond (1925–2008), an entrepreneur who, particularly during the 1970s, was credited with seeking to transform 'Britain's attitude to sex'.[3] Paul Raymond's personal story is hence linked in the narrative with a more public story concerning what some might term the growth of the 'sex industry' in Britain from the 1960s onwards.

As a way of considering the significance and importance of some of the developments Paul Raymond was associated with, in making sex a topic for open discussion and colourful explicit representation, this chapter will compare and contrast the treatment of sex as a vital part of a relationship in two films specifically concerned with this theme – *On Chesil Beach* (Dominic Cooke, 2017), set in the early 1960s and at a time when discussions, acknowledgements and representations of sex were not a prominent feature of British society, and *9 Songs*, set in the 2000s, when such features were more readily identifiable as aspects of everyday British culture.

Gilles Deleuze and Félix Guattari, in their seminal study *Anti-Oedipus: Capitalism and Schizophrenia* (1972), investigate the complex links between 'political economy and libidinal economy' in our everyday lives, and note that those who emphasise the importance of the right to be lazy and non-productive, and 'to dream' and engage in 'fantasy production',[4] will always be subject to criticism from those who stress the importance of moderation in sensual pleasures and of living responsibly and dutifully within society. Tym Manley, in a 1975 *New Statesman* article on magazines such as *Penthouse*, *Mayfair* and *Men Only* and the ideas propagated by these publications about what constitutes a worthwhile and fulfilled life, argues that 'in Britain, in default of concrete, spiritual, social, or even obtainable materialistic goals, we have made of sex a quasi-religion'. Manley feels that, as a result, 'more has come to be expected of [sex] than it can possibly provide'.[5]

The films discussed in this chapter (in their distinctive and idiosyncratic ways) all explore these questions, issues and concerns regarding the importance and significance of sex, variations in sexual behaviour, attitudes and aspirations, alongside the difficulties of forging positive and productive connections between the worlds of work and play, sex and love in modern-day

British culture. The issue of total commitment to one person versus a freedom to interact sexually with many diverse people (as demonstrated by Emmannuelle in the 1978 film) is also a pertinent topic in many of these films. If characters in these movies generally move towards excess rather than restraint and caution in their personal and private lives, such choices ensure that their experiences within the narratives are generally captivating to audiences, as a great deal may be at stake in the characters' behaviour and attitudes.

Some of these post-2000 British sex comedy-dramas (perhaps partly because of implied connections with their 1970s predecessors in the field) did not receive favourable or flattering reviews from film critics in Britain upon their release. Deborah Ross claimed in the *Spectator* that *I Want Candy* was 'distasteful ... insulting to women' and to 'Eastern Europeans', and concluded in a damning summation, 'This is a British sex comedy that isn't sexy' or 'comedic which may ... make it very, very British indeed'.[6] Jonathan Romney, in his *Screen International* review of *Dogging – a Love Story*, argued that the film-makers had 'astutely' chosen 'a tabloid-friendly topic' for exploration, although he felt that the movie was ultimately 'as tawdry and tired as a British sex comedy of the 1970s'.[7] Nick Dawson, writing about *9 Songs* in *Empire*, declared that the only parts of the film he enjoyed were the nine musical interludes in the movie.[8] In a 2005 *Cineaste* article, Pawel Pawlikowski asked his interviewer, 'You saw [*9 Songs*], didn't you? It was a joke, wasn't it?'[9] Deborah Ross in the *Spectator* claimed that *The Look of Love* was 'so astonishingly uncritical' in its portrayal of Paul Raymond and his life that it made 'posing for porn mags or getting your kit off in some seedy Soho dive seem like the most fulfilling and joyful thing a woman can ever do'.[10] Such criticisms suggest that the films' treatment of their subject material could be considered offensive and distasteful, illustrating that the inclusion of implicit or explicit sex scenes in narratives, and the subsequent methods and strategies adopted by particular film-makers for engaging with the subject of sex in British feature films, were still matters capable of inciting controversy, concern and sometimes even condemnation from film critics and cultural commentators.

A different country? Aspects of sex and sexuality in late 1960s and 1970s British film culture

Reviewing a film depicting Oscar Wilde's rise and tragic fall, *Oscar Wilde* (Gregory Ratoff, 1960), Leonard Mosley in the *Daily Express* argued that one of the effects of the 'Lady Chatterley' trial in 1960 was to put pressure on what he termed the foundations of 'prejudice and prudery' existing within British culture during 1960s Britain. Mosley claimed that 'Striptease theatres thrive in Soho. Four-letter words sprinkle the pages of the latest novels. Emotional and sexual dilemmas ... crop up on practically every screen.'[11] The trial which Mosley refers to was the court case brought by the Director of Public Prosecutions against Penguin Books for publishing an unexpurgated edition of D.H. Lawrence's 1928 novel *Lady Chatterley's Lover*. As the trial unfolded, it appeared at times as if the fictional female protagonist was being treated as if she were a real person, on trial for 'committing adultery' and of being 'some kind' of deviant figure or 'nymphomaniac'.[12] Frank Kermode, writing in 1962, claimed that in Lawrence's novel 'Lady Chatterley is the Sleeping Princess and also England on the point of death'. In such a scenario, the kiss that 'wakes her' up,[13] and symbolically the nation, must be both powerful and uncompromising. The book, if thought of in such terms, therefore had to be provocative, polemical and uncompromising as far as Lawrence was concerned, if it was to have a significant, meaningful and lasting impact upon its readers. In the novel, Lawrence notably leaves the ultimate fate and future of Lady Chatterley and her gamekeeper lover, Mellors, unrepresented, perhaps because in late 1920s British society it was not easy to imagine what might become of an adulterous liaison between an upper-class woman and a working-class man (both without work at the close of the novel) who are expecting a baby outside marriage.[14] Lawrence died in 1930 with his book banned in Britain, and it was not until this 1960 court case, when a not guilty verdict was arrived at by the jury, that it was freely and legally available to be read in his native country.

Film-makers in Britain still faced restrictions in how far they could depict sexual relationships on screen in their films in ways which might echo the questing spirit of Lawrence in his tale of Lady Chatterley and her lover. Derek Hill, in an *Encounter* essay of 1960 about the work of the British Board of Film Censors, reported that the Film Board opposed 'nudity' in any forms, any 'suggestion of sexual fulfilment' on the part of depicted lovers, and forbade what he termed discussions of 'sexual ethics' or 'departures from accepted sexual conventions' in films passed for exhibition in British cinemas.[15] The landmark Lady Chatterley trial, and the sense that D.H. Lawrence had been belatedly vindicated and validated, nonetheless encouraged directors and writers to work towards pushing the boundaries of what could be permitted when setting out to depict and dramatise the sexual and emotional experiences of characters in British feature film narratives.

In *Here We Go Round the Mulberry Bush* (Clive Donner, 1968), seventeen-year-old Jamie (Barry Evans) declares to his girlfriend, Mary (Judy Geeson) in the woods, 'Now my Lady Chatterley, I'll show you why they put the game in gamekeeper!' Jamie finds, however, that his beloved Mary, unlike Constance Chatterley, is not willing to settle down to the prospect of sex with possibly just one man (i.e. him) for the rest of her life. At the close of the film, though, he is looking forward to the prospect of meeting new women when he starts studying at Manchester University, now that he and Mary have gone their separate ways. Pauline Kael, reviewing *Here We Go Round the Mulberry Bush* on its release at an American 'art house' cinema, was not enamoured of the film's stylised and casual approach to sexual relationships, claiming that 'the sex has no more character than the mating of penguins ... less, because that might have a certain authenticity ... When you come out, you want to see a movie with somebody in it.'[16]

It is not clear whether Pauline Kael saw later examples of British sex comedies from the 1970s in American cinemas, and if she did, her thoughts are not recorded in subsequent edited collections of her reviews. A fellow American, however, writer Bill Bryson, recalled that watching *Suburban Wife-Swap* (Derek Ford, 1972) in a Dover cinema in 1973 'provided a rich fund of social and lexical information'. Bryson wryly claimed that the film introduced him to such terms as 'dirty weekend ... au pair ... shirt-lifter and swift shag against the cooker, all of which have proved variously useful since'.[17] These sex comedies of 1970s British cinema have never enjoyed a high critical reputation and have been summed up by Julian Petley as 'ghastly British cinematic abominations',[18] and Andy Medhurst as 'a monstrously popular procession of titillation-fests'.[19] Matthew Street, in his 2005 study *Shepperton Babylon: The Lost Worlds of British Cinema*, argued, however, that such 'productions, irrespective of their poor quality and vulgarity, require restoration to the narrative of our national cinema', as they were 'engaged in the business of projecting Britain, and the British character'.[20] Ian Conrich, in a journal essay on 'The British Style of Sexploitation', has similarly argued that 'the British sex film ... can assist in explicating questions of Britishness and the national libido'.[21]

The 1973 comedy *No Sex Please, We're British* (Cliff Owen) appears to have been made with such an aspiration in mind. In this film, bank clerk Brian (Ronnie Corbett) finds that through the mistake of a 'Scandinavian import company' he keeps getting sent pornographic material, including photographs, blue films and a collection of hardback books entitled *1001 Perversions*. Trying to dispose of these items by flushing them down the toilet, setting fire to them in a public park or putting them down the waste-disposal unit proves to be of no avail. Brian's farcical and unsuccessful attempts to dispose of the material also perhaps testify to the impossibility of ridding British society of pornographic images and films from this time on. Brian declares to various representatives of law and order that the books are just packages 'full of nothing' and that the books he is anxiously holding are just items he is taking 'back to the library'. Brian's declarations are in part aimed at pacifying his employer at the bank, Mr Bromley (Arthur Lowe), a man who takes a firm stand against pornography. Bromley, however, would appear to be a secret frequenter of two high-class prostitutes (played by Valerie Leon and Margaret Nolan) who crop up in the narrative, making the point that some of those protesting most strongly about the so-called excesses of the permissive society may also be secretly enjoying some of its pleasures illicitly and hypocritically. This adaptation of a highly successful stage play features external scenes shot on location in Windsor, thus appearing to suggest that what Mr Bromley describes as the 'rising tide of pornography' is making its presence felt outside Soho. At the film's close, as Brian runs away from his pursuers in Windsor Park, he states that he is heading for a life of exile in Canada, following his apparent failure to sever the ties between himself and a seemingly never-ending gathering and accumulation of pornographic material. Paul Newland, in his 2013 study *British Films of the 1970s*, notes how the film gives a voice to those who are against pornography, as well as providing audiences with moments of farce, near nudity and potential 'titillation' as events proceed and unravel. Newland sees the depiction of such opposing elements as evidence of what he terms the 'sexual tensions pulling at an increasingly fragmented British society' at the time of the film's production and release.[22]

Such a proliferation of provocative sexual images within the public domain inevitably had an effect upon the kinds of films being produced for exhibition and distribution in British cinemas. Historian Dominic Sandbrook in a study of 1970s Britain claimed that between 1971 and 1975 'a staggering forty-three' sex comedies were released, without which, he claimed, 'the British film industry would have virtually disappeared'.[23] Hence, in his study of British popular culture in the 1970s, Leon Hunt was able to entitle a chapter exploring the phenomenon of the 'sexploitation' movie 'Can You Keep it Up for a Decade?'.[24]

Films and Filming described *Eskimo Nell* in 1974 as a 'warning to those who seek fame and fortune in the British cinema', focusing as it does on 'a young hopeful straight out of film school who becomes involved in the outrageous exploits ... of a disreputable film producer ... who has helped to put the British cinema where it is today'.[25] The film indeed offers a parody of what it perceives to be the state of the British film industry in the mid-1970s and of the genres and subgenres which were most popular in British cinemas during this period. These included kung fu movies, films produced as 'family entertainment', westerns, musicals and hard- and soft-core pornographic movies intended for screenings in 'specialist' cinemas. Owing to producer Benny Murdoch's (Roy Kinnear) dishonesty, newly graduated would-be film-maker Dennis (Michael Armstrong) is compelled to make four versions of the same film revolving around a poem about Eskimo Nell, each narrative version in turn drawing upon one of these types and modes of film production. Lady Longhorn (Rosalind Knight), of the Society for Moral Reform, is persuaded to finance a 'family entertainment' version of *Eskimo Nell*, and this film is subsequently selected as suitable viewing for the Queen (Connie Brodie) as a Royal Film Performance screening.

The director of *Eskimo Nell* is shown possessing the seminal film books *Losey on Losey* (1967) by Tom Milne, *Godard* (1968) by Richard Roud and *Stanley Kubrick Directs* (1972) by Alexander Walker among his collection, but these studies of masterful 'auteurs' who succeeded in making a distinguished reputation for themselves within British and French cinema are shown as not relevant to the commercial and cultural contexts pertaining to the production of *Eskimo Nell* in its varying forms. The narrative concludes with the wrong film, the pornographic version of *Eskimo Nell*, being shown to the very people whom it will offend most at the royal premiere. This version opens with a man and a woman stripping off, and the man immediately asking (in a way that activist Richard Neville would have approved of), 'Wanna fuck?' The couple then proceed to have frantic sex on a table. Consequently, Lady Longhorn faints and there are gasps from the audience, although we do not witness Her Majesty's reaction to events on screen. The film concludes with the film's producers in jail, revealing that the making of pornographic films in the 1970s could result in a loss of liberty for those involved in the process.

Eskimo Nell was a self-reflexive movie about sexploitation cinema and the state of mid-1970s British film culture, but a film such as *The Ups and Downs of a Handyman* (John Sealey, 1975) was more typical of the British sex comedy genre during this era. The film's title refers to more than fluctuations in employment. Bob (Barry Stokes) finds that his occupation regularly brings him into contact with women who wish to have sex with him, and his life subsequently develops into a series of sexual escapades and adventures. There is more nudity than would be found in a *Carry On* narrative, but one could still watch the film and not be entirely sure what the men and women are actually doing to each other when they are excitedly rolling around on the floor or in the middle of a haystack.

Cool It, Carol! (1970) was an example of a film offering a semi-realist, documentary-type account of a couple who find a way to make money in London through sex work and appearing in 'adult' films. Joe (Robin Askwith) arrives in London with no job and few real prospects of one. His girlfriend, Carol (Janet Lynn), is noted for her sexual attractiveness within the capital, and her lack of inhibitions and willingness to have sex for money ('It's only a fuck') lead to her being photographed nude for *Mayfair* magazine and becoming a much sought-after escort and prostitute, numbering Arab sheiks and a Member of Parliament among her clients (a shot of the Houses of Parliament is followed by a man embracing Carol, dressed in a school uniform). The demand for Carol's services becomes too much for the couple, however, and they finally leave London and return home to resume their original lives. This conclusion does imply, however, that British society, in about 1970, offers no real middle ground for characters such as Joe and Carol between a dangerous (particularly for Carol) world of sex for money in London and an unexciting, unadventurous, restricted life back home with their families in a countrified environment, perhaps evoking what Michel Foucault once referred to as 'the tyrannical bitterness of our everyday lives'.[26] This is the kind of life which Susan (Maria O'Brien) in *Escort Girls* (Donovan Winter, 1974) describes herself as having escaped from, a world and a culture in which people spend their time 'watching telly every night, [playing] bingo on Saturday and polishing the car on Sundays', instead of trying to create lasting sexual memories with lots of different individuals and partners …

Sex lives, 'animal fables', dogged spectators and making a pornographic movie on a low budget: *Sex Lives of the Potato Men* (2004), *Animals* (2019), *Dogging – a Love Story* (2009) and *I Want Candy* (2007)

The post-2000 films to be discussed and considered in this section of the chapter in one way or another feature characters who subscribe to Susan's view that human beings should seek out exciting sexual sensations and experiences, rather than submit themselves to what she sees as dull and essentially mindless (if respectable) passive leisure activities. In that sense, they appear to be very much influenced by trends and tendencies established by previous examples of film-makers in British culture engaging with themes of sexual desire and the search for sexual satisfaction. Each film is set in a different and distinct location – the Midlands, Dublin, Newcastle and Leatherhead, respectively, creating a sense of local specificity to their portrayals – and crucially moving outside London, the dominant setting for many British produced films. Two of the films explore the question of how to be artistically creative within a culture which may not appear to encourage such aspirations and two of them focus on characters whose urge for sexual fulfilment is, in part, driven by a feeling that only sex offers the prospect of some kind of transcendence and liberation in a world of low-paid and not especially fulfilling jobs.

Sex Lives of the Potato Men (2004) has been summed-up by I.Q. Hunter as 'the lowest of … low comedies',[27] and it is difficult to disagree with such an assessment. The film includes mordant (some might say morbid) attempts to find humour in some of the following incidents and happenings – a woman lies unconscious in a coma, while three men lift up her hospital blanket to see what she looks like naked; a mother-in-law repeatedly sexually propositions her son-in-law after he has separated from her daughter; a husband finds pleasure from watching his wife have sex with another man, while suspended from a ceiling and masturbating on the copulating couple below him; a woman sprays dog excrement from a blender around an ex-lover's house in an act of bitter revenge; a man threatens to kill his ex-lover's dog with a knife after kidnapping it. The inclusion of such events in the narrative can only be seen as deliberate attempts to be provocative and controversial, particularly as the credits reveal that *Sex Lives* was made with the backing of the UK Film Council and awarded funds from the National Lottery (which critics of the film saw as perhaps the ultimate joke of the whole enterprise). Clearly, the idea of British cinema as a national cinema had taken a new turn, which shocked and disgusted some film reviewers: for example, Mark Kermode in his round-up of films released in 2004 made reference to the 'horrors of *Sex Lives of the Potato Men*'.[28]

The film is based around the amorous activities and aspirations of four potato delivery men, Dave (Johnny Vegas), Ferris (Mackenzie Crook), Jeremy (Mark Gatiss) and Tolly (Dominic Coleman), who offer their philosophical views on life, sexuality, relationships, sexual fantasies and pornographic images throughout the narrative. Given that *Sex Lives* regularly cuts from the (s)exploits of one character to another, the film's storytelling methods might appear to be disjointed, fragmented and even somewhat demented (Dave's 'crazy paving' work in the garden may be symbolic of the film's desire to present a defamiliarised, unemotional and detached view of events as they unfold). The film's title seems to evoke those 1970s sex comedy films which featured lots of double meanings in their characters' dialogue with each other. Here, though, apart from such lines as 'Keep your hands off my gherkins' and Dave fancying a 'spit roast' because he 'only had a sandwich' for his 'dinner', such euphemistic and double-coded terminology is less in evidence, a sign of how *Sex Lives* wants to move on in certain respects from its predecessors in the sphere of sexual comedy. The film's commitment to extending and enlarging traditions of vulgarity in British humour may also serve to disguise the fact that some of the film's perspectives on sex and romantic love are singularly unusual and reflective; it could be argued that the film is seeking to offer perspectives on sex which suggest that the act can be both mundane and surreal, memorable and an ordeal. Poppy (Nicola Reynolds), a Welsh woman in her late twenties or early thirties, is prepared to engage in threesomes and group sex with Dave, but draws the line at going for a walk in the park with him because she hardly knows him, making a sharp and intriguing distinction between physical and emotional intimacy. Dave, in turn, finds that the group sex he has with Poppy turns out to be hard work and aesthetically unappealing, given that there is only one woman (Poppy) and a whole host of other men present (this also makes it very difficult for Dave to find a parking space in Poppy's street, a source of much irritation for him). Poppy prefers action to talking, but she can also present the prospect of communal sex involving herself and nine men to Dave in very formal, polite and straightforward terms ('I'm having a few people round next week for group sex if you're interested'). The film therefore implies that people might benefit from a more honest and direct approach when seeking to satisfy their particular sexual cravings and desires.

Sex Lives, though, does not present relationships between men and women as existing in a particularly harmonious, stable or promising state of being. When Dave, for instance, greets two attractive women passing his van with a cheery, 'All right girls?', he is simply told to 'fuck off' by one of the women. Ruth (Lucy Davis) and Jeremy's relationship reveals how discourses expressing a certain kind of love and affection between men and women can quickly turn to their contrasting opposites (Jeremy: 'She has turned away like the winter, my hibernating love. Fucking bitch.' Jeremy: 'I'll always love you.' Ruth: 'Fuck off'). Fantasy and fantasising may be necessary in the film for successful sexual acts to take place (the wife of the voyeuristic husband tells an alarmed Ferris that it is all 'just a game'), but fantasy in the form of lying about what you do for a living to your partner is shown to be deceitful and disturbing. Jeremy has told Ruth that he is a dentist, but she and her parents discover to their horror that he is involved in the potato delivery business and not a dentist at all. Jeremy does subsequently find love with Shelley (Julia Davis) whom he meets in a park, she of the terrible blender revenge on an ex (Ferris ironically and unknowingly describes her as the kind of 'nice sensible girl' whom he would like to meet). When Jeremy admits to Shelley that 'I'm a potato man. That's what I do', this can be seen as a positive development which involves him taking some pride in what he actually does for a living, rather than taking refuge in a dangerously unreal world of his own making. Equally, the film does not present its predominantly white, working-class characters – two black characters without back stories play brief roles in the film's narrative – as living within a vibrant community or thriving local culture and social milieu. Dave's raucous karaoke rendition of *Come on Eileen* at a working men's club, for instance, is not much appreciated by its small audience. Television and radio presenter Adrian Chiles is shown trying to bring people together by hosting a 'towel' sex party, but we are not offered an extensive or extended picture of what might be occurring at this celebrity's sex-based gathering.

Life (as in the early 1960s social realist films set in the north) often seems to revolve around getting by and making do, without hopes of any great change or improvement in the lives of its characters. Like a number of the 'new wave' dramas, the film concentrates on the behaviour and attitudes of its male (rather than female) characters. Vicky (Angela Simpson), Dave's wife, is worn down by running a household and bringing up a daughter without help from her husband, but the film does not seek to explore her life or situation in any detail or depth. We do witness Ferris, however, having to regularly move from one inadequate and unsavoury place to another in search of a bed for the night, finally enduring the indignity of sleeping on the gherkin man's shelf in the Fishy Fingers shop.

In a concluding scene involving three of the main male characters, Ferris claims that '99 per cent of people would rather watch hard-core pornography than any other kind of film.' Ferris, in his commitment to what might be termed the 'Pleasure of the Text' above all else, cannot understand why people ever bother watching any kind of film which does not revolve around continuous and uncensored sexual acts. (The money spent on creating spectacular lavish special effects in blockbuster movies is, in his view, quite wasteful and unnecessary from such a perspective.) *Sex Lives*, despite its title, and Ferris's claims about mass consumer demand for pornography, does not, ironically enough, feature extended or explicit sex scenes. Instead, the camera tends to focus on Dave and Ferris's faces as they fail to enjoy or withstand particular sexual encounters, rather than concentrating on naked flesh. Ferris's married lover (Carol Harvey), in fact, tends to keep on her chip shop uniform while having sex, even when she is not actually working at the shop (which may be tied in with her apparent enjoyment of role-playing and sex games). This represents an interesting change from 1970s British sex comedies, which tended to intersperse scenes of characters chatting with some subsequently quite explicit sequences featuring sexual interactions between these same characters. Poppy at one point in the narrative sceptically wonders about Dave's intentions – 'That's your game is it, talking?' – and one might ultimately wonder if such a quizzical observation might be applicable to the film as a whole, which in many ways prefers to talk about sex without graphically representing it (as in the scene where men are queuing up to have sex with Poppy in her bedroom).

Scenes in *Sex Lives* involving different characters are punctuated and separated by a series of innocuous high-angle shots of housing estates, parks and clubs before the film proceeds to enter yet another indoors setting, where sex in thought or deed invariably becomes the central theme of a particular sequence. But while the various women characters in the film are depicted as being sexually ravenous and open minded, such assertive behaviour is not always appealing or appetising to Dave or Ferris. Dave in the end is pleased that his wife, Vicky, is prepared to take him back, so that he can avoid the kind of life apparently on offer to him as a single man. This is presented as an optimistic and hopeful yearning, as the work culture of the potato men seemingly does not hold out much promise for a fruitful future if left entirely to its own devices. It should be noted, however, that the film does not conclude with the reconciliation scene between Dave and Vicky, which a more conventional (or sentimentally inclined) narrative would surely have done. Instead, the film concludes with a round-table discussion between the potato men, which involves Ferris admitting to a desire to 'kill' a 'giant panda' and then 'fuck it'. This luridly monstrous and murderous fantasy is interrupted by Jeremy urgently asking his co-workers if they have seen his missing dog, suggesting that nothing is ever quite settled or totally out of the question in the subculture of the 'Potato Men'. It is presumably not accidental that the headline of one magazine glimpsed in the film declares that 'There is no cod.'

Animals (2019), like *Sex Lives*, seeks to explore the hedonistic desires of characters who have rather mundane and not especially lucrative or exciting jobs ('Fuck it. It's only work') and believe that life should be actively enjoyed rather than passively endured. If *Sex Lives* focuses on a group of male characters, *Animals* explores the lives of two women characters who are never shown at work, but are continuously depicted 'on the lash' in Dublin's bars and clubs. Irish Laura (Holliday Grainger) and American Tyler (Alia Shawkat) reject what they see as the societal pressures put on women to live safe, predictable and organised ways of life. Instead, they emphasise the importance of the spontaneous, the accidental and the transient. Both Laura and Tyler are in their early thirties, and while they apparently work as baristas in coffee bars, white wine is their drink of choice – and copious consumption is favoured over imbibing in a moderate or restrained fashion. Laura's sister, Jean (Amy Molloy), has settled down to a life of marriage and motherhood, and believes Laura needs to think about doing something similar, accepting that the 'party' cannot go on forever. Laura, equally, has literary aspirations and for ten years has been trying (unsuccessfully) to write a novel. Tyler believes that creativity is dependent on 'inspiration'; Laura is conscious that hard work and dedication may also be crucial factors in being productive. Laura's life is also complicated because she has to decide whether to wed her pianist boyfriend Jim (Fra Fee), a move which Tyler vehemently opposes. Jim rationalises Tyler's doubts by suggesting that Tyler is in love with Laura ('I get it'), but makes a case for himself as offering a calm and collected environment where Laura can 'focus' on her writing. To add to her dilemmas, Laura is acutely aware that her father, Bill (Pat Shortt), has been diagnosed with cancer and could be anxious to see what she does with her life before his own is possibly extinguished ('You all think I'm going to die').

The film consequently presents Laura with a series of difficult and complex choices which the narrative will explore in some detail, making the film an important text about modern relationships, sexuality and society. Should she marry Jim, who is kind, modest, thoughtful and talented, even though the abstemious, refined and meditative musical culture in which he lives his life is quite different to her own world of incessant partying and consuming large amounts of alcohol and drugs? (Cultural commentator Terry Eagleton wryly observed in 2013 that 'Drinking, dancing, cursing ... are not only tolerated in Ireland but sometimes compulsory.'[29] Such a claim would make Laura symptomatic of a whole way of life in Dublin, although the bars she frequents tend to be sparsely populated, and American-born Tyler is clearly Laura's equal in what Eagleton sees as characteristic features of Irish life.)

Both women are depicted engaging in sex outside committed relationships in the film. Tyler engages in sex between drinks in the toilet of a Dublin bar with a musician, but we do not witness this sexual act, and it takes place as Laura meets and flirts with Jim for the first time, which becomes the more significant narrative event. (Tyler will subsequently be keen not to let Laura out of her sight so easily again, after what transpires in her eight-minute absence from the bar.) After Jim's solo public piano recital later in the narrative, Laura will sexually seduce Jim outside the venue for the event, initiating a very different kind of performance and mood to that associated with the formal recital. Laura's literary aspirations and sexual curiosity both seem to be stimulated by poet Marty (Dermot Murphy), who finds her attractive and interesting. In something of a first for a British mainstream film, we witness (and this term seems particularly appropriate here) Marty engaging in cunnilingus with Laura after they both take cocaine, until Laura feels that this scenario (played out in a room full of stuffed animals and unfolding in 'real time') is possibly neither sexually satisfying nor fitting behaviour for a woman who has just announced her engagement to another man. In a coke-induced monologue, Laura will later talk of trying to 'nail' the work/play/life balance, but the film's many close-ups of her face suggest that the endless partying may be becoming more painful and draining than pleasurable and engaging.

Finding some kind of balance between unbridled hedonism and teetotalism, plenty and nothingness is not easy for Laura, however. In an evocative and resonant sequence, Laura and Tyler walk down the middle of the road in the housing estate where Jean lives, the two of them apparently the only people who are out and about. As they walk, Tyler asks Laura what she can hear. 'Nothing,' says Laura. 'Exactly,' replies Tyler, who sees life in such an eerily silent and somewhat deserted British suburb as symbolising 'death closing in on us'. For American Tyler (and possibly for many international and British audiences), such a setting is not conducive to the production of memorable and vivid personal narratives imbued with passion, excitement and unpredictability. Raymond Durgnat, in his study of *Eros in the Cinema* (1966), would seem to agree with such a notion and interpretation. Discussing the central female character in *Brief Encounter* (David Lean, 1945), also named Laura, he describes her final fate in the film as involving being banished to what he describes as 'darkest suburbia' and 'a passive and mawkish hubby',[30] the kind of narrative and iconic outcome which Tyler would see as a form of punishment and state of purgatory from which the only release is death.

In *Animals*, Tyler's drug-fuelled thirtieth birthday party becomes an event where many of these questions and concerns around the city versus the suburbs, sensuality versus sublimation and conformity versus the carnivalesque rise to the fore, and finally have to be confronted in a direct fashion. As time seems to slow down in the drug-fuelled atmosphere of the party, Marty in one scene unzips his trousers and engages in a sex act in Tyler's bathroom just after Laura has made herself sick. The time has been identified as 11am and Laura is shortly due to attend Jim's formal musical event. She suddenly gets a glimpse of herself and Marty in the bathroom mirror, amid the debris on the floor and in the centre of what her sister and family would probably view as a somewhat sordid and unbecoming situation.

Composing herself, she arrives at the afternoon event, where Jim is competing for a musical scholarship. Music, though, takes a back seat when Laura learns that Jim has been sexually unfaithful to her with a woman musician whom Jim has earlier praised for playing a 'mean flute'. Memories of her own behaviour with Marty come to mind when she asks Jim, 'Did you eat her pussy?', a question and an accusation which he does not deny. Laura and Jim subsequently drift apart, as Tyler has predicted (and hoped) would be the case. If sexual fidelity is still a desired feature in modern relationships, *Animals* suggests that men and women may always run the risk of their relationships being suddenly and traumatically exposed as resting on precarious foundations. Laura might be accused of hypocrisy in her insistence on Jim not entering into sexual relationships with others after she has behaved in a similar fashion (she does, admittedly, break off her sexual encounter with Marty and leave his flat, clutching the wedding dress she purchased earlier that day). Tyler would, of course, insist that all this emphasis on the importance of sexual fidelity within relationships is life-denying and pointless, particularly in a world where we all end up dead eventually (Tyler's unseen father dies during the course of the narrative, while Laura's father is suffering from cancer, and said to be looking 'sick' at the end of the film).

The boldness of the narrative, perhaps, lies in the way it sees a kind of happy ending in Laura living alone, without either Tyler or Jim in close proximity. This comes about through Laura's sister, Jean, who apparently owns some sort of 'property empire' in Dublin and is able to provide Laura with a new place to live. Tyler, it emerges, has lost her job after being found taking drugs at her place of work, so one might wonder how much longer she will stay in Dublin, having now neither employment nor the immediate and constant company of her best friend.

In *Withnail and I* (Bruce Robinson, 1987), a film which might be considered something of a male companion piece to *Animals*, the two close male friends in the former narrative have to part because one of them, I (Paul McGann), fears that he may suffer serious psychological damage if he continues to live with his extrovert and emotionally extravagant partner, Withnail (Richard E. Grant). Withnail is left alone at the close, reciting Hamlet's famous speech about man delighting not him, nor women either, to some animals in a zoo-like setting. Tyler is not left in quite such a bereft and reflective state at the close, but a sequence near the end of the film features her singing the Lorde song *Royals* to a sparse audience attending a karaoke evening in a city bar. Laura is shown leaving just as Tyler sings the line from the song 'Let me be your ruler, you can call me Queen B'. Laura, it will transpire, wants to put down her own original thoughts on paper and to avoid being trapped in the discourses of others. The film's final image of Laura reveals her set up in a new apartment, at one remove from Tyler, tapping away on her computer keyboard, still working on that elusive first novel. Laura's desire to be creative in her use of language and to write a work of fiction is presented as a positive aspiration, and it is interesting in these multimedia times that she gravitates towards the writing of a novel, rather than a screenplay or an internet blog, suggesting that she is concerned with preserving valuable cultural and literary traditions established over the centuries.

Animals reveals that even in a setting such as contemporary Dublin, where Tyler and Laura can enjoy a carefree and self-determining existence, life is not always easy for the modern woman. When Laura and Jean exchange wedding and baby magazines in the street, this moment indicates how women can still feel driven into adopting particular ways of living and being, which men (such as Withnail and I) are not subject to in a similar fashion. Laura's sister is married and a mother, but the only insight we glean about her life is that she is on anti-depressants following the birth of her baby. The friendship of Laura and Tyler does not extend into a sexual relationship (as happens in *Disobedience* and *My Summer of Love*, to be discussed in the next chapter). This may be something of a disappointment for Tyler, who appears to be open to such a development and is described by Jim as Laura's 'wife'.

What might be termed *Animals'* complex and contrasting perspectives on sex, sensibility and gender roles in a modern-day British setting are, arguably, the result of the film drawing upon a range of transnational funding sources (including Screen Australia and Screen Ireland),[31] and having an Australian director (Sophie Hyde) and an American actor (Alia Shawkat) in its cast and crew. Shawkat is able to recreate the fast talking, wise-cracking heroines of classic Hollywood romantic comedies of the 1930s and 1940s, while imbuing her character with a (literal) thirst for sensual experiences which make her life experiences interesting for audiences to follow. English-born Grainger makes Laura a sympathetic, lively and reflective character, who does not settle for straightforward ways of living. In ways that fellow Irishman Oscar Wilde would surely have appreciated, Laura and Tyler see evenings as times for indulging in heady pleasures, days as suitable for reclining and recovering, and all occasions as fit times for laughing and joking. Tyler (like her male counterpart Withnail) strives to turn her life into what might be termed a continuous piece of performance art, while Laura, through the power of the written word, tries to leave some more lasting record of her thoughts, sensations and emotions. For each woman, though, life and art are both works-in-progress, the only end of which is death itself.

Dogging – a Love Story (2009), like *Sex Lives of the Potato Men*, features multiple protagonists who are looking for novel sex experiences whenever possible. The film's title may appear to be oxymoronic (some might say moronic), but it alludes to how people of varying ages and backgrounds may develop a love of the practice of 'dogging', having sex in public places such as car parks and secluded woodlands, while possibly inviting others to watch, join in or record what is occurring. The second part of the title alludes to how a young man and woman move towards embarking on a romantic relationship out of their shared interest in finding out more about dogging, but, in doing so, will seek to move on from this particular subculture and way of life.

Dan (Luke Treadaway) is a university graduate in journalism, but being currently unemployed in Newcastle, he hopes that by researching and writing a story on dogging activities in the local area he might come up with a story which national newspaper editors would be interested in printing; thus kickstarting his career. In a sign of how young people in the 2000s were increasingly meeting, Dan corresponds online with Laura (Kate Heppell), who describes herself as a 'horny Geordie lass', but in fact is a rather lonely sensitive woman with an overbearing father and no mother.

Dan meets Laura by chance at various dogging sites, without knowing that she is the person he has communicated with online. Dan introduces his actual girlfriend, Tanya (Sammy Dobson), to dogging activities as a change from supposedly romantic dates involving meals in restaurants, which both acknowledge have become rather tired and formulaic get-togethers. 'You said you wanted excitement,' he tells her when she is initially appalled by the idea. But he is subsequently surprised and somewhat shocked (as Dave and Ferris are by the women they encounter in *Sex Lives*) when Tanya appears to anticipate the prospect of engaging in outlandish transgressive activities and possibly having sex with strangers much more enthusiastically than he had imagined possible. Dan's cousin, Rob (Richard Riddell), is an estate agent and keen 'dogger', as is his girlfriend, Sarah (Justine Glenton), a forty-year-old divorced woman with several children, whose house is up for sale. Rob will find that Sarah's commitment to dogging is in the end stronger than her sexual desire for him, and by the close of the narrative both Dan and Tanya, Rob and Sarah (these modern-day equivalents of 'Bob, Carol, Ted and Alice' or 'Rita, Sue and Bob Too') have split up, the women (unlike their male partners) refusing to be tied down to just the one sexual partner.

Dogging deploys a number of differing filmic styles within its narrative, including scenes shot in black-and-white night-time vision featuring brief (almost subliminal) moments of couples having vigorous sex in cars and men ejaculating on car-windscreens. Events move towards a kind of *Midsummer Night's Dream*-type conclusion in which the various central characters (minus Tanya) are transported to a forest setting where comical chaos and confusion over identities and roles can be unleashed. The pretext for this location is that the Newcastle-based doggers meet up for a nationwide dogging event held in the Lake District and advertised online. Here Sarah befriends an unemployed young man adept at stealing cars, whom she takes home to meet her children after he agrees to drive her back to Newcastle. Dan rescues Laura from the clutches of a rather dubious group of middle-aged men, the leader of whom turns out to be the council employee who interviews Dan about looking for work, so that he can qualify for his job-seeker's allowance. This revelation provides Dan with the kind of exposure story which he has been seeking, an example of reputedly low behaviour from a person in authority, who it is argued in a subsequent newspaper article should be setting an example and know better. The film has shown, however, that dogging involves people from all sorts of life, especially those who are not sexually successful in their daily lives, but who may gain some kind of sustenance or satisfaction from treating dogging as an activity akin to 'trainspotting' in which details about cars, makes, registrations and sexual practices can be jotted down, logged and noted. Dogging in the film is depicted as something of a response to the invisibility of sex in everyday life, with participants and voyeurs rejecting the notion that sex is not a fit activity (unlike sport) for spectators to watch and cheer from the sidelines. If Laura and Dan appear to be removing themselves from this subculture at the very end (hence the 'love story' aspect of the title), the film suggests that for some the activity brings pleasure, relief, excitement and spectacle to lives that may otherwise be devoid of these particular features on a day-to-day basis, especially if they are unemployed (like Dan) or employed (like Tanya) in mundane administrative jobs. The film offers glimpses into a sexual subculture not often represented in mainstream British films, and charts how romance may still blossom out of what appear on the surface to be quite unromantic and unsentimental settings, scenarios and situations.[32]

I Want Candy (2007) seeks to bring love and sex closer together, but also stresses that both may prosper from obtaining a more public, communal and less sheltered place in everyday society. Leatherhead University film production students Joe (Tom Riley) and John (Tom Burke) have been under the impression that they can submit a feature-length film for their final project. Therefore, they are shocked to learn from the course convenor, Mr Dulberg (Mackenzie Crook), that they have to make a film on the subject of 'Uncovering the language of a visual event' which lasts no more than two minutes. Encouraged by their friend Lila (Michelle Ryan) to avoid being knocked back by a person she describes as a 'bitter, jealous, dead-end college lecturer', the pair propose a project to Working Title films before becoming involved with a producer of 'blue movies', Douglas Perry (Eddie Marsden). He is prepared to finance their making of a feature-length film, *The Love Storm*, if as Anna Smith put it in her *Time Out* review of *I Want Candy*, 'they tweak it a bit ... insert some lesbian scenes, a bit of anal'.[33]

The Love Storm ends up being filmed in Joe's parents' house while they are at work (perhaps alluding to how low-budget pornography may well be shot cheaply in ordinary houses) and features a glamorous American star of pornographic movies, Candy Fiveways (Carmen Electra), as the star of their film. A sense of comic absurdity is generated by the film production team always running the risk of being discovered by Joe's parents and the inherent difficulties of producing an erotic movie in unexotic British suburban surroundings. Thus, we see how the unexpected appearance of an elderly male neighbour in a wheelchair can spoil the filming of an outdoor scene featuring Candy in a striking black dress and handcuffs, encountering her lover-to-be and seeking an escape from her mysterious 'chains'. This collision of the young and the beautiful with the aged and the infirm provides a striking contrast, and reveals how the two groups may normally never come across each other. The conclusion to this sequence, however, sees the disabled observer lending his wheelchair to facilitate the filming of a tracking shot, while enjoying a cup of tea with the film's production manager, Lila, a former waitress (Michelle Ryan, who plays Lila, may have had this scene in mind when she described it as 'a really sweet, wholesome film about two friends just trying to make a film').[34] *I Want Candy*, as perhaps befits a modern-day Ealing film production, therefore demonstrates how the communal efforts needed to make *The Love Storm* can also lead to an enhanced sense of community, transnational integration and shared purpose among those involved in the process; the communal nature of film-making is quite different to the more solitary and individualistic nature of novel writing in this respect.

If *Eskimo Nell* features several versions and variants of the same story, *I Want Candy* leads to the making of two films – one a two-minute avant-garde film in which Candy in a red leather jumpsuit and a slowed-down film speed takes a hammer to three pieces of red fruit; the other, an extended narrative which includes scenes of a sexual nature of which we see only a glimpse. Inevitably, the two films are shown to audiences for whom they were not intended. The financier of the sex film (John Standing) is shown the experimental two-minute short, leading him to declare that Doug Perry is a 'dead man'; while the sexually explicit film is mistakenly presented to the film production students and their parents. Here, though, the result is not as catastrophic as in *Eskimo Nell*, which suggests how graphic sexual images in British culture may have lost some of their ability to shock audiences compared with mid-1970s Britain. There are gasps from the audience watching *The Love Storm* and Joe's parents are surprised by the locations chosen for the film ('That looks like our house'), but no one goes to jail in the end and the spectators appear not to have been overly traumatised by the experience. Even so, as in *Eskimo Nell*, we never see more than an extract from the finished sex film and so are unable to come to any strong conclusions as to whether *The Love Storm* deserves the epithet bestowed upon it by Jimmy Carr's video shop assistant ('a masterpiece'). *I Want Candy* culminates with an awards sequence in which the contenders for the best adult entertainment film at the so-called *Golden Cockerel* awards include such titles as *We Know Who You Did Last Summer* and *There's Something Up Mary*. Joe and John win for *The Love Storm* and, accepting the award, John declares, 'God bless Erotica.' In *Eskimo Nell*, Lady Longhorn declares, 'I do so love [cinematic] adaptations from the classics', and in the coda to *I Want Candy*, Joe, John and Lila are working on such a film in the tradition of 'British literary/heritage cinema', suggesting they have moved on from a popular but disreputable subgenre (the British 'sex film') to one which is a much more respected and valued feature of British film production in a modern age. Like Laura and Dan in *Dogging – a Love Story*, Joe and Lila also appear to be a couple at the close, romantic harmony having emerged from a comically chaotic set of circumstances revolving around sexual desire and sexual frustration. If, as we shall see, Michael Winterbottom may have provided too much sex and not enough story and characterisation for some critics of *9 Songs*, we can only be sorry that we don't get to see more of what has (reputedly) been achieved in *The Love Storm*, beyond witnessing Candy Fiveways in handcuffs outside a suburban house and wondering how she got into (and out of) this situation. If nothing else, the title, *The Love Storm* has a pleasing link with the trailer for *Flames of Passion – All Next Week*, which Laura (Celia Johnson) and Alec (Trevor Howard) watch in the cinema while waiting for the main feature in *Brief Encounter* (David Lean, 1945). As Raymond Durgnat, in his study *Eros in the Cinema* (1966), noted, this title and trailer 'confirms' Laura and Alec's 'assumption that lust is too ridiculous for belief' and leaves them laughing 'heartily'.[35] Whatever the differences between the films discussed in this section of the chapter, they all agree on the importance of maintaining a sense of humour and a sense of the ridiculous when it comes to sexual matters. Such a belief is pertinent to a discussion of the next two films to be considered, where the central male and female characters have many varied qualities, but are somewhat lacking in a sense of humour and perspective, which may affect their abilities to deal with situations and scenarios which do not go according to plan.

Sexual frustration and failure in *On Chesil Beach* (2018) and sexual liberation and experimentation in *9 Songs* (2004)

On Chesil Beach is the story of Edward (Billy Howle) and Florence's (Saoirse Ronan) courtship, honeymoon in Dorset, their short-lived marriage (they only live together for a few hours before separating) and subsequent divorce. The film is set in the years between 1961 and 1962, and reveals that sexual difficulties and an inability to talk openly about sexual matters are at the root of the problems that lead the couple to separate, a traumatic situation which is accentuated by the ways in which sex is not seen as a fit subject for public discussion or explicit representation in British films and television programmes at this time. The narrative plotline of *9 Songs* has been wryly summarised by Melanie Williams in *Film Quarterly* (2006) as a film in which 'A couple meets, has lots of sex, goes to lots of concerts, and then splits up.'[36] The couple in question consists of Lisa (Margo Stilley), an American living and studying in England on a temporary basis, and Matt (Kieran O'Brien), a climate researcher, who lives in London (the film provides no indication as to what subjects Lisa may be studying). Both of the central characters in *On Chesil Beach* are intelligent, well-meaning, university-educated graduates, Florence specialising in Music and Edward in History. By forming a quintet with fellow musicians, Florence is able to find an outlet for her creative talents within British culture; Edward is less fortunate, not finding or pursuing work either as a writer or teacher of history (the film, however, presents him as a kind of historian narrating and interpreting his own personal history as it enters the final sections of its narrative).

9 Songs intersperses scenes of sexual abandonment with musical performances taking place at the Brixton Academy. *On Chesil Beach* also features a range of music from classical to jazz and the emerging 'popular' music of the early 1960s. *9 Songs* appears to be set around the time it was made (2004), but as the pair of lovers spend most of their time naked with each other indoors, the social and historical context within which their lovemaking takes place is not stressed. *On Chesil Beach* moves between specific periods in British culture centred around 1961, 1962, 1975 and 2007. When *On Chesil Beach* was released in British cinemas during May 2018, Britain was involved in the difficult and contentious situation of seeking to extricate itself from membership of the European Union, a reversal of the situation in 1962 when Britain was exploring the possibility of joining the European Economic Community.[37] Ian McEwan, who wrote the screenplay (based on his 2007 novel) and was doubtless aware of the irony of these contrasting national goals, sets the couple's disastrous wedding night in the summer of 1962, six months before 1963, the year that Philip Larkin famously designated as the time when 'Sexual intercourse began' in Britain,[38] something that historian Dominic Sandbrook has described as a 'tiresome and sadly invincible myth'.[39]

If *9 Songs* shows a couple enjoying a vigorous and varied sexual life together, *On Chesil Beach* presents the completely opposite situation, with Florence and Edward struggling and failing to have even one successful sexual encounter with each other. In *9 Songs*, Lisa talks of having had lovers from Colombia, Brazil, Argentina and Germany ('Isn't this romantic?' jokes Matt on being informed of these previous liaisons). Edward, however, when asked by Florence to name his previous lovers, embarrassingly has to admit that there aren't any ('There are no names'). Florence, in turn, is keen to put off their moment of sexual consummation for as long as she can, and so the present tense of their wedding night is broken up by flashbacks detailing how the two met and conducted their courtship.

One of the flashback sequences reveals the couple going to see *A Taste of Honey* at the cinema, a seminal movie about sex and relationships in modern Britain which was released in British cinemas in the autumn of 1961. The extract from the film features mother, daughter and the mother's boyfriend witnessing the would-be sensationalistic seaside attractions on

Blackpool pier. Malcolm Muggeridge, writing in the *New Statesman* in 1958, claimed that a film executive had told him that 'cinema audiences were slumping' because people were now living in better housing conditions and so were less tempted to go out at night, preferring to stay in and watch television. According to Muggeridge, one category of film-goer for whom the cinema would continue to cater, however, would be 'young lovers in search of relative privacy' as such spectators would not be overly concerned 'about the quality' of the film being shown.[40] Echoing a similar scene from *A Kind of Loving* (John Schlesinger, 1962), Florence and Edward are presented as being the only young couple actually watching *A Taste of Honey* – all the others are engaging in passionate kissing, seemingly confirming Muggeridge's point about the indoor venues, rather than the films themselves, being the most important feature of the cinematic experience for young people during this period. Edward takes some encouragement from the behaviour of those around him (and possibly from the sexual content of *A Taste of Honey*), and dares to put his hand on Florence's lower thigh. His behaviour is met with a firm rebuff, though, and he is forced back into concentrating on the film.[41] (Interestingly, *A Taste of Honey*, *On Chesil Beach* and *9 Songs* all feature scenes in which the central protagonists visit the British seaside – but only in *9 Songs* is the trip successful.)

9 Songs does not include any scenes featuring Lisa and Matt's parents or relatives (Lisa being from America – where she returns at the end of the narrative – may be one reason for such an absence). *On Chesil Beach*, by way of a contrast, is keen to place Florence and Edward's relationship in juxtaposition with that of their parents. Marjorie (Anne-Marie Duff), Edward's mother, has been injured by a reckless and thoughtless railway passenger who opened a train door too soon at a station platform, resulting in her being knocked unconscious and consequently suffering permanent brain damage. (This shocking sequence points out how changes in train carriage construction involving locked doors have made Britain's railway platforms safer places to be.) Marjorie is an artist who works on with difficulty, sometimes working naked, much to the consternation of her teacher husband (Adrian Scarborough). When Florence visits, she is able to engage with – and encourage – the mother's art, something that Edward's father and his two daughters much admire. Such glimpses of Florence's empathy with the family lead us to see that she is a naturally kind and helpful person.

Edward's visits to Florence's parents are not quite so successful or convivial. Geoffrey (Samuel West), Florence's father, is a somewhat cold and distant figure, liable to explode into rage at certain moments. There is some suggestion in the novella and the film that Florence's unease about sex may stem from incidents which occurred during the sailing trips and holidays she spent with her father while growing up: the narrator in the novella states, 'They never talked about these trips. He had never asked her again, and she was glad.'[42] This is, however, hinted at, rather than spelt out. Florence's mother (Emily Watson) is a university lecturer in Philosophy (who apparently speaks with Iris Murdoch on the phone), but she is also rather distant from Florence and her character plays no significant part in the narrative. Therefore, the film evocatively and economically reveals that children's experiences of their own parents' marriages may have a decisive and sometimes negative impact on their subsequent experiences of love, desire, sex and marriage.

On Chesil Beach, like *One Day*, also points out that relationships cannot exist in a social and economic vacuum. Edward has studied History but accepts a job with Florence's father at his electronics factory, as this will enable himself and Florence to get married. Such an arrangement (with Edward becoming one of the family in an additional way) will add to the underlying tensions in Florence and Edward's relationship.

If *9 Songs*, as noted earlier, depicts a couple engaging in a series of diverse and accomplished sexual encounters, *On Chesil Beach* shows the complete opposite; a couple who are unable to have successful sex together when they first try. Edward is revealed to have difficulty in undressing Florence, and when he fails to succeed in the act of making love, he ends up ejaculating over Florence's leg, an event which Florence subsequently describes as 'revolting'. She flees the honeymoon hotel in her striking turquoise dress and runs off into the vast expanse of pebbles known as Chesil Beach. Here, in an angry, tense and sad encounter, their relationship completely unravels. In T.S. Eliot's 'The Waste Land' (1922), the narrator observes, 'On Margate Sands/I can connect/Nothing with nothing'.[43] In *On Chesil Beach*, the couple's conversations on the beach lead to them making all kinds of connections between such topics as sex, money, class, family and work, connections which will quickly doom the marriage. Edward declares that he is no longer willing to work for her father and accuses Florence of being a 'bitch' and 'frigid'. He also rejects Florence's accommodating offer of being allowed to sleep with other women while they are married to each other (a radical proposal, which she defines as living by their 'own rules'). Edward is equally unimpressed when she cites the example of two homosexual men living together as a sign that unconventional relationships can work, arguing that they are man and wife, not a couple of 'queers' living together in Oxford (thus evoking the British Board of Film Censors' refusal to accept 'departures from accepted sexual conventions' at the beginning of the 1960s, mentioned in the *Encounter* article quoted earlier). Edward quotes the part from the marriage ceremony about the wife worshipping the husband 'with [her] body', suggesting that Florence is not fulfilling her side of the marriage contract as sanctified by the Church and state authorities.

What this confrontational scene brings out very forcefully is the unpleasant nature of a relationship when it becomes embittered and tormented, leaving one partner (in this case Florence) desperate to find a place of escape and refuge. The sequence also shows how sexual failure and disappointment can lead to a sense that a relationship as a whole may be flawed and beyond saving. Love here turns to bitterness, as traces of desire, adoration and familiarity are replaced by feelings of resentment and dismay. The vastness of Dorset's Chesil Beach as a location is contrasted with the short-lived nature of their marriage as the ebbs and flows of Florence and Edward's relationship is seemingly echoed by the tide endlessly moving the pebbles in and out of the ocean. In a lengthy sequence in which Florence's red hair and arrestingly coloured dress stand out amid the elements, Florence and Edward keep changing their position in relation to each other on the beach, until Edward finally turns his back on Florence (for ever), and she returns to the hotel on her own – to a life which does not include him.

This could have been how the film chose to conclude the story of Edward and Florence's time together, but in the spirit of a nineteenth-century novel, we learn something about the ultimate fate of each character. Florence has continued (and flourished) with her musical quintet. She is also shown at the end of the film to have married the only male musician in the group, Charles (Mark Donald). Charles, at least, shares Florence's expertise in performing classical music, so their relationship is possibly based around a shared interest rather than a grand passion (we learn that she has three children at the end, so some of her concerns and dislikes about sex must have been eradicated). Edward also gravitates towards a career in music, running a record shop in the mid-1970s. During a glimpse of his life during this period, we see him draped by two women and apparently enjoying the supposed greater sexual freedom and licence of the 1970s, but by the time we see him again in 2007, he appears to be living alone and possibly rather sadly; a *Sight and Sound* synopsis of the film described his final state as that of a 'morose recluse'.[44] As a man in his sixties, Edward hears Mark Lawson on the radio announcing that Florence's group will be performing for one last time at Wigmore Hall before they retire from public events. Edward and Florence have earlier cherished the idea of Florence performing at this venue, with Edward present. When their eyes briefly meet in this valedictory section of the narrative, the mood is not one of celebration, though. Instead, a feeling of loss and melancholy pervades the sequence, as the sight of Edward brings back what for Florence are painful memories of what might have been and what was. The very last image in the film goes back to their break-up on the beach in 1962, with Florence asking Edward to walk back to the hotel with her and Edward refusing, out of a feeling that he has been humiliated and duped.

Both *9 Songs* and *On Chesil Beach* in some ways appear to privilege the male voice and perspective in their respective concluding sections. Matt's voice-over at the end of *9 Songs* tells us that Lisa is leaving for America, but Lisa has no corresponding narrative voice to share her thoughts. *9 Songs* is based around Matt's recollections of his relationship with Lisa, but does not seek to portray the two characters when they are much older and separated. In *On Chesil Beach*, the film-makers' decision to significantly age the actors at the close and to emphasise that this is in the end a rather sad story about emotional and sexual failure and Englishness was critiqued and questioned by some British film reviewers. Deborah Ross, in the *Spectator*, described the film as 'literary and tasteful and sad and English', but then, deliberately using the kind of language not used in the film, wondered about how the couple come to part so quickly and irrevocably: 'One crap shag and that's it, it's over?'[45] Nigel Andrews in the *Financial Times* felt that *On Chesil Beach* illustrated that 'education, like class, can thwart passion's spontaneity', alongside 'parental warping, malicious or accidental'.[46] Peter Bradshaw, in the *Guardian*, felt that the film served to point out what he termed the 'silly, tragic pointlessness of the virgin-wedding-night business'.[47] The author himself, Ian McEwan, was keen to emphasise that this tale had contemporary relevance for our own drastically changed times. McEwan was quoted in the *Daily Telegraph* as declaring that 'online athletic pornography is completely warping [young people's] expectations of what the act of love could be', leading to what he termed 'vulgar pressure that must be very intimidating'.[48]

On Chesil Beach illustrates the difficulties sometimes involved in reconciling our sexual, physical desires with a sense of ourselves as thinking, rational and possibly sensitive and reserved human beings. When they are together, Florence and Edward cannot connect the sexual and the social, the physical and the cerebral sides of being human, and this is compounded by what Ian McEwan suggests is the sexually repressed nature of British culture in the early 1960s. Anthony Crosland, writing in *Encounter* on what he saw as the state of British culture in the year in which *On Chesil Beach* is principally set (1962), accused Britain's ruling classes of having an 'antiquated ... attitude to homosexuality' and of organising society around an 'oppressive' structure of 'class relations'. The one sign of optimism regarding the future as far as Crosland was concerned lay in young people: 'Eventually, one hopes, a rebellious younger generation, aided by much increased intercourse with the outside world, will shatter the present mood.'[49] *On Chesil Beach* takes two such positive representatives of a 'younger generation' from 1962 as its focal point, making their failure to make a success of their marriage all the more poignant and disappointing.

From a modern perspective, we might feel that Florence and Edward marry at too young an age. They find themselves in an all-or-nothing situation where sex looms large in their minds but not in their lives; both soon regret their decision to wed. In interviews, Ian McEwan has suggested that the unhappy story of Florence is a tale with a distinct message to convey about sex, society and the individual to modern audiences: 'No one is talking on social media ... about the joys of cuddling, it sounds too feeble; but I think a lot of teenagers ... would probably be very relieved if they did.'[50] McEwan here stresses companionship, compassion and consideration in male–female relationships, alongside an acknowledgement that sexual relationships will not always be successful or satisfactory, particularly when first embarked upon.

To turn from Florence and Edward to Matt and Lisa in 9 *Songs* is not just to move from one particular era in British social and cinematic history to another, but to enter a vastly different personal, cultural and cinematic world where full-frontal male and female nudity and sexual activities can be explicitly shown and implicitly celebrated in a mainstream British feature film. Drawing upon the iconography of pornography and this particular subgenre's concern to focus on the depiction of uncensored sexual activity above all else, 9 *Songs* offered a challenge to the British Board of Film Classification and to the film's viewers. The two lovers in the film engage in mutual oral sex on separate occasions and sexual intercourse while one partner is blindfolded. Lisa is also watched by Matt while she pleasures herself with a vibrator. Lisa and Matt are also depicted taking cocaine together and visiting a lap-dancing club, where Lisa enjoys a lap-dance with a woman performer at the club more than her boyfriend does. The Board passed the film as suitable viewing in British cinemas for those aged eighteen and over, judging that the 'explicit images of sexual activity' were 'justified by the context',[51] and by the apparently serious artistic intentions underlying the project. For a film aimed at public exhibition in cinemas, the sex scenes are quite graphically presented and crucially are performed by the actors themselves, not by body doubles or performers who work in the British adult entertainment business. The structure of the film is unusual and unique – scenes of a strong sexual nature interrupted by musical performances by artists playing at the Brixton Academy in London. The nine songs featuring performances from the music venue are narratively explained as emanating from Lisa and Matt's attendance at the gigs, although the connection between the songs and the sex is a loose one, and the music takes the place of scenes featuring the couple doing more ordinary and mundane things, such as 'washing up or watching the news',[52] as well as stopping the film from being composed of non-stop sex sequences. In the opening section of the film, the musical sequences and the sex scenes are not entirely separate, as there is a sudden and unexpected cut from a musical number to Lisa and Matt having passionate sex.

As the film progresses, we observe Matt and Lisa engaging in differing forms of sexual activity, trying out different sexual positions, with their final sexual encounter taking place in a hotel featuring Lisa on top of Matt and moving up and down on his erect penis. This emphasis on sexual activity above all other considerations means that we do not learn too much about the couple and their lives when they are not having sex (the fact that we may crave to learn more about their characters than we do is possibly one factor which makes the film non-pornographic). Matt has a career which he practises in Lisa's absence from the narrative; Lisa talks of having a meeting with her supervisor and appears to work in a bar, although we do not see her at work, college or even her place of residence. The film is not entirely devoid of more typical or conventional romantic content. The couple go away for a weekend break and as Matt runs naked into the sea, he declares, 'I love you' to Lisa (her reply is difficult to make out). Although Lisa is younger than Matt, she is possibly more sexually experienced as she talks (as noted earlier) of having a number of lovers from different parts of the world. I.Q. Hunter, in his study of *British Trash Cinema* (2013), has ingeniously suggested that such information might lead us to believe that northerner 'Matt represents British realism and Lisa the complexities of foreign art-house films'. He feels, however, that as *9 Songs* proceeds, Lisa, with her willingness to combine prescription drugs (possibly for depression or anxiety) with illegal drugs such as cocaine, 'comes across as simply mad'.[53] Indeed, much of the adverse critical reaction to the film centred around the character of Lisa, who was accused of being extremely 'irritating' by Zoe Williams in the *Guardian*,[54] and of having an 'aggravating US drawl' by Rowan Pelling in the *Independent on Sunday*.[55] Some reviewers felt that Winterbottom had possibly taken his pursuit of a certain kind of realism too far, not by making the sex scenes too explicit, but by not giving the characters more interesting, meaningful and intelligent lines of dialogue. Sukhdev Sandhu in the *Daily Telegraph* argued that the dialogue scenes most probably reflected male–female conversations of a real-life nature, which – as he put it – do not usually involve men and women speaking to each other as if they are characters in a 'Chekhov' play.[56] Nonetheless, if they were not depicting having sex together, we might be largely uninterested in Matt and Lisa as characters, which is another unusual (some might say revealing) aspect of Winterbottom's film.

Rowan Pelling, at one time editor of a British periodical entitled the *Erotic Review*, posed an interesting question about the film's aesthetic and ontological status, asking 'But is it art – or even enjoyable?' She anticipated that British cultural commentators would dislike the movie 'because they'll compare the film to Buñuel, rather than Ben Dover, and I'm not sure that's the right criterion'.[57] A 'Ben Dover' hardcore pornographic video would not have featured the various musical performances included in *9 Songs* (and one can see these as something of an irrelevance to Winterbottom's perceived aim of showing that there is nothing wrong with showing a woman and a man having real sex together). A 'Ben Dover' production would also be keen to vary the number of people involved in the sex scenes and to include, where possible, scenes of lesbian (but not male homosexual) sexual activity. His films (released on DVD, but not screened in cinemas) would also contain some elements of 'humour' in which, as I.Q. Hunter put it in a 2014 essay on British hardcore pornographic films, Dover cannot believe 'the sexual possibilities that come his way' from 'horny housewives and randy secretaries'.[58] Winterbottom, in contrast, focuses relentlessly on one heterosexual couple, so much so that when Lisa appears to be entranced by a woman lap-dancer, this heralds the end of her relationship with Matt and the end of the film.

Academic and discursive studies of cinema and sexuality have also not reached a consensus about the achievements and significance of *9 Songs*. In her seminal study *Screening Sex* (2008), Linda Williams concluded that Winterbottom's film represented 'one possible, lyrical direction for a new kind of hard-core art cinema'.[59] Mattias Frey's *Extreme Cinema: The Transgressive Rhetoric of Today's Art Film Culture* (2016) was particularly interested in how Michael Winterbottom emphasised (in his public statements about the film), its 'aesthetic' differences from pornography and his 'higher intentions'. This involved the director making 'assumptions' that the movie's spectators would not be sexually stimulated by events within the narrative, despite, as Professor Frey noted, the film devoting '40 percent of its running time to graphic sex'.[60] David Cooke, Director of the British Board of Film Classification when *9 Songs* was released, declared that the film was not an R18 film because the 'explicit scenes' were not intended to bring about 'sexual arousal',[61] which is the fascinating and somewhat subjective criterion for the Board deciding whether a work should be classified as pornographic or not.

Lisa and Matt's relationship lasts around a year, and Winterbottom has aimed to include what most British mainstream films about a couple's relationship over such a period of time would leave out, namely their sexual interactions and physical experiences together. Some viewers may feel that he goes too far in this direction, thus neglecting to imbue his film with a meaningful and engaging narrative arc or interesting and well-rounded characters. Whatever the perceived successes and failures of *9 Songs*, to some extent it still stands alone as an attempt by a relatively popular, prolific and imaginative British film-maker to present sex in an unmediated manner and to show that British cinema has the potential to be as sexy and unabashed as some of its European cinematic competitors, if it so wishes and desires.

Examining *The Look of Love* (Michael Winterbottom, 2013)

The Look of Love (2013) continued the director's desire to engage with themes of love, desire, relationships and sex, but this time in a wider social and cultural context. He sought to achieve this by exploring the life and fortunes of highly successful businessman Paul Raymond (1925–2008). A *Daily Telegraph* obituary of Raymond noted his description of himself as an 'honest entertainer', while recording that some dated the 'moral decline' of British society to 1958, the year in which he opened his striptease club, the Raymond Revuebar, in Soho. Describing him as an 'unhealthy man of vulgar tastes', the obituary claimed that in his later years he 'evoked Dracula lurking in the guise of an Oxford Street spiv'.[62] Steve Coogan portrays Raymond in the film as a pragmatic hedonist, a materialist pleasure-seeker and a wry observer, who becomes rich by providing entertainment in the form of stage shows and print magazines which emphasise the attractions of the female body when naked. The narrative begins, however, in a sombre fashion, with Raymond returning home from the funeral of his daughter, Debbie (Imogen Potts), who has died at the age of thirty-six after overdosing on heroin. Raymond is pictured looking intently at a video recording of a television interview featuring Debbie and himself, a reminder of a past happiness that now exists only on tape. *The Look of Love* is therefore imbued from the start with a loss of love, which no amount of 'excessiveness' in terms of sex, drugs or money can assuage. (An obituary of Paul Raymond in *The Times* described Debbie as 'An alcoholic and cocaine addict' whose death led to Paul Raymond becoming a 'recluse, rarely venturing outside his penthouse flat'.[63])

The film, having outlined its tragic trajectory at the start of the narrative, then turns to the late 1950s and the years of Paul Raymond's beginnings as an impresario of what he termed 'erotic entertainment'.[64] Scenes shot in black-and-white feature Raymond and his wife, Jean (Anna Friel), pushing the boundaries of what is allowed in public entertainment in a show featuring two scantily clad women and a lion in a circus-type act. Raymond would later recall that when the two women subsequently appeared topless and the act was promoted as a *'Festival of Nudes*, the takings went up five times in one week',[65] leading him to see a way of becoming very rich indeed. A subsequent switch to colour in the film is associated with Britain itself supposedly becoming more liberal, sexually open-minded and colourful.

Raymond himself, although married, wishes to make the most of opportunities to have sex with the women who appear in his shows. Jean is at first shown to be understanding and tolerant of this behaviour, asking 'Was she nice?' when he returns home in the early hours of a morning. However, when he falls in love with the woman who will become known as Fiona Richmond (Tamsin Egerton), and leaves Jean and his two children for her, a more familiar dramatic scenario emerges. Jean rages at Fiona, and follows Raymond and Richmond to their new abode, accusing him of being a 'coward', walking out on his wife and family as Raymond's own father had done when he was growing up. Paul protests that 'It's not the nineteenth century' when Jean tries to stop him leaving. Subsequently, the couple divorce, and news of their divorce settlement is lapped up by journalists eager for details concerning their parting. Historian Dominic Sandbrook has noted that during the 1970s divorce rates 'doubled amongst people over 25 and trebled amongst those younger',[66] and the separation between Paul and Jean Raymond points to a tension between marriage and concepts of individual sexual freedom and liberation, which Paul Raymond's high-profile magazine publications of the 1970s, *Men Only* and *Club International*, had helped to intensify. (Bruce Manton, in a 1972 *New Statesman* essay, 'The Profits of Erotica', suggested that these magazines in particular promoted views which were 'anti-establishment' and 'anathema to good-old puritan consciousness'.)[67]

With Jean divorced, *The Look of Love* subsequently focuses on how Raymond is able to amass a fortune by buying up property in Soho and putting on financially successful stage shows featuring Fiona Richmond (who in 1975 described herself as playing the kinds of 'sexy' roles which someone such as 'Dame Flora Robson' would not 'relish').[68] Raymond's production manager and photographer, Terry Power (Chris Addison), tells him that by making the photographs of the women in his magazines even more sexually explicit, they can seek to rewrite the 'cultural history of this nation'. Raymond and Power embark on a way of life in which sexual fidelity to one partner is not a concern, and they are free to engage in sexual acts with large numbers of seemingly willing women, with copious amounts of cocaine being consumed. Winterbottom often films these group sex scenes from a high angle in contrast to his close-up shots of the couple having sex in *9 Songs*. The scenes find a kind of aesthetic beauty in the bodies of the copulating couples, although the sex act is less dwelt upon than in *9 Songs*, as if the director wished to avoid some of the critical controversy stirred up by the earlier film's more single-minded and intense gaze.

Paul Raymond, the film informs us at the close, was the richest man in Britain when he died of natural causes at the age of eighty-two in 2008. His life of excess was therefore both enjoyable and profitable for him. Terry

Power is shown introducing Raymond's daughter, Debbie, to cocaine and himself becoming addicted to the substance. He ends up being fired by Paul Raymond for losing the right balance between 'work and play', but the film shows how both men are drawn towards pushing boundaries in their life and work, so it becomes difficult to know what might constitute going too far. Academic Susanne Kappeler argued in a 1986 issue of *New Socialist* that 'Nobody knows where to draw the line' as far as pornography is concerned, because, in her view, it 'doesn't stop anywhere'.[69]

If Raymond spots that excessive drug use is harmful to Terry, he fails to stop his daughter heading in a similar direction. A key strand of the narrative focuses on Debbie's desire to make something of her life and to be creative, echoing Laura's ambitions in *Animals* and those of the university would-be film-makers in *I Want Candy*. Debbie is expelled from her boarding school for drug offences – an indication of how drugs will prove to be destructive in her life – and pursues a singing career in a musical/burlesque review staged and financed by her father. When he cancels this show because of mounting financial losses (Raymond claimed to have lost £420,000 in the venture),[70] Debbie is shown as becoming more and more reliant on cocaine to raise her mood and morale. The cocaine is provided by both her father – even when she is having her baby – and Terry, before he is dismissed from his employment. Debbie survives breast cancer, but not a final lethal mixture of alcohol and drugs, administered (the film implies) by a young man whom she barely knew. Early in the film, Raymond has joked, while watching young women in his club covered in gold paint, that everything or enough things that he touches, turn to gold and become lucrative. The loss of Debbie proves this not quite to be true, and the film suggests that in losing Debbie he loses that which he valued most, leaving him a broken man.

Amid the overall downbeat conclusion, the film, in line with its transitions between past and present throughout, conjures up two happier utopian-type moments at its finish. The principal guests at Debbie's wedding to musician Jonathan Hodge (Simon Bird) are shown dancing joyously together in a slowed-down montage sequence emerging from a scene featuring Debbie's coffin being cremated. The guests include the Vicar of Soho, Edwyn Young (David Walliams), dancing with Fiona Richmond, Terry dancing with Fiona, Paul dancing with Debbie and ex-wife Jean in turn. The accompanying music creates a sense of mutual enjoyment and joyful happiness among the participants. The film has earlier shown the actual wedding to be a somewhat fraught and unhappy occasion; Debbie suggests Jean is flirting with her new husband and retires to take cocaine in a lavatory, while the unorthodox vicar, chaplain to the Raymond Revuebar, describes the wedding as more 'like a fucking funeral'. In this brief moment of communal joy, however, we get a sense of what life might have been like for the central characters if resentments, divorces, dismissals and overdoses had not intruded upon their lives and blighted their quests for happiness.

In this spirit of what-might-have-been, *The Look of Love* concludes with Debbie singing the title song, movingly and eloquently, as part of her bid to become an established singer, to an audience which includes Paul and Fiona (Dave in *Sex Lives* and Tyler in *Animals* both have similar moments where they sing someone's else's song to a small group). In this conclusion, as the credits unfold, Debbie's virtuoso rendition provides a moment of grace and epiphany. As the audience applauds, Paul Raymond looks on, proud of her achievement. For all its emphasis on the importance of sex and of gratifying the senses, this moment constitutes what one might term the real 'look of love' in the film. At Debbie's funeral, the chaplain quotes the familiar words 'Death, where is your victory?', a reference to the Christian belief in resurrection after death. Paul Raymond has certainly privileged the life of the body over the importance of the soul, and his final despair does not suggest that he holds out much hope of being reunited with Debbie in some form of afterlife. Raymond, in fact, has been depicted throughout the film as seeking to create his own kind of 'heaven on earth', based around the willingness of particular women to display their naked bodies for money and exposure on stage, screen and the printed page.

Concluding thoughts

An earlier film, *Mrs Henderson Presents* (Stephen Frears, 2005), had presented a case for women appearing naked on stage in British culture based around the eponymous Mrs Henderson's (Judi Dench) regret that her own son, who died in the First World War (1914–1918), probably went to his grave without ever having seen a naked woman. When she becomes the owner of the Windmill Theatre in London, business is boosted when naked women (appearing in the form of non-moving statues) are included in the stage reviews that are mounted. When the Second World War breaks out in 1939, the theatre becomes renowned for never closing, despite the bombing that is taking place all around it. Mrs Henderson sees the female nudity on stage as contributing to the war effort by boosting the morale of soldiers who are waiting to be shipped abroad to fight, many of whom being fated to die in the process. From her perspective, the Windmill becomes a symbol of a free society, a celebration of an open, democratic community standing up against fascist, life-denying authoritarian forces committed to nihilism, death and destruction. Mrs Henderson does not live to see the end of the war, but she bequeaths the theatre to an impresario (Bob Hoskins) who ensures that her work continues in post-war Britain. Paul Raymond would later become an owner of the Windmill Theatre, staging among other productions *Let's Get Laid*, 'twice nightly',[71] in 1975, thus creating another link between these two cinematic biographical studies of idiosyncratic pioneers in the field of naked entertainment.

Sceptical commentators might note that both Mrs Henderson and Paul Raymond concentrate on the promotion of female rather than male nudity in public performances and magazine publications, an imbalance which they don't seem to question or seek to redress. There have, of course, always been cultural observers and commentators who disapprove of what is termed 'pornography' and who question the inclusion of sex scenes, simulated and real, in film productions. Barbara Ellen, writing in the *Observer* during the worldwide COVID-19 pandemic crisis in August 2020, felt that the change in social circumstances necessitated by the virus opened up opportunities to cut down and move away from explicit or suggestive sex scenes on screen. Noting that Directors UK had updated its 'directing nudity and simulated sex guidelines', Ellen felt that now was a time to stop the practice of what she termed forcing 'actors to remove their clothes and simulate sex to liven up a dreary film'. She concluded that it ought to 'be possible to portray unbridled passion without showing a couple rutting'.[72]

Paul Raymond would probably not have agreed with such a viewpoint, which is parodied in the figure of Lady Longhorn in *Eskimo Nell*. *The Look of Love* presents Raymond as a man of his time and era, but also as someone who seeks to alter British attitudes to sex and the display of female nudity, seeing these both as aspects of humanity which should be cherished and affirmed, not hidden or shied away from. Certainly, a film such as *On Chesil Beach* shows the harm that can be done to a couple whose marriage is destroyed by living in a culture which is bereft of public images of sexuality and treats sex as not being a suitable subject for discussion or analysis, and essentially as an act (particularly for women) to be endured, rather than enjoyed. D.H. Lawrence, in his essay 'Pornography and Obscenity' (1929), referred to this phenomenon in British life as 'The grey disease!', leading him to argue that 'Only a natural fresh openness about sex will do any good, now'.[73] *Sex Lives of the Potato Men* may depict a society which has gone to the other extreme, where, to cite Lawrence again, what comes across in moments of the film is a picture of a world where 'the psyche deteriorates' and sex becomes synonymous with 'dirt' and 'something slightly obscene, to be wallowed in, but despised'.[74] The film does not entirely endorse such a world, however, and, at the close, Dave wishes to escape from its grip and be allowed to return to the family home by his wife. A final image of the film, however, is of some crazy paving he has constructed in the form of a giant penis at the front of an ex-lover and landlord's house, an image which even Sigmund Freud might struggle to interpret at this endpoint of the narrative, suggesting that his character will always have something of an anarchic sexual impulse about him, one that will not be easily incorporated into 'polite, everyday' society.

Michael Winterbottom's *9 Songs* was an attempt to take the sniggering and 'dirty little secret' aspect of sexuality in British film culture out of the picture by offering a film containing explicit actually performed sex acts, which nonetheless did not come under the category of pornography. It may be that Winterbottom's artistic and polemical intentions in so doing have been more celebrated than the actual film which eventually emerged from the process. Geoff Brown and Pamela Church Gibson's entry on the director in an authoritative reference book on *Directors in British and Irish Cinema* (2006), for instance, suggests that 'there are few rewards for the viewer' of *9 Songs*.[75] This may be an over-statement, but it is notable that the director does include a series of musical interludes (from which the film takes its title), which arguably belong to a different film altogether. From that perspective, *The Look of Love* might be viewed as a greater achievement for the strong roles it provides for the three most important women in Paul Raymond's biography: wife Jean, who has to try and rebuild her life after being discarded by Paul; Fiona, who becomes a sex symbol and a symbol of sex in the 1970s; and daughter Debbie, who becomes a victim of a desperate search for 'highs' which seemingly only drugs can provide (we never witness her having sex in the film). If the film has a 'message', it might be seen as a warning that drugs, rather than sex, can damage your health irrevocably. Paul Raymond proves able to make a personal fortune out of female nudity, and his playboy life can seem like a specific kind of male fantasy. But in the end, he appears alone and disillusioned, as if having found out the possible truth of Emma Morley's claim in *One Day* that an orgy is all well and fine, but it won't keep you warm at night.

Relationships and pairings in the post-2000 British films discussed in this chapter feature both couples who stay together and couples who part. Paul and Fiona go their separate ways in *The Look of Love* after an evening involving group sex in Raymond's apartment. Fiona's departure from his life also leads to her departure from *Men Only* and later debates about who 'sacked' whom. Lisa goes back to her native America at the end of *9 Songs*, while Matt, perhaps 'burned out' by his love and passion for Lisa, heads off for the 'purifying' cold of the Antarctic. One of the potato men finds a companion with similar views of life and love as himself, and in *I Want Candy*, a couple can find love and creative work through their shared love of making films. Laura in *Animals*, conversely, finds that she must move away from characters who demand a kind of total and draining commitment from her in the form of unending marriage or friendship.

Such nuanced conclusions are illustrative of how British cinema and society may have changed and developed since the 1970s. In *Eskimo Nell*, scenes and characters exist in isolation from each other and the narrative concludes in the dead-end of a prison cell. In *I Want Candy*, both individual scenes and characters exist in a much freer and open fashion, and the film concludes with its central characters finding new creative and productive possibilities are open to them, following the success of *The Love Storm*. Dan achieves some kind of professional satisfaction from his exposes in *Dogging – a Love Story* and is possibly able to build a loving and lively relationship with Laura, whom he meets during his sexual investigations. Carol and Joe, by way of a contrast, appear to have little left to say or do with each other once their sexual adventures come to a close in *Cool It, Carol!*

Marriage in the 1970s sex-oriented *Carry On* films was not always presented in a positive light, but Dave in *Sex Lives of the Potato Men* becomes an unlikely advocate for the stability and security of marriage at the close. Laura in *Animals* recognises that being creative in a literary manner may be dependent on being by oneself, and that indeed a process of meaningful self-realisation might only be possible on those terms. Paul Raymond, following the death of daughter Debbie, withdraws from public life and some of his previous excesses, but his loneliness is also the result of an acute awareness that aspects of the past involving his family cannot be rewritten or revised. His detractors might feel that this is also true of the legacy of explicit sexual images involving naked women which he helped to pave the way for and generate. *The Look of Love* does suggest, however, that if Raymond had not created and facilitated such changes in British culture and society, then someone else may have come along and done so. Raymond saw an opportunity and sensed a demand which he was pleased to satisfy. He is shown as a believer in the sanctity of sex (if not marriage) and an admirer of the aesthetic pleasures inherent in female nudity and the act of sex. Alongside several of the characters discussed in this chapter, he saw himself as championing sexual honesty and openness, celebrating the human body and its pleasurable sensations, urges and instincts. The cinema is driven by a desire to see and know more, and the films discussed in this chapter revolve around characters searching for sensual joys and an urge to learn more about themselves and other individuals in the process. Sex is seen as a basic human desire, but the films also show that the search for sexual happiness can be a difficult and complicated journey, and one which is never quite concluded or complete.

Notes

1 Author not identified, review of *Carry on Loving*, *Monthly Film Bulletin*, 37:443 (December 1970), p. 250.
2 Richard Neville, *Play Power* (Jonathan Cape, 1970), p. 73.
3 Jack Malvern, 'The Man who Owned Seedy Soho', *The Times* (4 March 2008), p. 3.
4 Gilles Deleuze and Félix Guattari, *Anti-Oedipus: Capitalism and Schizophrenia*, trans. Robert Hurley, Mark Seem and Helen Lane (London: Bloomsbury, 2015 [1972]), pp. 431–2.
5 Tym Manley, 'Back in the Centre Fold', *New Statesman*, 89:2306 (30 May 1975), p. 716.
6 Deborah Ross, review of *I Want Candy*, *Spectator*, 303:9319 (24 March 2007), pp. 51–2.
7 Jonathan Romney, review of *Dogging: A Love Story*, *Screen International*, 1678 (13–19 February 2009), p. 27.
8 Nick Dawson, film review of *9 Songs*, *Empire*, 190 (April 2005), p. 36.
9 Richard Porton, 'Going Against the Grain: An Interview with Pawel Pawlikowski', *Cineaste*, 30:3 (Summer 2005), p. 41. Pawlikowski suggests that 'people like Michael Winterbottom just assume airs as if they've got something to say' (p. 41).
10 Deborah Ross, 'Women of Substance', film review of *The Look of Love*, *Spectator*, 321:9635 (27 April 2013), p. 54.
11 Leonard Mosley, film review of *Oscar Wilde*, *Daily Express* (20 May 1960), page number not listed, consulted at the BFI Library in London, South Bank.
12 These phrases are taken from the 'Closing Speech for the Defence' by Gerald Gardiner in the Regina v. Penguin Books Ltd trial on 1 November 1960. Mr Gardiner asked the jury, 'it is not really right, is it, to convict Constance as if she were some kind of nymphomaniac?'. C.H. Rolph (ed.), *The Trial of Lady Chatterley: Regina v. Penguin Books Ltd* (Place of publication not identified: Privately Printed, 1961), p. 192.
13 Frank Kermode, 'Lawrence in his Letters', *New Statesman*, 63:1619 (23 March 1962), p. 422.
14 Katherine Anne Porter, writing in *Encounter*, felt that the conclusion to the story, with Connie and Mellors facing an uncertain future was a melancholy ending, promising only a 'long, dull grey, monotonous chain of days, lightened now and then by a sexual bout', a life, she felt, without 'laughter', peace or 'love'. Katherine Anne Porter, 'A Wreath for the Gamekeeper', *Encounter*, 14:2 (February 1960), pp. 72–3.
15 Derek Hill, 'The Habit of Censorship', *Encounter*, 15:1 (July 1960), pp. 58–9.
16 Pauline Kael, film review of *Here We Go Round the Mulberry Bush* (March 1968), reprinted in Pauline Kael, *Going Steady: Film Writings 1968–1969* (London: Marion Boyars, 1994), pp. 63–4.
17 Bill Bryson, *Notes from a Small Island* (London: Black Swan, 1998 [1995]), p. 21.

18 Julian Petley, 'There's Something about Mary ...', in Bruce Babington (ed.), *British Stars and Stardom from Alma Taylor to Sean Connery* (Manchester: Manchester University Press, 2001), p. 210.
19 Andy Medhurst, *A National Joke: Popular Comedy and English Cultural Identities* (Routledge: Abingdon, 2007), p. 131.
20 Matthew Sweet, *Shepperton Babylon: The Lost Worlds of British Cinema* (London: Faber & Faber, 2005), p. 293.
21 Ian Conrich, 'Forgotten Cinema: The British Style of Sexploitation', in Alan Burton and Julian Petley (eds), *Journal of Popular British Cinema*, 1, 'Genre and British Cinema' (1998), p. 87.
22 Paul Newland, *British Films of the 1970s* (Manchester: Manchester University Press, 2017 [2013]), p. 57.
23 Dominic Sandbrook, *State of Emergency: The Way We Were: Britain 1970–1974* (London: Penguin, 2011 [2010]), p. 449. He states that the titles of the *Confessions of ...* and *Adventures of ...* films 'were almost beyond parody', but notes that not all professions and job titles were equally represented: 'thankfully nobody had the courage to make *Confessions of an Academic*' (p. 449).
24 Leon Hunt, *British Low Culture: From Safari Suits to Sexploitation* (Abingdon: Routledge, 1998), pp. 91–113.
25 Author not identified, 'Picture Preview': *Eskimo Nell*, Films and Filming, 21:242 (November 1974), p. 40.
26 Michel Foucault, 'Preface', in Gilles Deleuze and Félix Guattari, *Anti-Oedipus: Capitalism and Schizophrenia*, trans. Robert Hurley, Mark Seem and Helen Lane (London: Bloomsbury, 2015 [1972]), p. xiv.
27 I.Q. Hunter, 'From Window Cleaner to Potato Man: Confessions of a Working-Class Stereotype', in I.Q. Hunter and Laraine Porter (eds), *British Comedy Cinema* (Abingdon: Routledge, 2012), p. 168. Hunter notes that despite featuring 'numerous sexually active working-class bodies' in its narrative, no one in *Sex Lives of the Potato Men* appears to be 'having much fun' (p. 166).
28 Mark Kermode, 'Film 2004: Heroes and Villains', *New Statesman* (13–27 December 2004), p. 68.
29 Terry Eagleton, *Across the Pond: An Englishman's View of America* (New York and London: W.W. Norton & Company, 2013), p. 166. In this study, Eagleton describes the Irish character as 'deeply unsentimental' and possessing a 'keen sense of the ridiculous' (p. 116). Eagleton also suggests that Ireland is a 'country' which by 2013 has reverted to what he describes as 'third-world status again' (p. 125).
30 Raymond Durgnat, *Eros in the Cinema* (London: Calder and Boyars, 1966), p. 67.
31 Production details taken from Al Horner, 'Call of the Wild', *Empire*, 365 (August 2019), p. 89. Horner sums up *Animals* as a 'debauched ode to female friendship' (p. 84).
32 Anna Smith, reviewing *Dogging – a Love Story* in *Empire*, 243 (September 2009), described it as offering 'an original subject for a romantic comedy ... [and] a seemingly authentic insight into a peculiarly British scene' (p. 43).

33 Anna Smith, film review of *I Want Candy*, *Time Out* (21–27 March 2007), p. 67.
34 Matt Holyoak, 'Michelle Ryan: Sweet as Candy', *Empire*, 215 (May 2007), p. 21.
35 Raymond Durgnat, *Eros in the Cinema* (London: Calder and Boyars, 1966), p. 67.
36 Melanie Williams, '9 Songs', *Film Quarterly*, 59:3 (Spring 2006), p. 63.
37 In a response to a survey of writers' views regarding Britain becoming a member state of the Common Market in the near future, John Gross commented that he was in favour as entry would remind British citizens of an insular disposition that they were 'living in the world, and not just in Coronation Street or Little Gidding'. John Gross, 'Going into Europe: A Symposium', *Encounter*, 19:6 (December 1960), p. 60.
38 Larkin's famous 1967 poem 'Annus Mirabilis' claims that sex began in 1963, 'Between the end of the Chatterley ban/And the Beatles' first LP'. Anthony Thwaite (editor), *Philip Larkin Collected Poems* (London: the Marvell Press and Faber & Faber, 1988), p. 167.

In a 1960 letter to Judy Egerton, Larkin wrote, 'I went to *The Nudist Story* tonight, which is the sort of thing I do when alone.' He concluded from this experience 'that bad films aren't so bad when the characters haven't any clothes on'. Anthony Thwaite (ed.), *Selected Letters of Philip Larkin 1940–1985* (London: Faber & Faber, 1992), p. 319.
39 Sandbrook, *State of Emergency*, p. 425.
40 Malcolm Muggeridge, 'Diary', *New Statesman*, 55:1405 (15 February 1958), p. 191.
41 In the original novella, Edward recalls having 'misread the signs ... at the showing of *A Taste of Honey*', a misinterpretation which leads to Florence jumping 'out of her seat and into the aisle like a startled gazelle'. Ian McEwan, *On Chesil Beach* (London: Vintage, 2018 [2007]), p. 90.
42 *Ibid.*, p. 50.
43 T.S. Eliot, 'The Waste Land' (1922), reprinted in T.S. Eliot, *The Waste Land and Other Poems* (London: Faber & Faber, 1940), p. 167.
44 Andrew Osmond, synopsis of *On Chesil Beach*, *Sight and Sound*, 28:6 (June 2018), p. 72.
45 Ross also criticised the 'ending', declaring that 'whoever signed off on this deserves a good thrashing'. Deborah Ross, 'This Will End Badly', film review of *On Chesil Beach*, *Spectator*, 337:9899 (19 May 2018), p. 40.
46 Nigel Andrews, film review of *On Chesil Beach*, *Financial Times* (17 May 2018), p. 8.
47 Peter Bradshaw, 'Virgin Territory', film review of *On Chesil Beach*, *Guardian*, G2 (18 May 2018), p. 14.
48 Ian McEwan quoted in Jake Kerridge and Anita Singh, 'Ian McEwan: The Young Know Nothing of Sex', *Daily Telegraph* (18 May 2018), p. 3.
49 C.A.R. Crosland, 'On the Left Again: Some Last Words on the Labour Controversy', *Encounter*, 15:5 (October 1962), p. 3.

50 Ian McEwan quoted in Kerridge and Singh, 'Ian McEwan: The Young Know Nothing of Sex', p. 3.
51 Derek Malcolm, '9 *Songs*: 'Next Stop: Classification', *Screen International*, 1454 (28 May–3 June 2004), p. 28.
52 Catherine Shoard, film review of *9 Songs*, *Sunday Telegraph* (13 March 2005), review section, p. 6.
53 I.Q. Hunter, *British Trash Cinema* (London: Palgrave Macmillan/British Film Institute, 2013), p. 121.
54 Zoe Williams, 'Sex without the X Factor', film review of *9 Songs*, *Evening Standard* (7 March 2005), p. 27.
55 Pelling, 'Oh Yes! Oh Yes! Oh my God, No!', *Independent on Sunday* (6 March 2005), p. 27.
56 Sukhdev Sandhu, 'The Naked Truth', film review of *9 Songs*, *Daily Telegraph* (11 March 2005), p. 19.
57 Pelling, 'Oh Yes! Oh Yes!'.
58 I.Q. Hunter, 'Naughty Realism: The Britishness of British Hardcore R18s', in Julian Petley and Duncan Petrie (eds), *Journal of British Cinema and Television*, 11:2–3 (2014), pp. 160–1. Hunter reveals that Dover's real name is Lindsay Honey. He stars as Ben Dover in his films, which he directs as Steve Perry (p. 161). The 'laddish' producer of pornographic films in *I Want Candy* is named Doug Perry, possibly in reference to Honey's directorial alias.
59 Linda Williams, *Screening Sex* (Durham, NC, and London: Duke University Press, 2008), p. 266.
60 Mattias Frey, *Extreme Cinema: The Transgressive Rhetoric of Today's Art Film Culture* (New Brunswick, NJ, and London: Rutgers University Press, 2016), p. 179.
61 David Cooke, 'The Director's Commentary', in by Edward Lamberti, Jason Green, David Hyman, Craig Lapper and Karen Myers (eds), *Behind the Scenes at the BBFC: Film Classification From the Silver Screen to the Digital Age* (London: Palgrave Macmillan/British Film Institute, 2012), p. 162.
62 Author not identified, obituary of Paul Raymond, *Daily Telegraph* (4 March 2008), p. 25.
63 Author not identified, obituary of Paul Raymond, *The Times* (4 March 2008), p. 60.
64 David Taylor, 'Naked as Human Nature Intended', interview with Paul Raymond, *Punch* (11 June 1975), p. 1024.
65 Clare Colvin, 'Roots: Paul Raymond', *Sunday Express* (28 July 1985), p. 38.
66 Dominic Sandbrook, *Seasons in the Sun: The Battle for Britain, 1974–1979* (London: Allen Lane, 2012), p. 402.
67 Bruce Manton, 'The Profits of Erotica', *New Statesman*, 84:2179 (22 December 1972), p. 940. Manton claimed that the titles of *Penthouse* and *Mayfair* indicated their 'right-wing' editorial tendencies aimed at celebrating the 'glories of the consumer society', whereas what he saw as the more anarchic qualities of *Men Only* and *Club International* had led to 'the police' in December 1972

seizing and burning sufficient 'copies and proofs' of these magazines 'to cripple a smaller organisation'.
68 Fiona Richmond, commenting on her part in *Let's Get Laid* in a photo spread in *Men Only*, 39:10, original publication date not listed when reprinted in *Men Only*, 84:3 (2019), p. 75.
69 Susanne Kappeler, 'Censored – the Porn Debate', *New Socialist*, 36 (March 1986), p. 20.
70 Taylor, 'Naked as Human Nature Intended', p. 1024.
71 *Ibid*. In this interview, Raymond describes his idea of 'light entertainment' as taking place in a 'friendly' environment with a 'few laughs'. He also states that he dislikes the term 'striptease', preferring the phrase, 'erotic entertainment'.
72 Barbara Ellen, 'Enough of the Explicit Sex. Do Put some Clothes on, for All our Sakes,' *Observer* (23 August 2020), p. 45.
73 D.H. Lawrence, 'Pornography and Obscenity', reprinted in Edward D. McDonald (ed.), *Phoenix: The Posthumous Papers of D.H. Lawrence* (London: Heinemann, 1967 [1936]), pp. 174–7.
74 *Ibid*. Lawrence describes this as the 'condition of the common, vulgar human being whose name is legion' (p. 176).
75 Geoff Brown and Pamela Church Gibson, 'Michael Winterbottom', in Robert Murphy, Geoff Brown and Alan Burton (eds), *Directors in British and Irish Cinema* (London: British Film Institute Publishing, 2006), p. 629.

5

'The way we live now': Narratives exploring relationships in modern British society

This chapter will explore the ways in which a significant number of directors and writers working in the British film industry during the 2000s sought to examine and investigate the social and personal relationships, sexual yearnings and hopes and desires of a range of characters in a series of contemporary settings and situations. British cinema has developed a reputation for providing thoughtful dramatisations that concern what Thomas Carlyle once formulated as the question of the 'Condition of England'.[1] Chapters in Raymond Durgnat's *A Mirror for England: British Movies from Austerity to Affluence*, entitled 'The State of the Nation', 'Points of View' and 'Our Glorious Heritage',[2] reflect such ways of identifying and interpreting trends and tendencies in British film history. Such a focus on particular movements and subgenres can be helpful in locating important changes in how filmmakers have sought to depict sexual, emotional and romantic relationships within British culture during particular periods of British social history. In his monograph *The Day Britain Died* (2000), Andrew Marr goes so far as to argue that 'one could construct an entire history of twentieth-century British consciousness' out of a study of significant film cycles in British film culture.[3] Movements in British film-making highlighted as especially important and influential have included the emergence of the British 'new wave' social realist mode of film-making and the 'social problem' film in the late 1950s and early 1960s; the move towards examining British society and sexuality in a 'Swinging London' setting from the mid-1960s onwards; the 'sex comedies' and 'sexploitation' films of 1970s British cinema; the 1980s comedy/dramas depicting personal relationships as experienced by British citizens under a Conservative government led by Margaret Thatcher between 1979 and 1990; and the Richard Curtis romantic comedies of the 1990s and 2000s, which presented a more generally benign and optimistic view of the possibilities for individuals and couples to find happiness in their personal relationships within British culture than perhaps was implied or evident in several of these earlier film movements and cycles.

Before proceeding to examine how film-makers explored and probed themes of sex, love and desire in British cinema during the 2000s, this opening part of the chapter will consider the significance and importance of a number of these earlier cinematic engagements with such themes and subject material. This will provide a historical context for what follows and an opportunity to see how modern-day writers and directors have sought to draw, build upon and go beyond (where possible) earlier treatments of emotional, sexual and loving relationships in British film-making.

Looking for something to watch at the cinema in the play *A Taste of Honey* (Shelagh Delaney, 1959), Helen finds nothing which appeals, only a horror film, *I Was a Teenage Werewolf*, and *The Ten Commandments*, which she does feel, however, might be good for her daughter's moral education.[4] Neither of these films seems to speak directly to Helen's experiences as a single mother living in an industrial northern city and struggling to make ends meet. If she had been following the film career of Sylvia Syms, Helen might have come across a number of film dramas which explored the diverse range of experiences a woman might conceivably face in the contemporary sexual climate of the late 1950s and early 1960s. In *My Teenage Daughter* (Herbert Wilcox, 1956), Syms is Janet Carr, a seventeen-year-old woman who rebels against her upper-class, female-dominated household, preferring the frenzied atmosphere of the jazz club to sedate ballroom dancing and the company of a rebellious young man (Kenneth Haigh) to more conventional companions. Janet's transgressive conduct leads to her becoming implicated in her boyfriend's manslaughter charge and her mother (Anna Neagle) being publicly castigated by a judge for failing to effectively curb her daughter's 'wild' behaviour. In *Woman in a Dressing Gown* (J. Lee Thompson, 1957), she is another quietly subversive figure, the 'other woman' in a 'love triangle', seeking to break up her work partner's marriage which he feels has become stale and atrophied after twenty years of togetherness. Having been Janet Carr earlier, in Basil Dearden's *Victim* (1961) she is Laura Farr, a barrister's wife trying desperately to understand and comprehend her husband's sexual and emotional yearnings for another man and the implications of this intense desire for their marriage. The narrative of *Victim* unfolds within a largely all-male environment as it explores the tortured lives of male homosexuals facing prosecution and blackmail for pursuing their desires and inclinations, but the film also illustrates how Laura can feel as if she, too, is a kind of victim in this culture, which ruthlessly suppresses homosexuality and does not encourage open discussion of sexual issues in a public forum. Issues of race and sexuality were to the fore in *Flame in the Streets* (Roy Ward Baker, 1961), in which Syms plays a schoolteacher entering into a relationship with a black Jamaican man of whom her racist mother vehemently disapproves. In both of these latter films, Syms's character pledges to emotionally support her male partner, despite pressures from society and family members to bring about a separation. *Honey's* Helen in time might, therefore, have found much to be intellectually stimulated and emotionally moved by in Sylvia Syms's performances and characterisations in these four films that explore complex and troubled sexual and social relationships.

A Taste of Honey was made into a feature film in 1961, following *Room at the Top* (Jack Clayton, 1959) and *Saturday Night and Sunday Morning* (Karel Reisz, 1960), two dramas which privilege the desires and behaviour of youngish male characters in their particular narratives, alongside a depiction of male–female relationships seen as existing in an uncertain and sometimes tormented state of being. *Room at the Top* focuses on Joe Lampton (Laurence Harvey), a young man who believes that the 'loosening up' of the British class system has created opportunities for someone such as himself to attain the woman of 'his dreams' and a higher place in the social class system, while the latter focuses on Arthur Seaton (Albert Finney), a less socially ambitious figure, a factory worker living for the eponymous weekend of the title, gulping down drink and sexual experience in a concerted effort to celebrate life in the present. Both of these films conclude tentatively with Lampton and Seaton contemplating life as married men, with mixed (in Joe's case, tearful) feelings about what the future may hold. American film critic Pauline Kael felt that Arthur's future was likely to revolve around such non-transcendental activities as getting 'drunk' and arguing 'with his wife'.[5]

What is generally seen as having replaced these lively but occasionally sombre realist-orientated dramas was a move by film-makers to explore issues of sexuality and national identity in a South of England setting and context (in his study of film-making changes and developments in the 1960s, Geoffrey Nowell-Smith entitles one chapter 'Britain: From Kitchen Sink to Swinging London').[6] *The Servant* (Joseph Losey, 1963) has Dirk Bogarde's man-servant from the north of England arriving in London, alongside his 'girlfriend' (Sarah Miles) posing as his sister, to wreak havoc on a complacent 'gentleman' employer (James Fox). The film, with its allusions to possibly incestuous and bisexual relationships and sexual pairings unfolding in a potentially endless series of permutations, intimates in its final 'orgy-like' setting how a servant might rise to become a kind of master, if the latter is to let his guard down and give into his previously submerged desires for sensual and seductive pleasures of different kinds. *The Servant* also illustrates how black-and-white photography could lend itself to suggesting malign forces might be at work just out of sight in the shadows, and that a film can stretch the bounds of realism by demonstrating that characters are capable of constantly changing their personality and outlook (rather than generally acting in the same manner) throughout an entire narrative.

Darling (John Schlesinger, 1965) is another film that pointed to changing times and the multifaceted nature of individuals, but one which focused this time on female sexual and social ambitions and aspirations. This movie also sought to go beyond the enclosed London setting of *The Servant* to include scenes in Italy and Paris. In the narrative, Julie Christie is Diana Scott, a model who becomes known as the 'happiness girl' in 1960s London advertising circles, but ends up rather unhappy by the end of the narrative. Scott leaves her husband for a married man, Robert Gold (Dirk Bogarde), who in turn leaves his wife and two children to be with her, demonstrating just how quickly these particular marriages can be dissolved and partners deserted. Gold and Scott's relationship, however, proves to be equally precarious, and Diana subsequently has an affair with an advertising executive (Laurence Harvey) who is dedicated to sensual pleasures and opposed to settling down. Harvey's character tells Diana to put away her 'Penguin Freud' when she seeks to reflect on whether their free-spirited sexual behaviour is bringing them any real happiness. Diana at one stage tells Malcolm that she doesn't 'really like sex', although she is aware that her sexual attractiveness and openness is key to her social mobility. In a 1985 *Screen* essay, Carrie Tarr notes that by the film's end, 'Men, marriage, romance, friendship, and family life have all been held up to scrutiny and found wanting' in the course of her emotional journey.[7] The film-makers appear to find the mid-1960s British advertising and media outlets which make Diana everybody's 'Darling' rather shallow and lacking in substance, and Diana ends up in a lonely and soulless marriage to a rich widower in Italy, who turns out to be a rather distant and absent husband. Robin Griffiths, in an essay in *British Queer Cinema* (2006), sums up the overall drift of the narrative as indicating 'a rather conservative cautiousness towards these new sexual attitudes that were emerging'.[8] Alexander Walker was not entirely convinced or satisfied by this gloomy conclusion to Diana's life, however, and felt that 'Within five minutes of the film's ending ... she would have had the spare Ferrari on the road to Rome to have herself a little *dolce vita*'.[9] In certain ways one can only hope this was so, but as there was no sequel to *Darling*, we can never be sure what finally became of Diana Scott.

If Diana Scott's life goes awry in *Darling*, the destinies of three central female protagonists in other significant 1960s and early 1970s movies (directed by Polish and American directors) exploring sex, class and culture in a British context were scarcely more hopeful. In Roman Polanski's *Repulsion* (1965), Belgian beautician Carol (Catherine Deneuve) finds herself so alienated from her London surroundings that she turns murderous and becomes clinically insane. In Joseph Losey's *Accident* (1967), the presence of an attractive Austrian female student, Anna (Jacqueline Sassard), in the male-dominated environment of an Oxford college creates an atmosphere of such competitiveness and destructiveness that no one emerges entirely unscathed. For two Oxford dons (Dirk Bogarde and Stanley Baker) and a student (Michael York), the life of the mind is as nothing compared with the possible sensual satisfactions to be gained from attaining sexual intimacy with Anna. The poster advertising *Accident* for its initial run in London included a picture of Jacqueline Sassard's face in close-up, juxtaposed with the phrase 'A sensuality which not only contradicted the surface respectability of their lives but damned it altogether',[10] and the final scenes have Bogarde's mild-mannered, but frustrated and disappointed don forcing himself sexually upon Anna as his wife has a baby in hospital and Anna's husband-to-be lies dead in a morgue, thus combining life, death and desire in a particular morbid and unsettling manner and style. Film historian Brian McFarlane has suggested that films such as Losey's *The Servant* and *Accident* reveal how in a 1960s British context 'Class can be brutal and sex can be destructive', but the films themselves offer what he terms a 'darkly poetic treatment' of their themes,[11] resulting in them being endlessly fascinating dramas to re-watch and study.

For much of its narrative, Jerzy Skolimowski's *Deep End* (1970) creates a picture of sexual desire as subject to disappointments and mishaps, often of a farcical nature. Susan (Jane Asher), a beautiful baths and swimming pool attendant, provides fifteen-year-old Mike (John Moulder-Brown) with a reason to enjoy going to work, but his fascination with her leads to tragedy and Susan's sudden and unexpected death at his hands in the municipal swimming baths. The film combines an expatriate's eye for the bright colours, uninhibited sexuality and seedy settings of late 1960s London, with an uneasy sense that too much rushing about in a manic search for sexual and material gain may lead to people getting badly hurt, resulting in dead ends rather than deep ends or new beginnings.

American Stanley Donen's *Two for the Road* (1967) features Audrey Hepburn and Albert Finney as a British married couple (Joanna and Mark), who find that though the French holiday setting to which they return every year remains essentially the same, they as a couple are constantly changing and altering in ways which make them less happy and settled in their relationship. This film, with its vibrant colours and fragmented time structure, shows that film-makers could be influenced by cinematic techniques and approaches associated with the French 'new wave' and illustrates that married couples build up a series of shared memories which, in retrospect, can appear elusive, 'dream-like' and difficult to make sense of. The film provides the character of Frenchman David (George Descrières) with a speech which suggests that the mid-1960s constituted a revolutionary time for relationships between the sexes: 'The whole world is changing. There is no such thing as permanence', he tells Joanna, his married lover. Joanna returns to her husband by the film's close, though not without some misgivings, and with a nagging feeling (as David has earlier claimed) that concepts of sexual faithfulness and fidelity within marriages are going to be more difficult for couples to adhere to and consider sacrosanct from this time in history onwards.

British cinema in the 1970s (as noted in Chapter 4) was keen to explore such perceived changes in sexual relations within Western culture, while taking advantage of accompanying changes in film censorship regulations. Heterosexual relationships remained the predominant focus, but one should note that British cinema of the late 1960s and 1970s did, on occasion, engage with gay relationships and seek to go beyond a depiction of homosexual and lesbian characters as essentially victimised and marginalised figures within British culture. An American–British film, *The Killing of Sister George* (Robert Aldrich, 1968), explores a gay relationship between a heavy-drinking middle-aged woman, June (Beryl Reid), about to lose her part in an ongoing BBC television serial, and her attractive and much younger lover, Alice (Susannah York). *Sister George* is a strange mixture of tragedy and farce, bawdiness and sadness, with Aldrich parodying British 'soap opera' conventions and traditions which present a sentimentalised and sanitised view of British society and culture, which the film itself is keen to undermine and unsettle. *Sister George* includes an (at the time controversial) extended sex scene – separate in style and mood to the rest of the narrative – in which a BBC producer played by Coral Browne provides Alice with a degree of sexual satisfaction which succeeds in prying her away from Reid's character. June is thus effectively 'killed' twice in the narrative, each time by ruthless television producers.

A critically highly regarded film released three years later, *Sunday, Bloody Sunday* (John Schlesinger, 1971), explores the theme of bisexuality by focusing on Bob (Murray Head), who enters into simultaneous relationships with Alex (Glenda Jackson), a divorced woman, and a gay Jewish Doctor, Daniel (Peter Finch). The pervasive mood of the film is one of melancholy, however, as Bob eventually leaves both lovers to experience life in New York. Daniel feels alienated from both the Jewish religion and his family, who are keen to see him settle down with a woman partner and have children. Daniel equally finds it difficult to meet gay men with whom he might have a meaningful relationship (a chance re-encounter with a man (Jon Finch) whom the film implies Daniel has formerly slept with, leads to him being robbed by this particular individual of his surgical equipment). Walker suggested that the film posed the questions 'What does it all mean?' and 'Is this all there is'? in a specifically early 1970s British context,[12] without suggesting that there were any easy answers or solutions to such pressing and troubling questions and concerns.

Nighthawks (Ron Peck/Paul Hallum, 1978) also poses many questions about the possibilities for sexual fulfilment in British culture, many of them addressed to the central character, Jim (Ken Robertson), a gay geography teacher working in a London school. Jim decides to explore human geography and homosexuality in a frank, no-holds-barred discussion during one particular lesson. 'Is it true? You're a wrong un. Admit it,' he is challenged by one pupil. Another defiantly declares, 'We're not working for a queer.' Two female pupils, who seem disappointed by Jim's admission that he is attracted to men, say they thought he 'was going out with Miss Pritchard, the supply teacher'. Other questions that follow thick and fast – this soon becomes one lesson that has the full attention of the entire class – include 'What do you do in bed?' 'Aren't you ashamed of it?' 'What do your family and close friends think [of your homosexuality]?' To which Jim replies that his family do not know, leaving the pupils in the position of knowing more about Jim than his own family. 'What's wrong with it?' asks a more liberal-minded pupil, who is quickly shot down by another asking 'What's right about it?' Another pupil states that if all men had the same inclinations as Jim, the human race would die out in time. Later, Jim is called in by the headmaster to explain what occurred during this lesson, and states that he felt he had to respond to their 'stupid questions' and to try and counter prejudices about gay people in society. The headmaster, however, is more concerned about such open discussions possibly affecting the school's reputation in the London area. The film concludes with Jim heading out in search of new sexual partners and potential relationships. He may not succeed in convincing his more sceptical and unruly pupils about the validity of his way of life and sexual preferences, but the film suggests, via the intense and extended question and answer sequence, that such concentrated and open discussions may be necessary to break down ingrained prejudices in British culture and to open up dialogues for freer and happier gay relationships to potentially emerge and flourish in future decades. *Nighthawks* was an important contribution towards realising such aims.

Another seminal, but not well-known,[13] British film, *Pressure* (Horace Ove, 1975), also sought to highlight problems and prejudices in British culture, this time in connection with social, sexual, economic and emotional interactions between black and white characters in mid-1970s British society. Tony (Herbert Norville), the son of parents who emigrated to Britain in the 1950s from Trinidad, seeks meaningful work and fulfilling personal relationships, but the only job he succeeds in finding – working as a hospital porter – brings him into contact with dead bodies, which serve to evoke the deadness of his personal and social relationships with others. A possible relationship with a friendly young white woman (whom he knows from school) is cruelly and brutally curtailed when her landlady refuses to let Tony enter her house because he is black. Tony's brother, Colin (Oscar James), and his black activist girlfriend from America, Sister Louise (Sheila Scott Wilkinson), see a pattern to all this quenching of hope and desire for black communities and advocate a form of resistance based around the privileging and promotion of what they term 'colour, culture and consciousness'. Colin's political activism based around the concept of 'black power' leads to his arrest, though, and the film concludes with Tony and his brother's friends and supporters valiantly trudging through London with placards to protest against his arrest and the treatment of black communities in 1970s Britain. Even the weather seems to be against the protestors, however, with heavy rain dampening their banners and spirits, leaving no one around to take notice of their pleas and demands for justice, recognition and a better way of life. Just as we do not know whether Jim's open-ended discussion in *Nighthawks* might cost him his teaching job (or how his sexual and emotional life will eventually work out), we do not know in *Pressure* whether Colin will be released from jail, or whether Tony will finally achieve a sense of cultural belonging and sexual and social fulfilment within British society.

As the 1970s drew to a close, British politics moved rightwards when Margaret Thatcher became the Prime Minister of Britain from May 1979. As her time in office extended across the whole of the 1980s, filmmakers took to exploring and examining sexual, social and economic relationships within the context of what became known as 'Thatcher's Britain'.[14] During the 1980s, the characters of Elaine (Alexandra Pigg) and Teresa (Margi Clarke) in *Letter to Brezhnev* (Chris Bernard, 1985), Rita (Siobhan Finneran) and Sue (Michelle Holmes) in *Rita, Sue and Bob Too* (Alan Clarke, 1987) and Johnny (Daniel Day Lewis) and Omar (Gordon Warnecke) in *My Beautiful Laundrette* (Stephen Frears, 1985) succeeded in becoming much-discussed figures in British culture, as their characters' behaviour and attitudes towards love, sexuality and society were seen as going 'against the grain' of traditional conservative beliefs and guiding principles during this period when Margaret Thatcher was in office.[15]

In *Letter to Brezhnev*, one of the central characters, Elaine, is pictured heading for Moscow at the close to reunite with her Russian lover (of one night), leaving behind her family and her close friend Teresa. This is seen as both a romantic and pragmatic move on Elaine's part, with neither the men of Liverpool, nor the current state of Liverpudlian life, offering compelling reasons for her to stay (reviewer Peter Ackroyd pertinently noted, however, that 'the Russian sailors' (notably played by non-Russian actors) 'seemed to have done nothing to earn the girls' undying devotion'.[16] Alexander Walker stated that this was the 'first British film to assert that life in the Soviet Union couldn't be worse than life in Liverpool', leading him to ponder, 'Swinging England, where are you now?'[17]

The Yorkshire setting of *Rita, Sue and Bob Too* provided the backdrop for its two central female characters, who were also looking for some kind of respite from their unprepossessing surroundings and situation. In this case, Rita and Sue find a temporary escape from the physical and psychological squalor of their circumstances not by meeting up with desirable men from abroad, but by engaging in illicit sexual encounters with Bob (George Costigan), a married man for whom they babysit. Sian Barber has revealed that the British Board of Film Classification awarded the film an 18 certificate at the time of its release in case it might be viewed as depicting 'teenage promiscuity' in a 'positive way' during an era of concern around the AIDS virus.[18] Hilary Mantel, in a *Spectator* review of the film entitled 'Bonkers in Bradford', felt, however, that it could work as an advertisement for safe sex: 'The Government ought to employ this entire film crew, to put the nation off [sex]', she suggested wryly. Mantel noted that *Rita, Sue and Bob Too* was promoted with the saucy tagline 'Thatcher's Britain with its knickers down', although she concluded that the film made no clear 'political point'.[19] The movie ends with Rita, Sue and Bob, too, in bed together, Bob's wife having left him and Rita and Sue having got over their rivalry for Bob's affection. This conclusion can be seen as unconventional or utopian (particularly from Bob's point of view), but also as an attempt by the film-makers to find some kind of humorous or slightly subversive note upon which to conclude events, the film, having elsewhere, depicted the local community as frequently at odds with itself and being far from a harmonious or enjoyable place in which to live and prosper.

If relationships are complicated and unpredictable in Alan Clarke and Andrea Dunbar's film, they are equally so in Stephen Frears and Hanif Kureishi's *My Beautiful Laundrette* (1985), a tale of a seemingly unlikely sexual and emotional alliance between two men – one, Omar, a British Asian would-be entrepreneur; the other, Johnny, an unemployed white male hanging out with a group of men prone to violent and racist behaviour in a run-down area of London. Alexander Walker felt that this was a film (like *Brezhnev*) which 'Social historians of the future [would] have to reckon with', as the narrative sought to stand 'the old imperial order on its ear'.[20] Johnny works for Omar – his physical strength coming in handy against the threatening elements circulating around the laundrette – and he also becomes his lover. This shared sexual desire and pleasure between the two men is shown as just about capable of withstanding the pressures all around that are working towards the destruction of both the laundrette and their relationship, but it is a close-run thing. The movie, which Kureishi described as 'an erotic', not a 'dirty film',[21] concludes with the two men splashing water at each other, following Johnny's beating at the hands of his former associates. This regression to a kind of childhood innocence on their part is shown as perhaps necessary given the kind of violence and nihilism which is shown to be prevalent within the local community. The film has sought to present events within the narrative in a kind of distanced and, at times, dreamlike manner, in order, perhaps, to encourage audiences to reflect thoughtfully and critically on what they are seeing. Melanie Williams has described such films as operating within generically fluid modes of 'social engagement and realism ... fantasy and fable'.[22]

Hanif Kureishi and Stephen Frears' follow-up to *Laundrette*, *Sammy and Rosie Get Laid* ('While the streets of London rage,' as the posters put it), was a film released in British cinemas during January 1988. This film also sought to evoke strong responses from its audiences by making a number of contentious points about sex, sensuality and British culture. However, it failed to achieve the commercial and critical success of its predecessor, and the obscurity into which *Sammy and Rosie* has subsequently fallen makes it appear that this movie's attempt to align itself with 'progressive' calls for sexual, political and economic change and emancipation was seen as too radical and extreme in its artistic and social aspirations by some critics and viewers. In particular, the film presented Sammy (Ayub Khan-Din) and Rosie's (Frances Barber) sexually 'open marriage' as a possible alternative to the more insular and less adventurous ways of living promoted and encouraged by Margaret Thatcher and her government.

Another Stephen Frears film, *Prick Up Your Ears* (1987), explored the dark, nihilistic humour of playwright Joe Orton (Gary Oldman) and his terrible death at the hands of his former friend and lover Kenneth Halliwell (Alfred Molina) in 1967. Orton's equating and mingling of sex and death, black comedy and tragic endings in his writing arguably seemed apposite again in a world shaken and troubled by the emergence of the AIDS virus in the 1980s. This film proved to be an early forerunner of the genre which more fully emerged in the 2000s that explores the sexual, personal and public lives of eminent writers in British culture.

The 1990s witnessed the emergence of an 'auteur-like' figure, Richard Curtis, who in a number of seminal and influential movies made romantic comedy dramas a key feature of modern British cinema. *Four Weddings and a Funeral* (Mike Newell, 1994) brought together, not without some difficulties and obstacles along the way, Charles (Hugh Grant), a diffident Englishman filled with self-doubt (Hugh Grant) and Carrie (Andie MacDowell), a confident, sexually experienced American woman. *Notting Hill* (Roger Michell, 1999) went one step further in promoting such

Anglo-American relationships by suggesting that Anna (Julia Roberts), a world-famous American actress, could be so enchanted by a similar kind of Englishman to Charles (once more played by Hugh Grant) that she is willing to put her career on hold and enter into a very different way of life with him by immersing herself in traditionalist British culture (an idea which possibly seems even more fantastical and unlikely to succeed nowadays than it did in 1999). *Love Actually* (Richard Curtis, 2003) has Hugh Grant becoming Britain's Prime Minister and presiding over what is presented as a nation of people constantly looking for love, either at home or abroad.

In terms of the films released in the 2000s that are discussed in this book, *This Year's Love* (written and directed by David Kane, 1999) was perhaps the most prophetic and perceptive about the mood and tone of many of the cinematic dramas and comedies to follow in the next decade. The film followed the fortunes of a group of characters whose love lives intersect in Camden Town, London. By the end, only one of the couples featured in the narrative is together – and the narrative actually begins with them splitting up just hours after getting married, when it emerges that the bride, Hannah (Catherine McCormack), has been sexually unfaithful to the bridegroom, Danny (Douglas Henshall). One of the characters in the drama, Liam (Ian Hart), is so undone by his failure to find a partner that he spirals into madness, while another, Mary (Kathy Burke), declares to Danny, who is still obsessed with Hannah, that she may be lonely, but not so lonely that she is prepared to spend time with him, listening to him endlessly going on about his ex. Danny and Hannah, two tough-minded Scots, belatedly go off on a honeymoon holiday to Corfu after he tells her in the unromantic setting of a supermarket queue (where she is a cashier) that she has taught him what love is: a state of being where 'You care for somebody more than you care for yourself'; you 'risk everything' to be with this person; and 'You forgive' their mistakes and errors of judgement. These are thoughtful, positive, encouraging definitions of what might constitute love and a meaningful relationship, but as the characters and films touched upon in this brief account have demonstrated, such sentiments can prove easier to achieve in principle than practise and promote on a regular basis in British cinema, culture and society.

The following sections of this chapter will seek to consider how key film-makers in the 2000s have sought to develop and expand upon these earlier treatments of romance, desire and sexuality in British film-making. In a range of varying styles and narrative forms, the post-2000 films to be discussed have continued to examine the themes and concerns explored in these previous cinematic treatments: the potential joys and disappointments of first loves and married lives; British characters seeking intimacy away from home; the pressures on women in changing times about whether to conform to traditional/conventional expectations about their lives and roles in society; the difficulties of finding lucrative, stable and satisfying work in the British economy; the problems which can be faced by gay men and women and couples in mixed-race relationships when various elements and factions within British culture disapprove of their getting together.

This chapter will consider the contributions made to post-2000 British cinema in relation to such themes and issues by Pawel Pawlikowski (*Last Resort*, 2001; *My Summer of Love*, 2004), Mike Nichols (*Closer*, 2004) and Lone Scherfig (*An Education*, 2009; *One Day*, 2011), films from non-British directors which Jonathan Romney welcomed as offering a meaningful alternative to what he termed the 'second-hand postcard pictures of home touted by so many of our own film-makers'.[23] Films such as *God's Own Country* (Francis Lee, 2017), *Pride* (Matthew Warchus, 2014), *My Summer of Love* (2004), *Disobedience* (Sebastian Lelio, 2017) and *Ae Fond Kiss...* (Ken Loach, 2004) will be examined for the ways in which they feature characters whose relationships are considered to be transgressive and possibly even shocking by other characters. *Notes on a Scandal* (Richard Eyre, 2006), also to be considered, focuses on a woman's illicit sexual relationship with an under-age boy and the traumatic consequences of her behaviour. This chapter will investigate the depictions of sex, love and desire in such films, alongside explorations of the work of Joanna Hogg and Noel Clarke and their quite different, but equally resonant and compelling portraits of relationships in a contemporary British cultural context. *Perfect Sense* (David Mackenzie, 2011) provides a chilling and disturbing coda to the theme of 'how we live now' in the modern world by focusing on a relationship between a young man and woman whose relationship is blighted and tormented by the emergence of a virus that gradually robs human beings of their senses and threatens their continued existence on earth.

The films will be examined for their thoughtful means of providing insights into how characters in the respective narratives experience the highs and lows of day-to-day relationships. The aim is to gain an enhanced understanding of how film-makers succeeded in creating distinct and diverse narratives about the lives, loves and desires of complex and charismatic contemporary characters in a series of moving and challenging films about the interactions between society, sexuality and the individual in modern-day British culture.

'One day' at a time and 'unsentimental educations'

Danish film-maker Lone Scherfig directed four strikingly innovative films in the 2000s that explore relationships between individuals and society in four very different eras in British social and cultural history. *Their Finest* (2016) looks back to what has been seen as Britain's 'finest hour', when Britain fought fascism and faced the threat of a Nazi invasion in 1940. *The Riot Club* (2014), by way of an extreme contrast, considers what could be termed one of Britain's 'worst hours', as the British upper-class members of the Oxford University-based 'Riot Club' destroy a publican's private dining room (nearly killing him in the process), in an attempt to demonstrate that they will not be part of what they see as a society ruined by greater social diversity and notions of 'political correctness'. Alistair Ryle (Sam Claflin), who is studying History at Oxford and is a leading member of the club, is shown railing against the establishment of the welfare state in 1945 for creating what he sees as a culture of dependency among the masses. He is also against people borrowing 'more money than they can ever afford to pay back', and believes that the upper classes have become too apologetic about flaunting their wealth and privilege. As Alistair is part of a group which treats women with contempt, destroys a restaurant and viciously attacks the kindly and tolerant restaurant owner, he is hardly a good advertisement for such views, but then he is opposed to the notion of positive images and representations in general. While he is heading for prison at the close, the film suggests that his political contacts in high places will lead to him attaining a well-paid and influential position in society upon his release.

Ironically, given this damning depiction of certain aspects of male-oriented life at the University of Oxford, the film which made Scherfig's reputation in Britain, *An Education* (2009), revolves around a young woman's hopes of gaining a place to study English there. Teenager Jenny Mellor (Carey Mulligan) dreams of escaping from her stifling suburban existence in London, in about 1961, via Oxford, but her ambitions are nearly derailed when she becomes involved with an older man, David Goldman (Peter Sarsgaard), who, it emerges, is married and occupied in conning people out of their money and homes. Jenny also worries about the possible future that is lying ahead for her, as she is unexcited by the prospect of becoming a schoolteacher or going into the Civil Service. Instead, Jenny is enthused about Paris as a city of love, music and culture, especially when compared with what she sees as the grey and boring England of the early 1960s. Jenny has her first sexual experience with her middle-aged lover in Paris on her seventeenth birthday (although this is not an event which is depicted on screen). Traumatically, though, Jenny comes to realise how close she has come to marrying a bigamist who lives in Byron Avenue, just around the corner from her. When she meets his wife (Sally Hawkins) and children, Jenny also has a glimpse of the cruel life such wives and mothers can be forced to live as their husbands seek younger single women in order to enjoy an illicit bachelor-type existence while actually being married.[24] In the end, Jenny achieves her ambition of studying at Oxford, having been helped by a sympathetic English teacher (Olivia Williams), whom she has earlier chided for what Jenny perceives to be her dull, unstimulating (single woman) existence.

We do not learn how Jenny fares at Oxford, but to some extent her character transmutes into the character of Emma Morley in *One Day* (2011), who similarly studies English at a prestigious university and finds it equally difficult to achieve happiness and fulfilment in her personal and private life. This romantic comedy-drama offers an irony-tinged portrait of a couple who meet just as their studies have ended, imbuing their relationship with a sense of belatedness from which it never quite recovers. If we do not know what becomes of Jenny, we do know that Emma will be killed in a tragic road accident while cycling in London. This is intimated at the start of the narrative when she turns left into a side road, but only truly emerges towards the end of the narrative.

Emma (like Bridget Jones) is involved with two different kinds of men, neither of whom can quite give her the emotional warmth, sensuality and stability which she seeks. Dexter (Jim Sturgess) is a friend and sometimes lover, who does not wish to be tied down in a long-term relationship, especially as he has a brief moment of fame in the late 1990s as a presenter on a late-night television programme aimed at young people. Ian (Rafe Spall) is a co-worker with Emma in a Mexican themed restaurant who has hopes of becoming a stand-up comedian. We never witness Ian's performances on stage, but in a way we don't need to as he consistently tries to be amusing in Emma's company, thinking that this is what will make her fall in love with him. This never quite works out, though, and, by the close, Ian is working for an insurance company and married to another woman. Emma's own career trajectory signals how, in the new kind of late capitalist economy of the 1990s and 2000s, a person may have several different kinds of jobs in one lifetime. Thus, she progresses from waitressing work to teaching and finally to becoming a published author of books for children. While Jenny dreams of visiting Paris in *An Education*, Emma, on money made from her writing career, actually gets to live there for a while with her French boyfriend. This is short lived, however, as Paris implies exile for Emma just as much as exhilaration, and a visit from Dexter is enough for her to abandon the city and lover in exchange for settling down with him. As Jenny might have suspected, however, none of these professional accomplishments appear to mean that much to Emma in the end, in comparison with the state of her love life and emotional affairs. This might seem a reductive point of view that is adopted by the film, but it does testify to the importance which people attach to their personal experiences of love, sex, desire and friendship.

In *One Day*, no happy-ever-after scenario is to be played out. Emma and Dexter get together in the end, but the final scene between them (while Emma is alive) is a sad one, as Emma is disappointed that she has not become pregnant and has concerns that she might have left it too late to successfully conceive (in the novel, Emma states that she will be 'thirty-nine next April, Dex').[25] In the parting scene in the novel, Emma and Dexter also have a serious argument about the ethics of the Anglo-American invasion of Iraq in 2004 and removal of Saddam Hussein from power, a discussion which does not feature in the Anglo-American film.[26] This adds to the poignancy of her unexpected and untimely death and possibly makes viewers wish that they had got together sooner. Melanie McDonagh, after viewing *One Day* in 2011, commented in the *Spectator* that, 'It's at times like this you hanker after the pragmatic approach to matrimony of earlier times, when men didn't have commitment issues and women didn't have cod-mystical ideas about the perfect mate, but both regarded settling down as the normal, grown-up thing to do.'[27] *One Day* perhaps testifies to a world in which children have witnessed their parents getting divorced and are therefore anxious about making similar kinds of emotional and legal commitments, which turn out in the end to have been misjudged. Dexter appears to get married largely because his girlfriend Sylvie (Romola Garai) is pregnant and they make a good-looking couple. These factors do not prove to be enough to keep them together, and she cheats on him with a university friend who has offered Dexter work in his crayfish restaurants, illustrating how work/sexual/romantic relationships are all intertwined in complicated ways for the couples in this film.

The final section of the narrative focuses on Dexter as he struggles to cope with the loss of his television career, the deaths of his mother, Alison (Patricia Clarkson), and Emma, alongside his failed marriage to a beautiful but distant, and ultimately sexually unfaithful, woman (an ironic development, perhaps, given Dexter's previous commitment to sleeping with as many women as he can, a fact noticed by Sylvie when they attend a friend's wedding). Regret and a sense of loss become pervading features of the narrative, and the film tries to find ways in which it might be possible to carry on after experiencing the loss of loved ones. (Dexter finds no solace in returning to a world of drink, drugs and strip clubs.) *One Day*, as the title suggests, implies that the only way to survive the deaths of loved ones is to try and remember and cherish the happier moments spent with these people when they were alive. Thus, the film closes by going back to the past and to Emma and Dexter's first meeting in Edinburgh. Here, Emma and Alison are alive again and everything seems possible and hopeful. Emma and Dexter exchange contact details, and Dexter is in the company of his loving mother and sceptical but caring father, Steven (Ken Stott). Emma and Dexter walk to the top of a hill with a beautiful view of the city at its highest point, and Emma notes that even if they were never to meet again, they will always have had this 'one day'.

This conclusion brings out the incontrovertible fact that all relationships will eventually be terminated by the death of one partner and that this is a terrible thing to contemplate and come to terms with. Those with religious faith (a subject to be discussed in connection with later films in this chapter) might find such losses easier to bear or to comprehend in that they can be seen as part of the process of God's design, with a possible spiritual dimension awaiting the deceased, thereby affording the prospect of some form of eternal life or continued sense of being. Those who do not accept or seek out such a religious perspective or framework (and Emma and Dexter do not discuss such matters in the narrative) must therefore find satisfaction and fulfilment in this world, or possibly not at all. From that point of view, Dexter and Emma's lives in Britain between 1988 and 2006 are a mixture of losses and gains. Dexter gets to partake in a world of hedonism, drug taking and casual sex, something the 'riot club' would applaud, but these pleasures do not bring him much permanent happiness or contentment. (The book's author David Nicholls has observed that he worried the implied message of *One Day* was overly moralistic, in appearing to suggest that 'if you ... take drugs and be promiscuous, you will be punished'.)[28] Dexter enjoys a brief period of fame (or notoriety) on British late-night television, but the programmes on which he works are not presented as having much substance or lasting value. Dexter graduates from working for others to being his own boss (at the close, he is the proprietor of a small café), but this inevitably lacks the excitement of live appearances on television with an audience of millions.

Emma's experiences of teaching are not dwelt upon – a brief curtain-call scene of a school production of *Oliver* stands for Emma's work in education – and we do not hear more than the opening sentences of her first novel. Her success in life, though, is to be a good person, witty, loyal, articulate, tolerant, forgiving and thoughtful. This makes her early death even more of an ordeal for viewers (and readers of the original novel). In killing her off, David Nicholls at once emphasises the 'power of the author' (despite what Roland Barthes might have said on this matter) in determining the ultimate fates of characters whom they have lovingly created.[29] Emma's demise raises questions which used to be a feature of academic literary studies about whether accidents leading to mortalities can be referred to as tragedies in the classical sense. Raymond Williams's *Modern Tragedy* (1966) argues that 'a broken career' and 'a smash on the road',[30] both of which can be said to affect Dexter and Emma, can also count as tragedies, but a later study of tragedy by Terry Eagleton, *Sweet Violence: The Idea of the Tragic* (2003), makes the perceptive point that the 'more everyday' our conceptions of tragedy become (a process which he described as the 'democratization of tragedy'), the harder it becomes to eradicate 'lethal accidents' and 'flawed relationships' from our daily lives.[31] One might conclude that Emma's death is both an accident and a tragedy. (This might not be part of Nicholls's intention, but her death does lead one to wonder how many cyclists die on Britain's roads each year and how this situation might be improved.) Anne Hathaway's warm, sensuous and humanistic interpretation of the role brings a luminous quality to the character. The film may also be seen as offering something of a moral imperative and a warning to its spectators, that we should try to live each day with a full consideration of others, because one day will eventually turn out be our last.[32]

Joanna Hogg: love and desire among the British upper middle classes

Joanna Hogg's films have sought to explore the personal, emotional and intimate lives and relationships of middle- and upper-class British characters. *Unrelated* (2007) and *Archipelago* (2010) are set outside Britain, and Hogg has suggested that holiday settings in films provide opportunities to witness characters acting in different kinds of ways because they lack 'the habits of home to fall into'.[33] Holidays, which in general can offer the prospect of possible exciting romances with strangers or fulfilling time with family members, in this director-writer's films turn out to be fraught and tense affairs, possibly suggesting that 'Britishness' does not always travel well.

Unrelated (2007) offers a portrait of the British upper middle classes abroad, holidaying in a Tuscan villa in what Joanna Hogg has described as a film about what it is like to be 'outside a family'.[34] The central character, forty-something Anna (Kathryn Worth), arrives late at night, pulling a suitcase on wheels, to stay with Verena's (Mary Roscoe) family and their friend George (David Rintoul) and his son Oakley (Tom Hiddleston). Anna, it transpires, is seeking respite from a troubled marriage and the narrative is punctuated with scenes in which she experiences difficult mobile phone conversations with her partner, who has declined to come on the holiday. (As the film does not show him, there is a sense that Anna is talking to herself during these frantic phone calls.) Anna starts to develop a kind of emotional connection with Oakley, who is young, good-looking and confident, and she does not conceal the fact that she finds the company of the teenage members of the families more inviting and lively than that of their parents. *Unrelated* raises interesting questions about age gaps between characters who enter into relationships which could be construed as 'unlikely' or undesirable. Anna is forced to wonder about issues of loyalty, obligation and trust after she is with the teenagers when they crash a borrowed car and decide to lie about what has happened. Should Anna go along with the subsequent cover-up or inform their parents about what has happened? Anna chooses (or is forced into) the latter option. This destroys her friendships with the teenage family members and just as the car may be written off, so is her burgeoning relationship with Oakley.

The 'documentary-type' observational nature of the film with its extended takes and sense of eavesdropping on 'real people' led some film reviewers to respond to Anna as if she were a 'real' person taking part in a 'reality' television programme featuring a group of individuals on holiday together. Jonathan Romney in the *Independent on Sunday* claimed that Anna was not someone you would 'want to get stuck next to at breakfast',[35] while Anthony Quinn in the *Independent* summed up Anna as 'Attractive without being a stunner', and someone who's 'still in good shape and senses her own allure'.[36] As the narrative unwinds, Anna is presented as someone who is somewhat disconnected and disappointed in life (hence, perhaps, the film's title), her spiritual loneliness accentuated by the unpeopled landscapes of Tuscany where she makes her phone calls, and the (understandable) sense of emptiness and boredom she experiences while having to listen to the families' dull and trivial conversations about drinks or take part in their party games. Despite the tedious elements of these family relationships and conversations – and the intense unpleasantness which emerges following the crashed car incident – the film goes on to suggest that Anna is predominantly unhappy because what she thought might have been pregnancy turns out to have been the early stages of the coming menopause. This plot development led to Sophie Mayer in *Sight and Sound* criticising what she felt was the film's explicit linking of 'women's identity' with conservative notions of 'family and fertility'.[37] In interviews, Joanna Hogg has stressed that she believes 'Having children is a very creative thing to do',[38] and that like Anna in the film, as a childless woman in her forties, she became conscious while making *Unrelated* that she was not going to become a mother. This realisation apparently fed into and helped to determine the eventual structure, content and mood of the film.

In all of her films, Joanna Hogg is keen to explore how various British characters interact with each other on a personal, social and linguistic level. Most of the conversations between the (presumably well-educated) characters in *Unrelated* have little depth or significance, but one key extended scene shot in medium close-up has Oakley and Anna in a piazza discussing intimate issues – what constitutes sexual pleasure, and emotional direction and purpose in people's lives. Oakley, as a single ex-public school pupil, appears keen to explore the dynamics of mature relationships with an older person. Anna, in turn, wearing a distinctive hat and seeming to be more relaxed and engaged than previously, responds to Oakley's questions about sex, commitment and children with candour and good humour. Anna admits that sexual attraction may fade in long-term relationships but argues that marriages are about 'making a bond with somebody', establishing an emotional rapport with a person which can be nourished and developed through a lifetime of togetherness. Oakley, however, believes that an ongoing and immediate sexual attraction between partners is central because sexless relationships are 'dead in the water'.

The denouement to this discussion takes place when Anna appears to offer herself sexually to this much younger man at the end of an evening out ('Oakley, you can come in if you like'). 'I'd better not,' is Oakley's polite reply, and the film leaves it open as to whether he is thinking that sleeping with Anna would be an improper act on such a family holiday or that he declines because he does not find Anna sexually inviting or alluring. (This might tie in with his earlier claim that a mutual sexual attraction is necessary for a relationship to begin and prosper.) Oakley, in fact, does not have sex with anyone in the course of the narrative, suggesting that Joanna Hogg is interested in the sexual thoughts which her characters have and in demonstrating how a certain level of sexual frustration may influence their behaviour (the film contains a number of shots showing Anna alone and naked in bed, unable to sleep). It is left open as to whether being sexually rejected by Oakley leads to Anna informing Verena (under pressure) of the true reason why the borrowed car was towed away to a local garage.

Writer-director Hogg does not, however, end *Unrelated* on an entirely sombre or pessimistic note, despite including scenes of Anna breaking away from the family, being tracked down by Verena and brought back somewhat reluctantly into the fold of the holidaying community (a moment shot from a high 'god-like' angle). At the close, Anna is shown as resilient, gracious and forgiving as the holiday eventually comes to an end. In a pleasingly symmetrical touch, she is shown as being the last person to actually leave the villa in contrast to being the last to arrive at the holiday destination. 'It's been a pleasure,' she tells the family (euphemistically? sincerely?), wishing Oakley 'good luck' as she bids farewell to him in a parting embrace and hug. We last see Anna in the back of a taxi en route for the airport, once more on the phone to her unseen husband and still trying to build emotional and spiritual bridges: 'Are you still there, Alex? I'm still here.' Anna appears more upbeat than on previous occasions, and states that she looks forward to being able to speak to him face to face, perhaps aware that the family life she has expressed a desire to experience may not be without its own disappointments and moments of extreme unpleasantness. *Unrelated* explores the kind of ties which may bind people to each other and the ways in which relationships can be conventionally based around notions of duty, obligation and routine, rather than being driven by spontaneity, empathy, passion, sincerity and attempts at understanding, something that leads many of the characters in the film to feel 'unrelated' to or unappreciated by those around them. As Oakley suggests, relationships between the body and the mind, the soul and the intellect, the cerebral and the carnal will always be complex and possibly, in the final analysis, slightly unfathomable.

Archipelago revolves around a family enduring a rather joyless break in the Scilly Isles. The son of the family, Edward (Tom Hiddleston), has decided to give up his banking job and to start teaching sex education and how to avoid becoming HIV-positive in Africa, much to the dismay and disapproval of his mother, Patricia (Kate Fahy), and sister, Cynthia (Lydia Leonard). The rainy and windy weather conditions and the confined spaces of the island appear to reflect the emotional constrictions of the family and their melancholy state of being. Edward appears to be fond of the hired live-in cook (Amy Lloyd), but nothing comes of their sympathetic talks with each other, and she leaves as soon as she possibly can after an argument between Patricia and Cynthia becomes extremely unpleasant. Patricia is studying painting with a tutor, but Hogg's film does not find in the family's experiences any painterly symmetry or pleasing aesthetic shape or artistic vision. As the holiday comes to an end, the family leave the island by helicopter, and cleaners are shown arriving to clean and tidy up the rented accommodation for the next set of guests. These concluding images imply that places exist and continue beyond the lives of individuals who may inhabit them briefly, while the ending also conveys a sense of the joylessness and possible futility of the family's time spent in this location. Edward's progression to Africa – and the very different climatic conditions, landscapes and relationships to those depicted in *Archipelago* – is not a development charted in the film.

Hogg's films – which include *Exhibition* (2014), her least emotional and narrative-driven movie about an artistic couple's unsettling relationship with their modernist house – are preoccupied with states of spiritual loneliness and disappointment among well-to-do characters, whom one might expect to be happier than they appear to be. Such thematic and conceptual concerns are to the fore in *The Souvenir* (Joanna Hogg, 2019), where the director focuses on Julie (Honor Swinton), a comparatively wealthy young woman living in London during the 1980s. Julie is studying at a film production school and has aspirations to make a social realist-type film about life in contemporary Sunderland. She is diverted from this aim, however, by her relationship with an older, upper-class man, Anthony (Tom Burke), who claims to work for the Foreign Office. The exact truth of this claim is never verified in the film, and it may be that this was once the case but is so no longer, because Anthony has developed a terrible and ruinous addiction to heroin which will kill him before the end of the narrative. In this respect, *The Souvenir* marks a step towards a more tragic perspective and outcome than in Hogg's earlier films. Anthony and Julie both speak a particular kind of upper-class English discourse which rejects (for the most part) too unmediated an attention on the less agreeable aspects of their lived reality and the uneasy nature of their relationship. Anthony's addiction to heroin leads to a distorted relationship between his body and his mind, turning him into a kind of alienated monster figure. He appears to have affectionate feelings for Julie, but he has no compunction about stealing her film-making equipment in order to fund his expensive drug habit. His upper-class distanced English perspective, perhaps honed to a fine art after years working for the Foreign Office, prefers not to acknowledge his terrible and terrifying behaviour, a failure which will lead to his own demise.

In an early scene in the film, Anthony expresses an admiration for the work of the film-makers 'Powell and Pressburger', and his own terrible end (dying in a public toilet) might seem to resonate with their 1947 film *Black Narcissus*, in which a character dies a painful and excruciating death, her mind having become unhinged through a dreadful obsession. When Anthony's conduct is at its most menacing and frightening towards Julie, he might also be seen as indirectly evoking the terrifying behaviour of Mark Lewis (Carl Boehm) towards women in Michael Powell's London-set *Peeping Tom* (1960), a film which appears to have heralded the demise of Powell's solo film career but is now viewed as a major directorial achievement.

Alongside such filmic allusions, Joanna Hogg seeks to place Anthony and Julie's courtship and relationship within the social and political context of 1980s 'Thatcher's Britain', as discussed earlier in this chapter. At one stage, after they have become sexual partners, Julie becomes very ill, pale, weak and confined to her bed in a moment that the director has described as having 'the shadow of AIDS' about it.[39] Julie recovers, but later, in a disturbing scene, her apartment is presented as being in close proximity to the real life IRA bomb detonated outside Harrods in December 1983. This explosion killed 'Five people including two police officers' and was, according to Prime Minister Thatcher, 'Even by the IRA's own standards ... a particularly callous attack ... designed to intimidate ... the British people as a whole.'[40] Anthony's desolate and debilitating activities around drugs can thus, in part, be seen as a doomed attempt to escape from such traumatic features of life in the 1980s.

In *Unrelated*, Anna journeys back to her difficult husband at the close, while Edward faces an uncertain future in Africa at the end of *Archipelago*.

In *The Souvenir*, Julie appears set on finding solace and a sense of purpose by becoming a serious film-maker. The final image shows her being dwarfed by the huge sound stage doors of a film set, the chance to be creative and imaginative opening up possibilities for her which are possibly denied to Edward and Anna (it is not clear what kind of work Anna is involved with). These three beautifully composed films imply that in emotionally reaching out to other individuals, characters such as Anna, Edward and Julie face having their feelings badly hurt and trampled upon by people who turn out not to be as sensitive, caring and empathetic as themselves. Nonetheless, one senses that Joanna Hogg admires Anna, Edward and Julie for their sincere and well-meaning efforts to make meaningful connections with other characters. Relationships, in any case, as Anna points out to Oakley, are never easy, straightforward or without some pain or complications, as the next film to be discussed in this chapter (*Notes on a Scandal*) will amply and disturbingly demonstrate.

The 'Shame of Sheba': *Notes on a Scandal* (Richard Eyre, 2006)

'I need to talk to you about Steven Connolly' (Barbara Covett to Sheba Hart).
'I need to talk to you about Mrs Hart' (Brian Bangs to Barbara Covett).

The film begins with teacher Barbara (Judi Dench) sitting alone on a park bench which affords a clear view of her immediate surroundings. Barbara subsequently goes on to provide an intimate voice-over of her thoughts, feelings and views on the characters, settings and situations within the milieu of the comprehensive school in London where she is the Head of History. Barbara is by no means an impartial historian and she does not hold back from offering views which are critical and dismissive of those around her. Watching the pupils stream in from her classroom window at the start of a new term, she comments that teachers used to have to confiscate cigarettes and pornographic magazines, but now it is 'knives and crack cocaine'; she observes ironically that this is seen as 'progress'. (In fact, knives and drugs, unlike in Noel Clarke's films, will not feature in this narrative, and the 'scandal' promised by the title will emanate fundamentally from the staff, rather than the pupils.) Barbara, while an effective disciplinarian in a difficult environment, has no time for the kind of detailed administrative research into how the school might do better that has been initiated by the headmaster. Given the social and economic conditions in which the pupils live, Barbara doubts that the school's results and behaviour problems can be radically improved. *Notes on a Scandal* will not prove to be a kind of *To Sir, With Love* (James Clavell, 1967) narrative in which a failing school is improved through the efforts of one dedicated teacher, but the ensuing drama will focus on the unexpected effects created by the arrival of new art teacher Sheba Hart (Cate Blanchett). Sheba is an attractive blonde woman in her thirties, who stands out from the rest of the staff even when wearing a long plain coat in the school playground. It transpires that she has entered teaching in order to try and make a useful contribution to society, and to feel that she is achieving something beyond being a 'good mother' and wife.

An invitation to lunch at Sheba's house introduces Barbara and the film's viewers to Sheba's husband, Richard (Bill Nighy), son and daughter. Barbara's caustic voice-over allows the film to re-create the first-person narrating style of the Zoe Heller novel (2003) from which the film was adapted. This reveals that Barbara is fascinated, if somewhat bemused, by the Hart household. She is surprised that the husband is 'nearly as old as' she is, and in a plot backstory, which has echoes of the relationship between Robert Gold and Diana Scott in *Darling*, we learn that Richard left his wife and children to set up home with the desirable Sheba. It is also revealed that Sheba has a son, Ben (Max Lewis), who suffers from Downs Syndrome, so that, to Barbara's surprise, Sheba's family life is not as perfect as she imagined it to be. (In a Christmas day entry in her diary, Barbara records that she feels sorry for Sheba being 'all alone with her awful family'.) The two women go on to form an emotional connection in what will later be referred to as Sheba's 'lair', her artistic/creative room, adjacent to the garden. Sheba entrances Barbara with her open and unguarded conversation, which in the novel is referred to as the 'pretty strong stuff she tells me in that newsreader's voice of hers'.[41] Sheba makes a point which Barbara can relate to about how there appears to be an unbridgeable gap as she gets older between 'life as you dream it, and life as it is', a gap between hopes and reality, aspiration and achievement, desires and actuality.

Barbara finds Sheba to be a deeper and much more interesting person than her other teaching colleagues; she will indeed turn out to be an exceptional teacher and individual, but not in the ways that Barbara anticipates or appreciates. Sheba's speech about disappointments in her life and a photograph of her with two women friends in 1980s hairstyle and make-up might retrospectively indicate that she is prepared to break out of her contained life as a 'good mother' and 'caring teacher'. But what she does embark on – sex with a legally under-age boy, who is a pupil at the school where she teaches – is relatively unprecedented as a subject for exploration in British cinema. *Term of Trial* (Peter Glenville, 1962) revolves around an alleged sexual relationship between a schoolteacher and a female pupil, but this is proved not to have taken place by the close of the narrative. In Zoe Heller's novel, Barbara reflects that unlike with male sexual transgressions, 'A woman who interferes with a minor is not a symptom of an underlying tendency ... People don't see themselves, or their own furtive desires in her,'[42] which might offer some explanations as to why this has not been seen as an appropriate topic for cinematic exploration. The boy involved in the relationship, Steven Connolly (Andrew Simpson), is of Irish descent, and he comes to prominence in the narrative when he is involved in a fierce fight with a fellow pupil in the library, the location for the school's 'homework club'. It emerges that Connolly claims to have been fighting to protect Sheba's honour after derogatory ('Bang out of order') remarks have been made about her. Only Barbara's intervention brings the fight to a stop and restores some kind of order (during her interrogation, she still finds time to briefly mimic Connolly's strong Irish accent).

From this point on, Barbara, Sheba and Steven's lives will be intertwined in ways which none of them can untangle. Barbara goes on to discover Sheba's illicit and illegal sexual relationship when Sheba does not turn up for the school's Christmas carol concert, ironically an occasion when the pupils as a whole seem to be pulling together in a positive fashion. Barbara is led to Sheba's art room by her desire to know Sheba's whereabouts and peers through a gap in the window. What she sees is Sheba, wearing a white bra, embracing a male partner and appearing to perform oral sex on him. As the words to the carol 'Hark the herald angels sing/Glory be to the new born King' are sung by an attendee leaving the concert (the film has something of a dark comic subtext underpinning the serious treatment of its themes), Steven Connolly is shown leaving the art room, revealing that it was he who was Sheba's sexual partner. Barbara is now in possession of some startling and shocking knowledge, information which she should pass on to the headmaster (Michael Maloney), who is in the building at the time.

As she likes Sheba and does not wish to immediately destroy her career, Barbara first gives her the opportunity to explain what has happened. At this point, Sheba takes over the narration of the story, and we see flashbacks of Connolly pursuing her in London, telling her she is 'beautiful' and speaking of his ill mother. Sheba and Steven are depicted meeting in a subway tunnel and having sex near a railway line. We witness them kissing and are privy to their post-sex behaviour, Steven smoking a cigarette, Sheba drinking from his can of beer and declaring in teenager-like language that he has 'done [her] brain in' (Barbara, drawing upon similar discourses, will later declare that the boy did Sheba in 'like a kipper'). The film-makers were presumably keen in such scenes to show no more of the teacher and pupil's sexual encounters than was deemed narratively necessary, but Thomas Sutcliffe, writing in the *Independent*, felt that the 'flustered embraces between Blanchett and her young co-star felt disconnected and underpowered as you watched', leading to a 'sudden drop in intensity'.[43] Sheba herself cannot really offer any truly convincing reasons for her behaviour, which may feed into Sutcliffe's failure to be convinced by the relationship, but this may also be indicative of how Barbara and Sheba's (non-sexual) relationship is, for all its trials and tribulations, probably the most dynamic and challenging relationship depicted in the narrative (and, arguably, the main focus of interest for the film-makers).

Barbara, disproving King Lear's famous declaration that 'Nothing will come of nothing',[44] announces that she 'could gain everything by doing nothing' (i.e. not reporting Sheba to the authorities and giving her a chance to end the relationship and save her career and marriage). The film, in fact, makes much use of such ironic uses of language, names and expressions in its narrative discourses: for example, key characters are named Covett, Hart and Bangs. Steven's father thanks Sheba for all the extra art lessons she has been giving his son after school, lessons which are helpful as Steven has 'special needs' (these classes will eventually land Sheba in jail). When Steven sees Sheba's husband looking for her, he asks, 'Was that your dad?' 'No, he's an uncle,' replies Sheba, in full Judas-like betrayal and denial mode. Steven wonders if the reason Barbara might not inform on Sheba is that she is 'giving her one' as well, a thought which will cross Sheba's mind. During their final time together, Sheba angrily asks Barbara if she wants to 'fuck' her, and Barbara asks Sheba not to 'demean' their friendship by talking in such a crude manner. Barbara tells Sheba that her close friend Jennifer became depressed and suffered from delusions, but instead of receiving medical help she got a job in 'Stoke'.[45] Her daughter Polly (Juno Temple) describes Barbara as being like a 'spectre at the feast' when she makes an unexpected appearance at the family home after the scandalous news has broken, a comment which is truer than she might imagine. Barbara expresses surprise that fellow teacher Brian Bangs (Phil Davis) wishes Barbara to find out if Sheba is 'inclined to commit adultery' with him, before taking rather special pleasure in informing the lovelorn Brian that Sheba's preference is for the younger man; in fact the 'surprisingly young' man. Earlier in their conversation, Brian's happiness following the 'mighty' Tottenham Hotspur's success at White Hart Lane causes Barbara to wryly reflect that her own father's lifetime commitment to Charlton Athletic did not seem to bring him much 'joy'.

Such a dry, throwaway remark, while not central to the narrative, sums up the mood and atmosphere of resigned disappointment which the schoolteachers experience. Derek Malcolm, in a review of *Notes on a Scandal*, wrote of the 'dreariness' of 'school life' as depicted in the film,[46] and this surely is one of the key reasons why the character of Sheba causes such a stir for the characters who surround her – her very presence offers an alternative to the grey, dispiriting, under-achieving ambience of their lives in London. In his *A Mirror for England: British Movies from Austerity to*

Affluence (1970), Raymond Durgnat comments on the 'constant procession of European' and 'American' actresses who made appearances in British films because they didn't have to 'grope for feelings, for their identity, through the fog of British reserve',[47] and one can note that several of the films discussed in this book feature non-British actresses in key roles, including *Notes on a Scandal*, where Sheba is played by Australian-born Blanchett, which perhaps makes her character stand out even more amid the very capable British character actors surrounding her as events unfold.

Having observed how the film uses language and phrases to comment obliquely on its narrative developments, we can also see how *Notes* does not shy away from the more direct sexual language used by Steven to Sheba. On Christmas Day, as she has lunch with her mother and family, Steven sends her a text which reads 'Happyxmas miss! Wish I woz fucking u blind rite now', both the spelling mistakes and the sentiments being quite at odds with the middle-class family festivities taking place. On another occasion, he rings Sheba from her garden (in a call which is intercepted by Barbara) and declares, 'I've been dreaming about your hot sweet cunt all morning' (the fact that he actually conveys this message to Barbara might be seen as part of the blackly comic aspect of the film, where with the exception of Sheba and Steven's illicit and illegal trysts, none of the characters – the headmaster, Brian, Barbara, Richard – really get what they desire and want).

The dramas which Sheba creates around her start to rise to an emotional climax when Barbara suggests to Sheba that they stroke each other's arms in Sheba's kitchen. This is a blissful moment for Barbara as she finally has Sheba to herself. The latter is wearing a low-cut blouse which is seductively attractive (it will emerge she is dressed this way because she is expecting to see Steven in her garden art room). What is heaven for one person may be an ordeal for another, however, and after a short time, Sheba makes it clear that she has tolerated the situation for as long as she can, forcefully declaring, 'I think that's enough' (Barbara will shortly declare that she has been humiliated at this point). Thomas Sutcliffe, cited earlier, was impressed by the emotional truth of this particular sequence: 'It's a moment at which [Barbara's] longing emerges into the open and it unnerves Sheba, who, after submitting for a few moments, recoils.' Sutcliffe felt that 'as a member of the audience you understand both sides of this exchange with an almost physical intimacy. You know why Barbara longs to touch Sheba and why Sheba doesn't want to be touched.'[48] Barbara feels insulted that Sheba is willing to be physically intimate with under-age Steven Connolly, but not herself in this most modest of ways. Sheba, in turn, would like to be kind and accommodating to Barbara, but does not find her attractive or desirable. Unhappiness and disappointment ensue, particularly as it emerges that Connolly is present in Sheba's own household awaiting the pleasure of her body (Barbara sees what appears to be a criminal intruder in Sheba's garden).

As things start to approach what Barbara refers to as the 'final act' of the opera, Steven becomes worried that if the affair is made public he will be expelled and the matter will become very serious indeed. Barbara uses Brian's infatuation with Sheba to suggest to him that Sheba is involved in a sexual affair with Connolly. The headmaster puts pressure on Barbara to take early retirement because he suspects (rightly) that she knew about the relationship but kept quiet about it. The head informs the police and the local authorities (at an earlier point of the narrative, Barbara has talked about teaching being an extension of the Social Services). Polly accuses her mother of having a younger boyfriend than herself; while Richard wonders why Sheba did not go off and have an affair with an adult, something which has been working for centuries as a way of breaking up marriages (ironically, this is how his own relationship with Sheba began). Sheba worries about receiving two years in prison. A newspaper front page headline informs us at the close that the thirty-seven-year-old 'Sex teacher' was 'sentenced to ten months' in prison. There is a picture of Richard literally standing by her outside the court, implying that he will do so during her incarceration. At the close, Barbara meets a young woman, Annabelle (Anne-Marie Duff), on the park bench where the film began. Annabelle is reading about the court case and the 'Shame of Sheba'. This provides Barbara with an opportunity to introduce herself and seek to make this stranger a new friend. Barbara claims (in a statement that might be seen as both true and untrue) that she 'didn't know [Sheba] very well'. The film ends with Barbara, now retired,[49] 'Thank goodness', she says, inviting the young woman to a music concert. This ending can be seen as both ironic and disturbing, given that in the past a former friend of Barbara's, Jennifer Dodd, got a restraining order against Barbara being in her presence at any time.

The novel ends with Sheba and Barbara together, and at each other's throats, having both lost their teaching jobs and with Sheba awaiting trial for statutory rape. Sheba has taken shelter from the frenzy of newspaper photographers outside her home and Barbara, the narrator of the novel, implies that they are now inextricably linked together, given Sheba's ostracism by British society and her husband's cold attitude towards her. The novel ends with Barbara's first-person narration stating, 'She seems quite steady and calm after her rest. And she knows, by now, not to go too far without me.'[50] Cate Blanchett has interpreted this as Sheba almost having 'given up' after becoming captured in 'Barbara's web'. The film contrastingly concludes with Sheba returning home and silently asking to be readmitted to the family home by her husband. Blanchett felt there was 'something noble in her bravery' about this action of seemingly seeking forgiveness and attempting some kind of reconciliation: 'She's got two children and has to face up to it and repair what she can.'[51] In an essay by Adam Sonstegard in *Queer Love in Film and Television: Critical Essays* (2013) comparing the film and the novel, he notes that the ending of the latter is inconclusive, not informing readers of what 'Sheba's sentence' from the trial will be and whether she and Richard will get back together again. He feels that, in contrast, the film 'assures us' that Sheba will be 'safe at Richard's home after her jail time is served', thereby formulating a kind of narrative closure which foregrounds 'heterosexuals, whose privilege encourages them to reach for everything they can'.[52]

Both the film and the novel illustrate that breaking the law by having sex with an under-age person is likely to lead to imprisonment, shame and torment, although the manic and uncaring news photographers reporting the story at the close are not presented in any kind of positive light (Lord Alfred Douglas once referred to the British press in relation to the coverage of Oscar Wilde's arrest as engaging in that 'fine old British sport of kicking a man when he is down').[53] Sheba's provocative cry to them – 'Here I am', while dressed in a heavily made-up 1980s style – is a challenge to what Barbara sees in the novel (and Oscar Wilde saw in real life) as the innate hypocrisy and sanctimonious self-righteousness of the British press. Sheba would like to believe in the sanctity of marriage and family life, but she chafes at being good, selfless and confined all the time, perhaps seeing these as unrealistic and debilitating expectations. Her chosen means of hitting back at these restrictions is a singular one, which some critics such as Thomas Sutcliffe have felt is a narrative device, rather than something which is convincingly dramatised. Cate Blanchett has stated that she feels both Sheba and Barbara are somewhat 'trapped' in the story, Sheba in her marriage, Barbara in her lonely life as a single person. Together, though, in her view, they provide opportunities for audiences to be 'exhilarated ... delighted, and surprised by the absurdity, hilarity, and vulgarity of the stuff they said and did'.[54] Barbara refers to the Gospels and Judas when she decides to 'betray' Sheba to Brian, but when she claims not to have known Sheba 'well' or to have had positive feelings towards her at the end, we know this is not really true. When Sheba sadly and slowly puts Barbara's diary (with its stylised and euphemistic account of the sensational goings-on in their times together) on to Barbara's table and states, 'I liked you. I wanted to be your friend,' this is a truly sad moment for both of them. Even more so is Barbara's poignant reply, 'I wanted more than a friend.' For all the emphasis on Sheba's transgressions and 'bad behaviour', the real emotional story has been between these two women, their friendship, their confidences, their feelings of affection, gratitude and deep resentment towards each other, and finally their parting (for ever?) from each other's company.

Intimacy and distance in *Closer* (Mike Nichols, 2004)

Larry: 'What would happen if I touched you now?'
Alice: 'I would call security.'

First performed as a play on the London stage in 1997 and adapted into a feature film released in British cinemas in 2005, Patrick Marber's *Closer* focuses on the lives of a group of intertwined individuals living in modern-day London (an invitation card for a 'Private View' of Anna's photographic exhibition is dated January 2002). Unlike Noel Clarke's studies of alienated and disaffected teenagers to be studied later in this chapter, *Closer* concentrates on characters whose ages range from the 'early twenties' to the 'early forties',[55] and who are employed in occupations such as journalism, writing, dermatology, photography, waitressing and stripping. Whereas Noel Clarke's 'hood' films offer a panoramic view of the lives of a subsection of figures involved in a wide range of activities (many of them of an illegal nature), *Closer* concentrates on the obsessional behaviour of four characters, two men and two women, who above all else are concerned with their personal experiences of sex, love and desire. If violent behaviour is a constantly lurking threat in the 'hood' dramas, *Closer* focuses on what might be termed psychological violence nearer to home, leading drama academic Graham Saunders to describe the mood and tone of the original play as 'brutal and pessimistic'.[56]

Theatre director Max Stafford-Clark placed the play *Closer* within the context of a changing world in the late 1990s, when he felt the previously authoritative institutions of parenthood, schools and religion had been 'questioned, demolished and disempowered'. For Stafford-Clark, Marber's play 'deals with a world where marriage is no longer a realistic possibility as a guide for relationships'.[57] In his *Daily Telegraph* review of the film, Sukhdev Sandhu drew attention to the play's emergence at a time when a long period of Conservative government had come to an end, following the election of Tony Blair as British Prime Minister in May 1997. Although neither the play nor the film specifically refer to such political events and changes, Sandhu felt that the film adaptation was rooted in notions of a 'Cool Britannia', where characters 'live in lofts, go to openings in art galleries' and treat London as a 'playground' for their 'interminable dance of relationship swivels'.[58] Robert Hanks, in his *Independent* review of Nichols's film, felt that it was a depiction of key aspects of 'our times',[59] and the drama which unfolds concerns itself with dating in the age of the internet and lap-dancing clubs, and features childless couples who place a great deal of importance on issues of trust, fidelity, sexual satisfaction and emotional happiness. These characters are older and more articulate than the Londoners of Noel Clarke's urban dramas, but (like the characters in Joanna Hogg's movies) they are not as happy or contented as one might imagine and the language used by the characters reflects their unease and anger. David Cooke, Director of the British Board of Film Classification, noted in 2004 that some viewers of the film, attracted by the big-name stars in the cast, expected something along the lines of *Notting Hill* (Richard Curtis, 1999) and were surprised by 'what they got' in the 15 certificate *Closer*.[60]

For Mike Nichols, directing and producing a film version of *Closer* offered an opportunity (following the casting of fellow Americans Julia Roberts and Natalie Portman as Anna and Alice) to present a contemporary account of troubled Anglo-American relationships, the subject of many of Henry James's most esteemed novels and short stories. *Closer* also adds to Nichols's own body of work in which he has portrayed couples who engage in bitter and brutal arguments (*Who's Afraid of Virginia Woolf?*, 1966) and focused on sexual relationships from what viewers might perceive as a cold, detached and non-judgemental perspective (*Carnal Knowledge*, 1971). In *Closer*, Jude Law plays Dan, an obituary writer who falls in love with what John Hazelton in *Screen International* described as two 'mysterious, sensual American' women, leading to conflicts with a rival for their love, Larry (Clive Owen). Much angst, anger and sadness will emanate from the four central characters, who all, at one time or another, experience feelings of 'sexual jealousy',[61] betrayal and abandonment. *Closer* does not flinch from portraying what the American director Joseph Losey (who made Britain his cinematic home in the 1950s and 1960s) once described as the 'destruction and anguish and waste of most sexual relationships, whether heterosexual, homosexual, bisexual or whatever'.[62] For all its graphic language in discussing sexual affairs, *Closer* (like the works of Henry James) tends to shy away from presenting sexual interactions between characters in any kind of explicit manner. Characters are thus preoccupied with something which is out of sight, creating a sense of sexual desire as a longing which can never quite be satisfied or brought completely under control (the literary theorist and philosopher Pierre Macherey has written of 'Desire lagging behind its own emptiness ... [and] never appeased', amid a 'Language in flight, running after a reality which it can only define negatively').[63] *Closer*, in particular, depicts its male characters as predominantly consumed by negative emotions, insisting on fidelity from their women lovers and becoming furious when this desire for fidelity is not met, even though they cannot be trusted to stay faithful themselves. Alice wonders towards the end of her relationship with Dan, 'Where is this love? I can't see it ... touch it ... feel it', and viewers might similarly wonder if the word love is being used to stand for other emotions around attempts by the male characters to control and contain the women in their lives (Dan talks of lurking and stalking Anna).

Dan is a writer and compiler of obituaries for a national newspaper, which may, in part, explain his quest for the truth (especially the sexual truth) of a person's life. Larry is a dermatologist who also possesses a psychological ability to get 'under people's skin' on a personal basis. Anna is a photographer keen to turn her pictures into works of art which merit public exhibition. Alice works as a waitress in a café and more notably (as far as the film is concerned) as a stripper in a lap-dancing club. Jude Law's character purportedly writes a story of a young woman's life which is based on Alice's experiences. When she is asked what the book has left out, Alice pointedly states the 'truth'. As we never see this book, or are privy to listening to an extract from it, we can never be sure what exactly has been unrepresented, but both the play and the film raise the question of what it might mean to 'know' a partner, or to have access to their inner life or being. (Alice, it should be noted, also acts as a source of creative inspiration for Anna in her photography work. Larry comes across a black-and-white postcard photograph of Alice, entitled 'Young woman, London', in a New York hotel lobby.)

Closer explores love and sex in a modern age and finds that they exist in an uneasy relationship with each other. Sex can be paid for (Larry tells Anna just before she leaves him that he slept with 'a whore' in New York), but love cannot be so easily purchased. Dan and Larry are traumatised by the prospect of Alice and Anna leaving them, but Dan is prepared to masquerade as a sexually enthusiastic and available woman to Larry. In the online sexual chatroom, Dan assumes the identity of 'Anna' (just as he will assume or appropriate the voice of 'Alice' in his fictional memoir), and this allows him to express a woman's sexual desires in an uncensored and uninhibited fashion. Larry, in turn, is stunned to come across a woman who appears to express her sexual feelings and wants in such a direct manner and style ('I want to suck u senseless'). This scene between the two men draws upon the language and imagery of pornography, and the bottom section of this sex chat website features a naked woman lying on top of a naked man (which is the closest the film comes to actually depicting heterosexual coupling). The use of classical-sounding music as the two men seek to encourage each other in the explicit stating of their sexual desires creates a sense of dissonance and irony in relation to this merging of 'high' and 'low' culture'. Dan composes on a laptop in his home; Larry responds while at work on a hospital computer (he even refuses to take a work call, so intrigued is he by this wanton woman he has discovered online). This is both the language of desire and deception (the two are closely linked in the film), and quite why Dan engages in this practice is not clear, particularly as he later berates both Alice and Anna for not being transparently honest with him about their sexual conduct and feelings. It also works against Dan's interests as his false identity and obscene language serve only to bring Anna and Larry together in the setting of the aquarium (which is also the rather strange and not particularly commercial title of his book 'about Alice'). Larry introduces himself as a doctor, but tells Anna she can call him the 'Sultan' if she wishes. She is confused by this, not being privy to Larry and Dan's online conversation. Anna will go on to marry Larry and is in bed with him at the close of the film, so in some respects she does apparently grow to admire and like him, but Dan doubts that she can really have feelings for him.

Dan's ability to change his behaviour and personality quite suddenly relates to *Closer's* wider desire to explore issues of identity and character in relation to the central figures. While Dan can effortlessly pretend to be someone named 'Anna' online, 'Alice' finds it more difficult to be both Alice and Jane in the flesh when she is confronted by Larry demanding to know her real – rather than her stage – name. Alice, it will turn out, is actually stripping under her real name of 'Jane', meaning that Larry could have saved a great deal of the money he offers her in exchange for the truth. (A close-up of Alice's passport as she arrives back in America towards the end of the narrative reveals that her real name is Jane Rachel Jones and that she was born in January 1980.) Appearances can therefore turn out to be misleading; names can be both fixed and shifting; history can end up (as in Dan's book about Alice) becoming a kind of fiction, more mystifying than clarifying.

Larry and Anna subsequently refer to the potential possibilities of the internet for improved meaningful communications and interactions between people across the world, but observe that it may end up being used predominantly for pornographic purposes and pleasures, leading to a more explicitly sexualised culture in modern societies. A 2005 *New Statesman* essay, 'Why porn is the new glamour', by Kira Cochrane, claims that by the mid-2000s in the Western world 'porn imagery' had 'become an established part of our culture', with work in the sex industry being presented as 'simply a lifestyle and consumer choice like any other'. As an example of this way of thinking, Cochrane cites a 2005 'survey of a thousand girls between the ages of 15 and 19', which found that '63 per cent aspired to be a glamour model, while 25 per cent plumped for lap dancing'. The author concludes that working in the sex industry is increasingly seen as 'not just a viable option, but a genuinely attractive one'.[64]

When Alice/Jane first meets Dan, she tells him that she used to work as a stripper in New York. She observes that Dan's 'little eyes' almost appear to be 'popping out' on being given this piece of information, suggesting that attractive, sexually confident women in this narrative can be enticing, alarming and possibly beyond belief. When she splits up with Dan (after he leaves her for Anna), she finds work as a stripper in a London lap-dancing club which Larry visits. Having previously met at Anna's photographic exhibition, they now meet as punter and professional stripper, connoisseur and performer in the so-called Paradise Suite. When Larry asks Alice how many Paradise Suites there are in the club, he is told there are eight; in the play, Alice states that there are six.[65] The term paradise in this sexualised context possibly evokes Philip Larkin's use of the word in his poem 'High Windows': 'When I see a couple of kids/And guess he's fucking her.../I know this is paradise/Everyone old has dreamed of all their lives.'[66] Larkin's poem presents the speaker as someone outside this world of young sexual relationships, half-envious, half-sceptical of this new world of liberation and freedom. Larry is struck by the twenty year age difference between himself and Alice and the fact that (as he sees it) he now has to pay to have a conversation between himself and Alice.[67] Whereas he once took the liberty of touching Alice's face at Anna's photo exhibition, he now faces being evicted by security if he touches Alice in her role as striptease artist. He also declares at one moment that this is not utopia at all, but a 'hell-hole'. Nonetheless, he is prepared to spend £500 to learn Alice's real name or, failing that, as close a view of her nakedness as can be arranged. In a line from the play (but one which is excluded from the film), Alice tells Anna that Larry 'spends hours staring up my arsehole like there's going to be some answer there',[68] suggesting that for men like Larry, venues such as the Paradise Suite can be places to try and find some sense of meaning and purpose in a life which may otherwise seem drab and disappointing.

When *Closer* was first performed in 1997, this scene set in a lap-dancing establishment was not necessarily alluding to the possible metaphysical implications of such clubs but was acknowledging the increased prevalence of such forms of entertainment within British culture. Nick Horley wrote in a 1999 *New Statesman* essay that lap-dancing clubs were a growth area in the late 1990s, with Britain likely to 'end up with a couple of hundred of these clubs'. Horley anticipated that 'Every big town will have one, cities will boast a handful.' He also claimed that lap-dancing clubs offered the possibility of 'no stigma' being 'attached to paying a woman £10 to give you a close look at her genitals', and he concluded that the growth of this industry was perhaps a sign that 'Britons are at last defeating sexual repression'.[69]

In the extended scene in the strip club, music in the opening section features the sound of the 1997 song by the Prodigy *Smack My Bitch Up* playing in the background. This controversial piece of music helps to create a mood of after-hours hedonistic behaviour possibly seen by the management as appropriate to such a setting. The later section of the sequence is accompanied by the playing in the background of the Smiths' 1984 song, *How Soon is Now?* This move from a carnal to more emotive and reflective piece of music parallels Larry's efforts to have a more personally intimate conversation with Alice. When she rejects such overtures to give him a glimpse of her inner self, he exerts his financial power to make her reveal more of her physical self to him. Key words in their dialogue exchanges are money, flirting, dermatologist, whore, security, identities, names and thank you. Larry pleads with her to come home with him for sex and companionship. She refuses, but later it will turn out that she does enter into a sexual relationship with him, illustrating that what characters say and do in the narrative may be at odds with each other.

Larry and Dan – once in sync with each other's discourses and desires on the internet – increasingly become at war with each other over both Anna and Alice. Each is capable of turning threatening and unpleasant when they receive news of the other's successful liaisons with their loved one. Anna is worried about being hit by Larry when she has to face up to telling him she is leaving him for Dan (he resorts to verbal violence, telling her she is a 'fucked-up slag'). Alice senses that Dan wants to hit her – in the ironically named Renaissance Hotel – when he learns that she had sex with Larry, telling him, 'Hit me, you fucker.'

This degree of unpleasantness raises questions about how we are encouraged to interpret and respond to the characters and the cool, observational, seemingly detached style adopted by Mike Nichols to portray this drama about love, sexual desire and betrayal. Richard Corliss, writing in *Time*, praised the film for its life-like quality of not dividing characters into 'clear-cut heroes and villains', leaving audiences to decide upon their own emotional and intellectual responses about who to 'condemn or justify'.[70] Patrick Marber, explaining the director's way of creating what he saw as the appropriate atmosphere for the film stated that Mike Nichols 'wanted to capture that strange feeling you have when you're in love', so the pervading mood of *Closer* was to be dream-like, reflective, 'isolated' and 'haunting'.[71]

This leads on to the question of how Marber and Nichols seek to conclude the stories of these unhappy and tormented lovers. Larry agrees to sign the divorce papers Anna presents him with, if she will 'give me your body' one last time. She agrees, and they have (off-screen) sex in his place of work. When Dan finds out about this liaison, Anna says it was a compassionate act on her part (Larry will later admit that it was part of an attempt to 'fuck up' Dan's relationship with Anna). Dan decides he can no longer be in a relationship with Anna because he cannot trust her. His resumed relationship with Alice is broken off for the same reason. She, too, has slept with Larry and he feels betrayed. Alice returns to America, and is last glimpsed causing male passers-by almost to trip over as they gaze in admiration at her sexual attractiveness as she walks along W47 street in New York. This mirrors the opening of the film when she walks through a London street and is hit by a taxi after being momentarily distracted by the sight of Dan walking towards her from the other direction. Those viewers familiar with the original play will have expected Alice/Jane to die at the end, 'knocked down by a car ... on 43rd and Madison'.[72] In the film version, however, she lives on, walking confidently to an unknown future. In the background, there is a theatre sign for the play *Thoroughly Modern Millie* as Damien Rice's 2001 song *The Blower's Daughter* is heard on the soundtrack, with its key refrain of 'Can't take my eyes off you'. Even so, Alice disappears from view just before the final image of the busy street and the screen fades to black. Kim Newman, writing in *Empire*, has suggested that these final shots showing Jane/Alice (as vividly portrayed by Portman) walking through Times Square imply that she has escaped, 'but the other three [characters] remain trapped'.[73]

In these concluding moments, we learn that Anna and Larry are back together; our final image of Larry (so assertive and abrasive throughout much of the narrative) is of him asleep next to a still-awake Anna. It is not clear whether this is some kind of a compromise or loss of hope on Anna's part (Larry has earlier claimed that she suffers from depression). Dan discovers that Jane has adopted the name of Alice Ayres from a commemorative inscription to a woman of that name who in 1865 'saved three children from a burning house' at the cost of her own life. Needless to say, no one in the film's drama has performed any similar kind of heroic or selfless action ...

David Bell and Jon Binnie, in *The Sexual Citizen: Queer Politics and Beyond* (2000), argue that 'marriage remains the centrepiece for models of romantic attachment, and the task of thinking love otherwise can be a tricky one. Finding a way to recast love outside of the couple form requires some creative accounting, some leaps of imagination.'[74] *Closer*, rather gloomily, suggests that this will not be easily achieved. Dan engages in sexual flirtation with Larry when he pretends to be a woman, but there is no sense that they may engage in a sexual or emotional relationship when they meet in the flesh. When Anna rearranges Alice's hair before taking her picture, there appears to be a brief moment of possible attraction between the two, but this is soon dissipated when they start arguing over Dan. The men do not appear to be worthy of the women, as Larry in his most honest moments seems to realise and acknowledge. Apart from Anna (and possibly Alice in the strip club), no one seems much energised or enthused by their work. Society is just a backdrop to their emotional traumas; desires, it turns out, can never be satisfied; relationships are valued, but their foundations are not strong. In some ways, each of the characters is left disappointed or despondent at the close. History seems to repeat itself as tragedy and farce ('I've been here before', as Dan states early in the narrative). In the final moments of *Closer*, we see that Larry (as the most ruthless and forceful character) has probably been the most successful at getting what he wants, but there is a price to be paid for this as Anna may only be with him reluctantly and somewhat fearfully. Dan, on reflection, might also start to wonder how well an obituary of his own life would read if someone had cause to write it. The passport official at a New York airport greets Jane's return to America with a cheery, 'Welcome back, Miss Jones,' this friendly and courteous remark perhaps suggesting that (like the film's American director after filming was completed) she has returned to her true home and national identity. Alice/Jane's destiny and ultimate destination is, though, left open in the film. In this mixture of lost loves, good and bad memories and only-half-fulfilled desires, the characters live on to search for someone to whom they can get closer ...

'Unlikely couples' and unexpected alliances

Two films which explored female sexual and emotional relationships against a background of contrasting religious beliefs and forms of worship are *My Summer of Love* (Pawel Pawlikowski, 2004) and *Disobedience* (Sebastian Lelio, 2018). In each film, the relationship between the women in question is tested by pressures from external forces which disapprove of the liaisons and seek to separate the couples. *My Summer of Love* is set in Yorkshire and features a relationship between two women, Mona (Natalie Press) and Tamsin (Emily Blunt), of very different social and cultural backgrounds, who happen to live near each other and meet by chance. Their friendship and subsequent relationship are opposed by Mona's brother, Phil (Paddy Considine), who has become a fervent convert to Christianity and sees Tamsin as a negative influence on Mona. *Disobedience*, in contrast, takes place in a London suburb and focuses on two older women. The setting is an Orthodox Jewish community, where the return from New York of Ronit (Rachel Weisz), the only child of a beloved Chief Rabbi (Anton Lesser), after his death causes tensions when she rekindles a relationship with Esti (Rachel McAdams), a Jewish woman who is married to Dovid (Alessandro Nivola), the Rabbi's chosen successor. In both narratives, the two central protagonists set themselves up in opposition to the customs and outlook of the local community with their nonconformist behaviour, and consider making their relationship to each other the most important feature of their lives. Both films feature scenes of sensual love-making between Mona and Tamsin, Ronit and Esti, sequences which are presented positively in relation to the scenes of heterosexual coupling depicted in the narratives (Mona's unromantic sex in the back of a car to a married man who tells her that he can't be 'bothered' with her any longer after they have finished having sex; Esti's dutiful sex with her husband as they try for a child in *Disobedience*).

During *My Summer of Love*, the two teenage women go so far as to pledge their undying love to each other. In a scene shot in close-up, with their faces in silhouette and shadows and flickering flames in the background, the two declare that they will spend the rest of their lives together. Mona declares to Tamsin, 'If you leave me, I'll kill you and then kill myself', an emotional declaration which does not register as much with Tamsin as possibly it should (upper-class Tamsin takes a less literal view of the connections between words and deeds, statements and actions than working-class Mona does).

Ronit and Esti's behaviour is less obviously dramatic and subversive than Mona and Tamsin's conduct in *My Summer of Love*, but intense difficulties are posed as questions of orderly succession within the synagogue and a Jewish marriage are put at risk because of their relationship. Both films set notions of freedom and individual liberty against spiritual matters and subordinating the self to Christian or Jewish beliefs, precepts, prayers and rituals. Phil's evangelical faith aims to take Christianity back into the hands of ordinary people, and he and his followers seek some sign that God is listening to the unorthodox congregation assembled in Phil's former public house, known as The Swan. In *Disobedience*, the synagogue is the more formalised and traditional venue for sermons and contemplation, with the men and women sitting in different sections of the building. Phil and his fellow Christians succeed in raising a giant wooden cross aloft in a Yorkshire valley and this event is witnessed by Mona and Tamsin. Mona remains sceptical ('I've no intention of coming to your crucifixion', she informs Phil), but Tamsin seems more impressed and interested in Phil's strong Christian beliefs (she states, possibly sincerely, possibly disingenuously, that she wishes she could believe in something).

In *Disobedience*, Jewishness is shown as being indelibly tied up with notions of work, the family and the home, but married women are expected to wear wigs (sheitels) to hide their natural hair and (in Ronit's view) to privilege motherhood over an independent life and career. Ronit has chosen to live and work outside this community (she is a photographer by profession), but nonetheless she is related to the Rabbi by birth (referred to as the Rav in the film) which his many admirers and followers are not. (Tellingly, both Mona and Ronit's mothers are dead, perhaps giving them a sense of feeling somewhat isolated in the world and of lacking someone to whom they can talk to both truthfully and deeply.)

The title *Disobedience* would appear to reference the Jewish community's view of Esti and Ronit's behaviour, but the title could also apply to the behaviour of Mona and Tamsin in *My Summer of Love* (interestingly, not *Our Summer of Love*). Out of the three central protagonists in this film, Mona is the character who is most sincere and least committed to the 'other worlds' revered by Christian Phil and 'fantasist' Tamsin. Tamsin's cultured and wealthy background is very different from Mona's impoverished and stark surroundings, and she is keen to educate Mona into a familiarity with the works and significance of Nietzsche, Freud and Edith Piaf. As the film proceeds, events start to take on a dreamlike quality as the lines between fantasy and reality (à la *Letter to Brezhnev*) become increasingly blurred. Mona wakes up on Tamsin's lawn in the evening to find that Tamsin has gone in to eat with her family without inviting or apparently waking her. Tamsin's idea of a suitable location for a day out by taxi is to take Mona with her to a modern housing estate (the kind of place where Bob lives in *Rita, Sue and Bob Too*) and sit outside the house where, she claims, her father is 'fucking his secretary up the arse'. We never learn whether what Tamsin claims to be the case is true or not, and the way that the scene ends – Mona picking up a garden gnome and thrusting it through what she thinks is Tamsin's father's car window – adds to the surreal sense of the narrative as a whole and this sequence in particular. The film also seeks to convey a sense of the women's enjoyment at throwing off convention and being bold, unruly and liberating. This shared search for ecstatic and sublime moments possibly reaches its peak when they dance together in a public hall where Mona's former (married) lover, Ricky (Dean Andrews), is singing. The dancers in the hall are unimpressed by the women dancing together and they end up being ejected by security, but not before they have publicly celebrated their unorthodox way of doing things and their feelings for each other.

From this point on, events become unpredictable and rather disturbing. Mona and Tamsin torment and taunt Ricky's wife for their own amusement (not really acknowledging that she is a victim of Mona's affair with her husband, which she doesn't seem to know about). Tamsin constructs a story about her sister, Sadie (Kathryn Sumner), dying a painful death, caused by her refusal to eat. Mona believes this story, which turns out to be untrue and may stem from some resentment of her sister on Tamsin's part. Tamsin decides to see if she can persuade Phil to discard his strong

Christian beliefs long enough to make spontaneous love to her. The result is, perhaps, inconclusive, but the 'test' does lead to Phil becoming violent towards Tamsin and seemingly ending up in a state of emotional confusion (he dismisses his fellow Christians as fakers and appears to close his unorthodox place of worship after Tamsin claims that he is a 'fraud', an 'Adam' too easily tempted by her impersonation of 'Eve'). Ironically, Mona will also turn violent towards Tamsin when she learns that Sadie is not just still alive, but capable of asking for her 'top back' when she materialises in the front hall of Tamsin's home. Sarah Street, discussing the film in *British National Cinema* (2009), notes that Mona's dreams of a new life with Tamsin are 'shattered' when she realises that 'she has been used for idle amusement' and 'erotic distraction'.[75] Such a feeling of betrayal will lead to Mona holding Tamsin's head under water in a kind of grotesque parody of a baptism ceremony, with Tamsin calling out that Mona is a 'crazy bitch'. Mona is shocked that Tamsin is prepared to return unprotestingly to school, rather than spend the rest of their 'lives together'. Thus, both Phil and Mona resort to physical violence when pushed too far by Tamsin, who may finally see that her made-up stories and provocative behaviour can be harmful and disturbing to others.

The film concludes (to the sound of Edith Piaf on the soundtrack) with a close-up shot of Mona as she walks out of the forest and an unclear future. Mona has felt that Phil's conversion to Christianity is a form of delusion and not something to be affirmed or welcomed (even if it stops him being violent). It is difficult to imagine what might happen to his character in the future. As regards Tamsin, she will probably go on to university where she might take a course in creative writing, given the enjoyment she finds in imagining fictional scenarios (and the whole of *My Summer of Love* is, of course, a fantasy – none of these characters actually exist, but we treat them as if they were real). Mona's own future as a working-class woman is difficult to predict or imagine. Earlier, she has conjured up a future for herself which is drenched in a form of pessimistic realism bordering on nihilism, evoking the famous keynote speech from *Trainspotting* (Danny Boyle, 1995) about 'choosing life': Mona imagines herself working in an abattoir, marrying a man who is a 'complete bastard', then bringing up children with mental health problems while waiting for the menopause and then cancer. Some or all of these eventualities may lie ahead for Mona. But one can also believe that she has benefited from this strange encounter with the beautiful, intelligent (if duplicitous) Tamsin, and that the relationship has suggested to her other possible ways of living and loving which she may be able to draw upon in the future.[76] Tamsin, one imagines, will not completely forget Mona either, even if one cannot imagine the two women keeping in touch after all they have been through together.

Disobedience is also crucially based around a sexual and emotional relationship between its two central female protagonists, one which is fraught with difficulties and dangers. Esti has been warned that her teaching job may be in danger if she enters into an inappropriate relationship with Ronit again. Ronit, however, waits for her as she leaves the school, and they book into a hotel room where they experience what Deborah Ross in the *Spectator* described as a 'passionate encounter ... shot in close-up' and involving 'spit-sharing, hands in pants',[77] mutual masturbation and Ronit performing oral sex on Esti. This intense sequence highlights what Esti's life could be like if she were free to pursue a sexual life with women. In this spirit of liberation, the two women joke about the Rav's shocked response to their initial act of intimacy many years ago and even share a cigarette in their hotel room (possibly contravening the laws against smoking in public places introduced in the 2000s by the Labour government). We have earlier witnessed Ronit having sex with a male stranger who works in a New York bar as a response to the death of her father, so we know that Ronit is attracted sexually to both men and women. In this highly charged and complex narrative, Esti will also shortly learn that she is pregnant with Dovid's child, making her decision about how to live her life in the future even more difficult.

Disobedience concludes in an open-ended manner, which might be seen as realistic and life-like in the circumstances, though Deborah Ross in the *Spectator*, however, found the ending to be 'plain baffling'.[78] In doing so, it is less definitive than the original 2006 novel, in which Esti decides to stay with Dovid and bring up his baby as part of the community.[79] The film ends with Esti being torn between her love and desire for Ronit (and potentially other women), and the need to bring her baby up in a secure, supportive and financially manageable setting and situation (Ronit is returning to New York, so living with her may involve moving there, with all the uncertainty and financial cost involved in such a transition). At the close, Dovid, shaken by what has occurred in his 'house', decides against becoming the new Rav. Esti is depicted sleeping downstairs on the couch, a symbol of how she is caught between staying and leaving. Esti and Ronit's sexual encounter has been a powerful and unforgettable occasion for both women, and one which is presented as having to exist outside the religious principles and familial practices of the Orthodox Jewish community to which they each have strong ties. This also makes the sexual encounter particularly poignant for Esti, who has to decide whether to pursue more intense and fulfilling sexual experiences like this, even though such a move would lead to her becoming excommunicated by the Jewish community and possibly facing a custody battle over her child.

The final image in the film is of Ronit taking a photograph of her father's final resting place in a large London Jewish cemetery, her professional life here merging with her personal life. It is not clear if she will return to London and the Jewish community she is leaving once again, but she does ask Esti to let her know where she is living. A tearful and extremely sad farewell takes place between Ronit and Esti (and over the credits a song heard earlier on the radio – the Cure's 1989 *Love Song*, with its key lyric 'I will always love you' – is played). The film ends with the camera panning up to the sky in the cemetery as Ronit pays her final respects. Spectators can suddenly see just how many people are buried in this plot of land. This image seems to convey a sense that this is how all our desires and dreams conclude – in death and entombment – and leaves open the question of how we should choose to live our lives in the face of this awareness of our impending and inevitable demise.

Another gay love story, but this time between two men, *Weekend* (written, edited and directed by Andrew Haigh and released in 2011), also ends with a couple separating at the close, with one partner heading to America. The title refers to a two-day encounter between two gay men, Russell (Tom Cullen) and Glen (Chris New) and probes whether this relationship can and should last longer than a 'weekend'. Russell quickly feels that in Glen he has found someone for whom he feels a great deal of affection, but Glen is sceptical of gay relationships which mirror heterosexual couplings and exclusive long-term partnerships; what he describes as 'The whole straight narrative ... to shape your foundations ... boy meets girl, they fall in love ... and that's how your life is set.' Instead, he wishes to 'redraw' and recreate his life on an ongoing basis, refusing to reciprocate Russell's declarations of love at the end of the narrative (what he terms the '*Notting Hill*' moment in their relationship). Glen ends up leaving for a new existence and set of experiences in Oregon, leaving the future of their relationship (if there is to be one) open and unresolved.

The point of view articulated by Glen in *Weekend* contains echoes of Lee Edelman's argument in *No Future: Queer Theory and the Death Drive* (2004) that gay men should learn to live and love provisionally and refute attempts to constrain their sexual desires in monogamous relationships, even if this results in somewhat nihilistic and hedonistic attitudes and lifestyles: 'the only oppositional status to which our queerness could ever lead would depend on our taking seriously the place of the death drive ... to insist that the future stop here ... we do not intend a new politics ... since all those fantasies reproduce the past ... in the form of the future'.[80] Edelman's beliefs might be linked with what became known as Queer Theory, a body of thought which reacted against what could appear to be heterosexual acceptance or tolerance of gay lifestyles in society providing they mirrored and emulated male–female relationships working towards some kind of established and ongoing status. Queer Theory, by way of a contrast, emphasised the importance of sexual pleasure and unrestrained desire, pursuing what Andrew Bennett and Nicholas Royle described as a determination to resist the 'bland, monolithic certainties of heterosexuality'.[81]

God's Own Country (Francis Lee, 2017) shows farm worker Johnny (Josh O'Connor) seeking out male partners for transient sexual encounters involving anal sex in workplace and public house toilets. Such sexual experiences are shown as brief sexual encounters in which Johnny seeks release for his sexual urges but resists becoming emotionally involved with his sexual partners. (The character of Poppy in *Sex Lives of the Potato Men*, as discussed in Chapter 4, makes a similar distinction between sexual and emotional intimacy.) Lee's film revolves around what begins as a sexual affair between two men – Johnny, the son of a farmer who is forced to take on responsibility for his father's farm, and Gheorghe (Alec Secareanu), a Romanian worker, initially contracted to work on the farm for only a week. Johnny works long, cold and lonely hours on the farm, doing work once done by his father (Ian Hart), who has had a severe stroke. Sex appears to be one of his few pleasures as he seems depressed and alienated from his surroundings. He is at first resentful of and contemptuous towards Gheorghe, who has left Romania because he thinks it is a 'dead' country. Johnny is a man of few words, but one gets a sense that he might sum up Yorkshire, Britain and his life in similar terms. When the two are forced to work together in isolation from the wider community to fix a broken wall, a brawl between the two gradually ends up as a sexual encounter in the open fields. Johnny has previously being shown to separate sex from any emotional commitments, rejecting opportunities to meet his lovers socially after they have had sex; Terri White in *Empire* refers to his 'wordless sex' and 'casual shagging'.[82] Gheorghe, though, ends up leaving Johnny and his farm to work in Scotland after he comes across Johnny having sex with someone whom he has just met in the toilets of a public house. What changes everything for Johnny is a subsequent awareness that he has fallen in love with Gheorghe. Johnny's father, who nearly dies in the narrative, unexpectedly thanks him for his help in giving him a bath after his stroke, possibly awakening in Johnny a sense that love involves wanting to help and care for those individuals important in one's life. Evoking memories of the closing moments of *My Beautiful Laundrette*, Johnny subsequently decides that Gheorghe is both an emotional and a sexual partner for him, as well as being someone who can help to run the family business in an efficient and effective manner.

If Russell and Glen are parted at the close of London-set *Weekend*, *God's Own Country* offers a more hopeful sense of closure, with two men from different countries finally bonding together in shared work and their mutual sexual desire for each other. Their romantic reconciliation takes place in a large-scale mechanised farming workplace in Scotland where Gheorghe has found work. Johnny tracks him down and hopes that things can go back to how they were. Gheorghe describes him as a 'freak'; to which Johnny replies, 'So are you.' This is not the most obviously romantic conversation to bring two ex-lovers back together again, but here it works in convincing Gheorghe to give up his job in Scotland and return to Yorkshire. The caravan where he previously lived is shown being towed away as he enters the family home, after Johnny indicates that new sleeping arrangements will prevail and that Gheorghe will (hopefully) be viewed as a more equal partner in the business from here on. Gheorghe and Johnny's bonding is especially important as it extends beyond national borders and offers the possibility of becoming a professional and a personal relationship, with Gheorghe's farming abilities and nurturing qualities offering the possibility of turning the ailing family farm's fortunes around. Anna Smith, reviewing the film in *The Amorist*, claimed that events do not take place within 'an obviously homophobic world',[83] implying that British society had changed significantly since the times when *Victim* and *Nighthawks* were released in the early 1960s and late 1970s. Indeed, in an essay on British sexual cultures, Clarissa Smith notes that two significant pieces of legislation were passed in the 2000s that were aimed at improving the lives and living conditions of gay men and women. The British 2004 Civil Partnership Bill allowed 'gay and lesbian' couples access to the same legal rights as those offered by marriage, and in 2001, the age of consent for same-sex relationships was lowered to sixteen, marking what Smith felt was a significant step in breaking down legal distinctions 'between heterosexual and homosexual activity'.[84]

However, *God's Own Country*, despite its title, does not present its area of Yorkshire as being in a particularly vibrant or happy state, and this may reflect some of the turmoil within British culture at the time of the film's release. 'Remainers' and 'Leavers' were both vehemently arguing their particular cases in 2017 as a Conservative government sought to end Britain's membership of the European Union. The film, in its union of Johnny and Gheorghe, would seem to argue a case for Britain maintaining close ties with Europe. As regards its sexual politics, Gheorghe appears to believe in the concept of sexual fidelity, so one is left to speculate whether Johnny will completely come round to such a point of view or whether this might lead to tensions and problems in their relationship.

A tale of romantic woe in modern Glasgow

Mark Kermode: *Ae Fond Kiss...* (Ken Loach, 2004): a story of a modern-day 'Romeo and Juliet?'[85]

Dilys Powell, reviewing Ken Loach's *Poor Cow* in 1967, claimed that 'Today the recommended background is the slum; the favoured action is rape or robbery; the heroes are dingy seducers or layabouts.' Powell went on to suggest that even though it was only seven years since *Saturday Night and Sunday Morning* was released, already that much-discussed film seemed to emanate from 'another world' and from a very different kind of Britain. Compared with the 'self-respecting family' lovingly depicted in *This Happy Breed* (David Lean, 1944), Powell concluded we 'are in another universe'. Nonetheless, she praised *Poor Cow* as 'supremely well done' and felt that Carol White's performance as the central character, Joy, made one feel 'sympathy and even liking' for this rather 'hopeless character'.[86]

Decades later, the films of Ken Loach were still receiving somewhat mixed reviews. A 2017 editorial in the *Daily Telegraph* acknowledged that his 'skill as a director ... cannot be denied'. The writers of the editorial took issue, however, with what they claimed was the 'image' of British society 'projected abroad' by his films – Britain as a 'dark, miserable land run by toffs and rapacious bakers who subjugate the downtrodden masses and heroic workers beneath the jackboot of oppression'.[87] His 1998 film *My Name is Joe*, for instance, depicted a series of relationships which are shown to be destroyed by heroin abuse, alcoholism, social despair, unemployment and violent and ruthless drug dealers. Such a narrative of blighted relationships and dark forms of sensual gratification was a long way from both the films of Richard Curtis and from the kind of social progress promised by Tony Blair after he became British Prime Minister in 1997. Loach was notably critical of how, as he saw it, Blair's premiership continued with the Conservative party's promotion of 'free market economics', refusing to acknowledge Loach's own belief (which has underpinned all of his work) that 'There are better ways to live.'[88]

Historian Dominic Sandbrook has argued, however, that in certain important ways Britain has changed for the better since the 1960s and 1970s. He claimed that in the 2000s, by 'every statistical measure, people in Britain' had become 'more tolerant, less sexist and less racist than they were', with 'most of us ... comfortable with gay marriage' and regarding 'overt racism as unacceptable'.[89] Not everyone would agree with Sandbrook's claims and Ken Loach's, *Ae Fond Kiss...* (2004), in particular, suggests that Britain still has some way to go in attaining the kind of social harmony desirable in a modern society between those of different faiths, religions and cultural backgrounds. *Ae Fond Kiss...* illustrates the difficulties raised by a relationship which emerges between a Scottish male Muslim, whose parents were born in Pakistan, and a Catholic woman from Ireland currently working in Glasgow. The film begins with what Ryan Gilbey in his *Sight and Sound* review described as a 'dreadful speech, passionately delivered' by the character of Tahara (Shabana Bakhsh) during a Glasgow school debate about whether the 'West's campaign against international terrorism is justified'.[90] She boldly declares to her fellow pupils that she is a 'Glaswegian Pakistani teenage woman of Muslim descent who supports Glasgow Rangers at a Catholic school'. The statement serves to highlight one of the central themes of the film: that in a modern world, people may have several personal, cultural, religious and social identities. What happens after Tahara's speech also illustrates that not everyone will be happy about the existence of such diverse forms of identity. The most provocative aspect of her speech, however, is probably the part about supporting Glasgow Rangers, and this leads to a flourish of racist and intimidating behaviour from some of those who have witnessed her speech: a male pupil spits on her brother's car windscreen and she is called a 'coconut'. This conflict creates a situation where the two main protagonists of the film will meet by chance and in unpropitious circumstances. Tahara chases her tormentors into the school's music room where Roisin (Eva Birthistle) is conducting a music lesson with a pupil. Her brother, Casim (Atta Yaqub), follows her into the fray and thus comes across Roisin. Having met as strangers in a disturbing manner, they will become friends and eventually lovers, much to the disapproval of Casim's family and the governing bodies of her school.

In his review of the film, Mark Kermode summed up the key question posed by the relationship between Casim and Roisin as being whether they are 'prepared to abandon their careers, families and religions on the basis of a possibly fleeting passion'.[91] While this opening scene refers to the possibility of having several identities, the question of which should have priority remains an important one. For Casim's family, the priority is to accept a marriage arranged by his parents to someone chosen by them. Casim's bride-to-be is Jasmine (Sunna Mirza), and quite late in the story she comes to Glasgow from Pakistan to meet her prospective husband, only to find that he pulls away from her. By this stage, he appears set on continuing his relationship with Roisin, despite the difficulties this has created for both of them. A trip to Spain provides an opportunity for the lovers to get to know each other better, and outside a café they discuss differences between their respective religions. Casim interestingly echoes a speech made by the dying Rav in *Disobedience* about the differences between angels, beasts and human beings when he says that the Muslim religion teaches that we can be 'higher than angels and lower than dogs'. Roisin, it emerges, is less attached to her Catholicism, and jokes about the 'Day of Judgment' lying in wait for us all. This discussion ends with her proposing a toast to 'Paradise'. Back at their apartment in Spain, they make love, and the filming of the scene, while not as graphic as Michael Winterbottom's *9 Songs* (2009), brings out the sexual desire they feel for each other. Paradise is not to be found in

Spain, however. Roisin reveals that she is married, but separated (not yet divorced) from her husband. This revelation prompts Casim to reveal the next morning that his life is going in the opposite direction to hers, as he is due to marry Jasmine in a few months' time. This leads to Roisin feeling that she has been treated as if she were a 'cheap fucking tart in a stag party', suggesting that she does not believe in what might be termed 'casual sex'. An uneasy reconciliation follows, but when the couple are spotted together arriving back at Glasgow airport by some pupils of the school at which Roisin teaches, the seeds are sown for their relationship to be severely tested by external forces deeply unsympathetic to their coupling. Casim twice asks Roisin to 'duck down' in his car to avoid being seen by members of his family. A Catholic parish priest (Gerard Kelly) refuses to 'rubber stamp' her application to prove that she is a suitable person to teach at a Catholic school, telling her provocatively that he suspects her of getting into bed with any 'Tom, Dick and Mohammed'. Catholicism, he warns her, is not a religion for the 'faint-hearted'. Casim's father, Tariq (Ahmad Riaz), refuses to accept the notion of him marrying a non-Muslim woman, claiming that a white western woman will leave him if he gets sick and old and loses his earning potential. So outraged is he by Casim's refusal to marry Jasmine after she and her family have travelled all the way from Pakistan that he smashes the windows of the extension he has had built for the prospective couple to live in.

After this highly dramatic and tragi-farcical conclusion to events, it seems that the lovers' relationship is doomed. However, Loach and his screenplay writer, Paul Laverty, end the film on a note of calm, meditation and wry humour, qualities notably absent from other parts of the narrative. Roisin is revealed playing the piano in her apartment when Casim enters the room. She announces that in her tormented mood she nearly went out and 'fucked a complete stranger'. Following his father's chain of thought, Casim asks if she will 'kick' him out when she grows 'tired' of him. 'Absolutely', replies Roisin, playfully. And if he becomes sick, will he be shown the door? 'Definitely', replies Roisin. And, extending the worst-case scenarios, what if he becomes bankrupt, penniless and depressed? She would 'send him a card'. This comic replaying of what has been presented as deadly serious and deeply disturbing in the previous scene, acts as a tranquil, witty and 'cautiously optimistic' conclusion to events.[92] 'I'll let you know' are Roisin's final words about if or when she may have had enough of Casim. This is said lightly and humorously, but the film has revealed that she has already left one marriage because it was not an 'equal match', so we cannot know if they will stay together. The fact that they can joke about relationships going disastrously wrong might be seen as a positive note on which to end. Mark Kermode, in his review of the film, described this as a 'bitter-sweet denouement', which left him wondering if it 'would have been better' if this particular couple had 'never met'.[93] If *Disobedience* shows a prospective couple parting at the close, torn apart by religious dogma and societal pressures, Loach and Paul Laverty's film depicts a couple daring to defy convention and religious and familial pressures for them to part. In a newspaper interview, Ken Loach stated that the film was about 'second-generation immigrants', families and what he termed the 'compulsions of attraction'. He hoped that *Ae Fond Kiss…* would have a positive effect on audiences, making people realise they do not exist in 'separate ghettos'. He is not critical of the unyielding religious figures depicted during the narrative in the interview, but he does state that he hopes 'younger generations' will become more 'integrated' as that will 'always be our best defence against racism'.[94] The religions featured in *Ae Fond Kiss…* are presented as honouring concepts of continuity and adherence to historical tradition, so the film's two lovers find themselves stranded in something of a 'No Man's Land' by the close of the narrative (it is perhaps significant that our final view of the couple is of them alone in a non-public space).

From the ambivalently named Joy in *Poor Cow* to Roisin and Casim in *Ae Fond Kiss…*, Loach's films have opposed what they see as social, economic, educative, psychological and sometimes familial forces working against the achieving of human happiness for many of Britain's citizens, past and present. He has always applauded and praised those who stand up for what he might term social and economic justice in the face of oppressive and possibly overwhelming forces. If particular Loach narratives move inexorably towards social tragedy, *Ae Fond Kiss…* ends with a moment of relative calm and the future of Roisin and Casim's relationship left open, if uncertain. In what may prove to be the director's final film, *Sorry We Missed You* (2019), delivery driver Ricky (Kris Hitchen) dramatically ends up losing his job after being beaten up and robbed. To the deep concern of his family, however, he insists on jumping into his van and driving to his former workplace the morning after he has been treated by hospital staff. The final shot in the film is of him driving on without a clear destination on a journey which could well result in his death. The film subsequently fades to black and we never learn what becomes of Ricky and his loved ones, but the image of him driving on against all odds can eloquently stand for Ken Loach's portrayal of characters in difficult and trying conditions, all desperately striving to keep afloat and fight on for another day and chance of happiness. To evoke a religious phrase used by Roisin in *Ae Fond Kiss…*, for Ken Loach, the 'Day of Judgment' is always already upon us in the here and now.

'A matter of life and death': desire, danger and a lack of love in Noel Clarke's 'hood' trilogy

'Oh, my days!' (Jay on hearing that Alisa is pregnant).
'So what, me and you on, or what?' (Jay's question to Claire) [*Kidulthood*, 2006].

Kidulthood (Menhaj Huda, 2006), *Adulthood* (Noel Clarke, 2008) and *Brotherhood* (Noel Clarke, 2016) are three London-based films emanating from the imagination and observations of writer, director and actor Noel Clarke. The trilogy follows the interactions between teenagers of differing racial, cultural and social backgrounds and shows how individuals in groups gravitate too easily towards negative emotions and actions which can destroy relationships and human lives (organised religion is notably absent from the films' portraits of modern British life). Women are shown struggling to find peace of mind and sexual and emotional fulfilment, suffering in particular instances from bullying (sometimes carried out by other women), being raped (in an off-screen back story) and becoming pregnant (as in *A Taste of Honey*) while still a pupil at secondary school. In his review of *Kidulthood*, Derek Malcolm noted that the film involved a suicide, characters taking cocaine and engaging in 'casual sex', sometimes for financial gain, while behaving generally in such a manner that 'no normal adult would want to be anywhere near them'.[95] *Kidulthood* thus has the same concerns about how young people are conducting themselves that were depicted in *My Teenage Daughter* released forty years earlier, where the eponymous daughter was shown quickly moving from coffee bar to jazz club to a prison cell on a suspected manslaughter charge. For all of the inevitable differences between British films released in 1956 and 2006, *Kidulthood* also shows how one ill-advised action or commitment can quickly lead to terrible situations which are beyond the control of both perpetrators and victims alike.

In his 1938 book *Studies in a Dying Culture*, Christopher Cauldwell claims that 'bourgeois culture' was 'held together, not by mutual love or tenderness ... but simply by profit'. In Cauldwell's view, this affects relationships between the sexes and lived experience of 'love itself': 'Because economic relations in capitalism are simply each man struggling for himself in the impersonal market, the world seems torn apart' by the negative energies of 'envy, covetousness and hate', he concluded.[96] Noel Clarke's 'hood' dramas can be seen as exploring life in modern-day British culture from such a perspective, in which society seems to favour competitiveness rather than co-operation and does not do enough to protect the 'everyday' person from the damaging behaviour of those around them who are prepared to realise their self-seeking aims and urges by deploying force and the most ruthless of methods.

Kidulthood appears to be a word created for the film's title (an online dictionary search for a definition might result in the query 'Did you mean Adulthood?'). Nor is kidulthood a term actually uttered by any of the characters in the movie. A glossary for *Kidulthood* provided in the *Sunday Telegraph* explains such terms as 'Banged' ('slept with'), 'Blood' ('Brother/friend'), 'Buff' ('Fit/attractive'), 'Beanie' ('Girl') and 'Breas' ('Guys/men'),[97] so that older viewers of the film might not feel mystified or excluded by the discourses at play in the narrative. Alan Franks in *The Times* felt that despite the exact meaning of certain phrases being obscure at times, the language was as 'charged with meaning' as that deployed by the warring factions in Shakespeare's *Romeo and Juliet* (1597), which similarly ends in social and personal tragedy.[98]

In an interview with writer Noel Clarke, Catherine Shoard concludes that he was right to conceive of *Kidulthood* as a potentially entertaining and stimulating film for young audiences, as well as a film with an implied message that the kinds of destructive and damaging behaviour indulged in by several of the characters can have fatal and lethal consequences. Young people, after all, were 'unlikely to cough up their pocket money for something they might be forced to watch in general studies',[99] observes Shoard, dryly. She also notes how the film-makers' heightened and imaginative approach to characterisation and storytelling led to the creation of scenes which were unpredictable, intense and often deeply disturbing. Acknowledging that this was all a long way from the world of Harry Potter and his experiences of school life and British culture, Shoard notes that 'the only time we see someone pick up a pen is to write a suicide note ... Playing fields are for sex, mobile phones for videoing fights ... cabbies for fleecing [and] babies for getting rid of in case they make you look fat.'[100] To such defamiliarising moments, one could add the moment in which Sam Peel (Noel Clarke), the school bully in *Kidulthood*, is felled by a blow to the head from his own computer keyboard, a striking example of modern technology being used for purposes not intended by its makers, and of how violence in this film – and its sequels – is an ever present prospect, often carried out by any means possible (including fists, feet, knives, baseball bats and guns).

In working against privileging any one character in the story of *Kidulthood*, Clarke and director Huda could be said to be developing a kind of 'Dickensian' view of London as peopled by groups of characters whose destinies turn out to be linked in certain ineradicable ways by the close. Even the titles of some of Charles Dickens's novels, *Great Expectations* notwithstanding, could be applied to the 'hood' trilogy – *Hard Times, Our*

Mutual Friend and *Bleak House*, in particular.[101] In formulating a narrative about relationships different to the others discussed in this chapter, Clarke's films also eschew the kind of London featured in Richard Curtis's movies and seek to portray a world which is gritty and stark, but also based around young individuals who are eager to experience stimulating physical sensations of a sexual or sensual nature and keen to make their mark on the world in one way or another. The production notes for *Adulthood* described the world of the films as one where 'sex is currency, drugs are easy to come by and violence is a way of life'.[102]

A dramatic emphasis on such aspects of life in British feature films was always likely to prove controversial, and this proved to be the case with *Kidulthood*. Liz Hoggard, in the *Independent on Sunday*, wrote that the *Sun* newspaper had 'called for it to be banned'.[103] James Bell, in *Sight and Sound*, reported that *Kidulthood* had been criticised by some commentators 'for glorifying violence, drug-taking, casual teenage sex and antisocial behaviour', while the film-makers were quoted as defending the film on the grounds that it presented a portrayal of 'real, harsh truths'.[104] Nicholas Barber in the *Independent on Sunday* claimed that *Kidulthood* depicted the 'teens of today as sex-crazed delinquents with knives in one pocket and pills in the other'.[105] Alice Thompson in the *Daily Telegraph* recorded that the characters of *Kidulthood* were 'up for everything from prostitution to happy slapping'; all this occurred, she suggested, because they had nothing very much 'to do'.[106] To what extent such perceived antisocial behaviour in British culture was a new phenomenon, and how far some young (and not-so-young) viewers of *Kidulthood* might applaud (rather than deplore) some of the behaviour depicted in the 'hood' films were debatable points for some critics.

Activist and writer Richard Neville, who supported teenage rebellion against what he might have termed bourgeois ethics, notes in his 1970 polemic *Play Power* that a 'report to a London teachers' association in 1969 revealed how classroom anarchy is driving out teachers'. Neville writes, though, that the various 'challenges' to authority and 'disturbances of lessons' were emblematic and symptomatic of the everyday violence inherent in competitive, life-denying capitalist-run societies (this discussion of anarchic classroom behaviour occurs in a chapter entitled 'Carry On Motherfuckers', which gives some indication of Neville's sympathies). 'In other words, it's goodbye to Goodbye Mr Chips' and the decline of a British way of life based around 'a limbo of chairman's reports, vicars on television' and a future based around the 'Positions Vacant columns',[107] he notes drolly.

F.R. Leavis, the prominent literary and cultural academic and critic, wrote two years earlier of the disturbing traits which he associated with the behaviour and attitudes of some young people in British culture – 'violence, wanton destructiveness, the drug menace, adolescent promiscuity, permissiveness' and praise for the 'young' and 'their "candour" about sex' – were all undesirable features of 1960s Britain as far as he was concerned.[108] Leavis discerned a nihilistic, anti-educational and anti-authority tendency among certain young people, which he deplored. He believed, however, that the young had been let down by a modern society which emphasised the importance of technological training over creative pursuits, low-level and undemanding leisure activities over the reading, appreciation and criticism of major literary works, and encouraged a desire for instant sensual gratification over the development of mutually sustaining and meaningful relationships and partnerships informed by participation in a meaningful and highly literate/articulate culture. Clearly, Leavis would have viewed the situations and scenarios of Clarke's films as demonstrating all too vividly that his concerns about the ways in which British youth culture was developing had proved to be only too accurate and well founded. Leavis acknowledged, however, that individuals lived in a 'world of complexities and ambiguities in which we have to determine what our sense of personal responsibility dictates',[109] comments which fascinatingly connect in certain ways with some of Clarke's stated intentions about his 'hood' trilogy: 'The key is that it all comes down to choices ... It's time to move on, to stop this thuggery and this street culture.'[110]

In the films, viewers are presented with a vision of everyday existence as a series of conflicts for the films' teenage protagonists in which sometimes only the fittest, the strongest, the most self-seeking and the most ruthless thrive and survive. In fact, survival is a key theme throughout the narratives. The first segment of *Kidulthood* concludes with the suicide of Katie (Rebecca Martin),[111] a white fifteen-year-old woman, and the narrative culminates in the murder of Trevor/Trife (Ami Ameen), a black male, also fifteen. The film's chief protagonists are also around the age of fifteen (although Noel Clarke, who plays sixth former Sam, was thirty when he played the role). The two main female protagonists, Alisa (Red Madrell) and Becky (Jaime Winstone) are depicted as being sexually active, and on Becky's initiative are shown as being willing to engage in sexual acts in exchange for money and drugs. Alisa, it turns out, is pregnant and has to decide whether or not to have her baby. There appears to be some question of whether Sam or Trevor might be the father, although according to Alisa, the baby's father is Trevor (who has also, it seems, had sexual relations with the late Katie).

Kidulthood begins with Blake (Nicholas Hoult), a middle-class pupil at the London comprehensive school which the young characters attend, giving out flyers inviting his peers to a party at his house while his parents are away. 'Anything goes' is the message accompanying his invitation, and this phrase could be described as an accurate prophecy of what is to follow. Thus we witness appalling and disturbing scenes of Katie being bullied, humiliated and punched by female classmates, scenes in which no teacher or pupil intervenes to help her. Sam is subsequently shown knocking her to the ground outside the school gates, while stating that he could 'make life so easy' for her (presumably if she agrees to go out with him). Her father, in fact, seems to confuse Sam with Trevor – whom she has gone out with – when he collects her from school. 'How was biology?' is his opening question to Katie (spectators have already witnessed the shocking examples of human biology and interaction on display in the film's opening segment). Fatally, while her father notices the bruises on Katie's face, he is soon distracted by a phone call and thinks that because she plays her favoured music in her room, everything is OK. Her mother subsequently expresses concerns that 'Katie is being bullied at school', but almost immediately afterwards, mother, father and brother are left staring at Katie's dead body hanging from the ceiling with a rope around her neck. So shocking is this opening to *Kidulthood* that one wonders (and slightly dreads) what the film will proceed to present on screen.

Out of a concern that the deceased's school year-group may be too traumatised to attend classes, Year Ten are given the following day off, presumably for a period of sad and thoughtful reflection. What follows, however, is a 'carnivalesque' day of sex, drug-taking, stealing, fighting and (ultimately) killing, rather than a time used for mourning Katie's tragic and avoidable suicide. Death is present at the beginning and end of *Kidulthood* and sexual activity is a feature of narrative events as they unfold, but expressions of love, companionship, regret and compassion are largely absent from the narrative ('Get over it' is a key phrase uttered by Becky).

In relation to depictions of sexuality in *Kidulthood*, Victoria Segal noted in the *New Statesman* that 'This loose group of comprehensive pupils is unabashed about discussing – or even having – sex in front of other people.'[112] We hear (but do not see) fifteen year-old Becky having sex with a man in his late twenties, but close-up shots reveal Becky and Alisa snorting cocaine in the film's attempts to break down taboos or restrictions about what can be portrayed and featured on screen. Events are presented in a deliberately stylised and heightened manner on many occasions, with scenes speeded up and slowed down as if to reflect the adrenaline rushes experienced by characters in their sexual and drug-taking activities, alongside the mood swings and emotional lows which characters might experience afterwards. The film proceeds to show that Becky and Alisa are in the end very different. Alisa eventually stands up to the bullies who drove Katie to suicide ('I ain't scared of you'), an important moral stance. Later, she decides to have her baby and distance herself from Becky, whose sexual frankness at the concluding house party shocks and stuns even such a hardened character as Jay (Adam Deacon). 'You can put it in my arse as well', she informs Jay, who declines to take her up on this offer. Jay, though, like other male characters in the film, appears ultimately to be more drawn to acts of violence against other males than to engaging in sexual acts or emotional and loving relationships with women. Sam's on/off girlfriend, Claire (Madeline Fairley), warns Sam prophetically that 'someone will get hurt' if all these acts of revenge and counter-revenge do not cease. But even her offer of continuous sex with Sam – 'We can fuck all night' – is shunned by Sam in favour of what Slavoj Žižek describes as a way of reconnecting 'with reality ... through raw violence'.[113]

The evening party is the destination where the central characters and the narrative as a whole have been heading, and this setting becomes the place where events will both escalate and reach a terrible tragic climax. Becky and Alisa have spent some time shopping for attractive-looking and expensive outfits to wear during the event. The host, Blake, appears to view the party as an opportunity for him to become a bit more accepted by the school community than currently appears to be the case. All will be disappointed by the outcome. Jay tells Blake to 'go away' at his own party. Becky says that she is 'sorry' for her behaviour, but Alisa tells her that she is a 'sorry' (i.e. pathetic) figure, and Becky will subsequently not feature in the two sequels. What might be described as the film's brutal sense of realism or pessimism is writ large in its closing segments. Alisa is briefly reconciled with Trevor at the close – having been estranged from him during the rest of the narrative – and just at this moment there appears to be some slight hope that they might strive to make some kind of life together for the sake of their unborn child. In a night-time setting with garden lights creating an appropriate romantic aura, Alisa declares to Trevor that 'We're going to have this baby. So we should try.' Trevor agrees, while adding that his mother 'will kill' him when she hears that he is going to become a father. This remark (like many of the dialogue exchanges in the film) is quickly revealed as ironic and multi-coded. Sam suddenly appears on the scene with the direct aim of physically punishing Trevor for daring to enter his domain and question his authority and power. What ensues becomes a fight to the death in which Trevor is killed. The final images of *Kidulthood*, after a prolonged absence from proceedings where their presence might have been expected or helpful, show the police and emergency services turning up to make arrests and to attend to the injured and the dying.

Adulthood (2008) is set six years later, and like *Kidulthood* focuses on an extended period of time in the life of Sam Peel and a group of surrounding characters whose lives are affected by him in one form or another. Catherine Shoard wondered in the *Sunday Telegraph* whether Clarke's character in

Kidulthood was something of an overdetermined pantomime 'villain',[114] and one can see what she meant by this. Despite Peel having been presented as a vicious and seemingly incorrigible bully who does great harm in *Kidulthood*, *Adulthood* seeks to illustrate that he is someone who is capable of trying to reform and become a better person, while having to accept there are a number of people around him who are not prepared to forgive and forget. From making other people victims in the first film, he graduates to becoming a victim and the target of violent hatred in the two sequels to *Kidulthood*.

Adulthood introduces a new female character in the guise of Becky's cousin, Lexi (Scarlett Alice Johnson). Lexi's view of life and human relationships, we soon learn, is a bitter and pessimistic one ('Fuck it. If they ain't gonna love you, make them pay'). She is seemingly seriously depressed after seven men have been acquitted of raping her for three hours in a gym after hours, a situation she has been led into by her cousin Becky, who has since disappeared. Lexi recalls that her attackers were acquitted because they 'had money', that the jury were persuaded that the sex was consensual and that Becky and Lexi had a reputation for being promiscuous.[115] Lexi, like Becky before her, has taken to drugs, but in her case dope and cocaine appear not to be consumed in a recreational manner, but more as a means of trying to block out the pain of an everyday existence which has become joyless and lacking in coherence (Lexi is shown taking an anti-depressant tablet and smoking a marijuana joint in quick succession). In one psychologically dramatic scene, the camera moves closer and closer to her face as she lies next to Sam following an unsuccessful sexual encounter and she relates just how unhappy and disillusioned she has become in adulthood.

One of the most significant differences between *Kidulthood* and *Adulthood* is that whereas the characters of the former focused their attentions largely on various ways of breaking the law (involving threatening, intimidating and antisocial behaviour, refusing to pay for a taxi, drug taking, under-age sex, extreme and ultimately lethal violence), in *Adulthood*, a number of characters are depicted studying law at a London institution ('Central University') as a means of potentially creating a better life for themselves. Robert/'Moony' (Femi Oyeniran) even declares to Sam that he is studying law so that people like Sam do not serve only six years in jail for killing someone. Apart from a female law student asking Robert in a flirtatious manner for some help with 'getting [her] head around … basic ethics in law' (a problem a number of the characters can be seen as experiencing in all three films), we do not witness – aside from a scene of note-taking in a lecture – any scenes of anyone actually studying in the narrative. However, the very presence of the university as a background feature of the story provides a glimpse of possible other ways of living than the numerous antisocial scenarios graphically depicted in *Kidulthood*.

Clarke does not, however, suggest in the two subsequent films that there is an easy route to finding a kind of ideal moral balance or social equilibrium in the spheres of work/life/leisure for the various characters.

Derek Malcolm's review of *Adulthood* in the London *Evening Standard* was captioned with the title 'From Bad to Badder', suggesting that he did not feel the sequel necessarily depicted the main characters turning over a new leaf and renouncing all their previous behaviour, outlooks and actions.[116] Cath Clarke in the *Guardian* felt that *Adulthood*, like its predecessor, was keen to present audiences with graphic images of 'sex, drugs and stabbings'.[117] However, the final segment of *Adulthood* works towards a conclusion portraying the central characters as part of an existing relationship or a potential couple, suggesting that even in this harsh and unforgiving landscape, relationships between men and women can act as a vital source of emotional sustenance and warmth, providing some kind of hope for a better future. Robert is shown giving his law-studying girlfriend, Kayla (Shanika Warren-Markland), a rose as a symbol of his regard for her. Sam receives a phone message from Lexi to say that she has booked two tickets for them to go to the cinema together the next evening, having recalled how he missed being able to partake in such activities when he was in jail. Given the extreme danger Sam faces when this message is sent, the booking seems to be in great danger of having to be cancelled. However, he survives the multiple threats to his existence from the representatives of both law and disorder, and the film closes with Lexi letting him into her apartment – and possibly her life – after we have witnessed her own possible near-death experience while consuming cocaine in an extremely depressed state.

In 2016, Noel Clarke returned with a third film in the series; this continued (and concluded) the story of Sam Peel, his family, friends, associates and enemies. Clarke admitted that coming up with an effective and pertinent 'hood' title this time round was difficult. He apparently contemplated *Parenthood*, *Fatherhood* or *Familyhood* as titles, but lamented that these were 'all terrible names', and finally settled on *Brotherhood*, a title which raises questions pertinent to the pledges of loyalty, allegiance and commitment made by characters in the narrative.[118] *Brotherhood* is a more generic film than the previous two – being rooted in a certain kind of British gangster milieu – but equally it resists straightforward classification and is possibly a more ambitious and probing film than it initially appears to be.

Sam Peel is very much the central focus of the narrative; Robert and Jay are absent from the narrative and Lexi, we will learn, is dead from a drugs overdose (a death that may have been murder presented as a form of accidental death). Sam is living with Kayla, Robert's girlfriend in *Adulthood* (it is not clear how these two became acquainted or romantically involved), and he is depicted as working in various cleaning jobs while living in a brightly decorated and seemingly affluent house (presumably largely paid for out of his partner's earnings as a lawyer before she took maternity leave). It soon becomes clear, however, that all is not well with Sam and his world; *Screen International* summarised the plot of the movie as the story of a 'former gang member struggling to adapt to a new way of life'.[119] The film begins with Royston Peel (Daniel Anthony), Sam's brother, performing a jazz swing number in a London club, which brings its multicultural audience together in a brief utopian moment of shared togetherness and joy. The shooting of Sam on stage by an assailant who is not arrested leads to a nightmarish scenario in which Sam is repeatedly drawn towards a mansion house in London, the kind of exclusive dwelling which ironically served as the setting for the terrible concluding violence in *Kidulthood*. The male occupants of this house appear to be wholly evil, and are seemingly forcing a number of women who are listed in the credits as 'semi-nude' girls or 'sex slaves' to reside in the house in a state of stunned subservience. Several years after *Kidulthood* and *Adulthood*, this appears to be a London which for all its seeming gentrification and social renovation is possibly even more ruthless, violent and corrupt beneath the brightly painted surfaces than it is in the previous two films.

Sam is criticised in the narrative for not spending more time with his children by his partner, and possibly feels unstimulated by the several cleaning jobs which he undertakes to help provide for his family (in a 2011 essay entitled 'Appetite for Destruction', Theodore Dalrymple claims that it is 'as difficult to employ a hoodie as to hug him').[120] He is soon driven back to violence and having sex outside the family by an old adversary, Uncle Curtis (Cornell John), who is still seeking revenge on Sam for his murder of Trevor in the first film.

As the plot unfolds, Sam is 'tricked' into having sex with Jenette (Tonia Sotiropoulou), an attractive and alluring woman, so their sexual encounter can be filmed and shown on a DVD to his wife, Kayla, thus forcing an emotional wedge between them. Jenette's guiles and flair for deception also extend to convincing Sam's mother, Mrs Peel (Adjoa Andoh), that she is the victim of violence as a way of gaining access to her home. This act of treachery on Jenette's part will conclude with the death of Mrs Peel, illustrating that this really is a world in which no act, however wicked or terrible, is totally off limits.

At this point, the odds against Sam surviving the attacks upon his person appear low. Sam is appalled by the prospect of having to fight the late Trevor's uncle (Cornell John) to the death (and, in the process, presenting to the world an image of 'Two black men fighting in the street', which is how *Kidulthood* concluded its narrative). Sam does not back away from the confrontation, however, and it is left to a police marksman to effectively bring the seemingly never-ending male violence on display in the films to a possible close. 'All of the drama, is it done?' asks Kayla when Sam belatedly joins her and his family for Sunday brunch. 'It's done', declares Sam, while Detective Lynch (David Ajala) advises Sam to 'Be good' in the film's closing section, a message which we have seen is not as easy to live up to as it might seem.

Sam, through the extended storylines, finds a kind of peace and happiness at the close with his partner and two children, and he speaks up for the importance of family life throughout the final film. The politicised speeches which pervade *Pressure* (1976), Horace Ove's important film about black culture and experiences of London life in the 1970s, are nowhere to be found in the 'hood' trilogy, perhaps a sign of how times have changed and of how extensive political and social change might now be viewed as an impossible dream. Slavoj Žižek has written that 'The sad fact opposition to the system cannot articulate itself in the guise of ... a coherent utopian project ... is a grave indictment of our epoch. What function does our celebrated freedom of choice serve when the only choice is effectively between playing by the rules and (self-) destructive violence?'[121] Noel Clarke tends to emphasise the importance of his characters making the right kind of moral choices in his narratives, while Horace Ove's film might be seen as indicating the need for a kind of shared black/white working class politicised consciousness to emerge if better times built around more loving and productive desires and ideals are to manifest themselves and be allowed to flourish.

The 'hood' films present a remarkable view of the energies of its young characters as a whole, while suggesting that this energy may often be misdirected and misjudged. Characters who are seen as sexually promiscuous or mercenary in their outlook (Becky) or over-dependent on drugs (Lexi) tend to fall by the wayside. Equally, characters who are too enamoured with violence or violent behaviour may eventually get their comeuppance. Sam, who begins as a character without any redeeming qualities whatsoever, ironically ends up as a kind of moral figure in the stark and threatening worlds depicted in the later films (when Sam meets his old associate Desmond, formerly a community support officer, now a police detective in *Brotherhood*, they rather pointedly meet in a café named 'Le Pain Quotidien').

Jay's question to Claire in *Kidulthood*, 'So what, me and you on, or what?' with its convoluted syntax and multiple clauses, receives a positive response, despite Jay having just knocked her boyfriend, Sam, unconscious with his own keyboard. This may be an extreme (if not necessarily that unusual) occurrence in the world of *Kidulthood,* which indicates how male libidinal energies can all too easily find an outlet in violence. But as in *Romeo and Juliet* (1597), characters are conscious here that time may be running out and that declarations of love and desire may have to be expressed briskly or risk not being expressed at all.

One can only hope that the success of the trilogy leads to more British films exploring relationships with black characters as central figures. The 'hood' films, as a whole, pay testimony to what Paul Gilroy has described as vivacious youth-based countercultures in which a 'new style of dissidence is being reproduced in which discrepant forms combine, conflict, and mutate in promiscuous, chaotic patterns which require that the politics of influence, adaptation and assimilation be rethought'. Gilroy leaves open the question of what will be the end result of such ongoing social, sexual, ethnic and cultural changes occurring among young people in British society, pondering, 'Who, after all, is now being assimilated into what?'[122] The 'hood' films suggest that only by presenting and delving into what some viewers might describe as exaggerated or extreme situations can we gain a deeper and more informed sense of what may be taking place right now in some of our schools, communities and homes.

Loves, livelihoods and communities: lesbians and gays support the miners

Pride (Matthew Warchus, 2014) takes its creative inspiration from an earlier period in British social, economic and political history – the coal miners' strike of 1984–1985 – and seeks to show a range of diverse characters working together to achieve a common goal. If the 'hood' films graphically represent members of a community at war with each other, *Pride* celebrates (to use Thomas Wartenberg's term) 'unlikely couples' and communities coming together for a worthy purpose. The film's title refers both to the concept of 'gay pride' and to the miners having pride in their occupation. *Pride* explores the support given to the miners and their families by an organisation known as LGSM (Lesbians and Gays Support the Miners). Jeffrey Weeks, writing on sexual politics as the strike drew to a close in the winter of 1985, notes that 'Support from lesbian and gay activists for the striking miners and their communities' resulted in the raising of '£10,000', with 'some miners' coming out as gay and what he termed 'old boundaries' being 'undermined'.[123] The film commemorates a historical moment when identity and sexual politics are seen as coterminous with class politics as a Conservative government led by Margaret Thatcher is virulently opposed to the striking miners and determined to defeat them. A cinematic biography of Margaret Thatcher's life, *The Iron Lady* (Phyllida Lloyd, 2011), tellingly references the strike only by showing striking miners clashing with police. Over one such montage, Mrs Thatcher pronounces, 'They believe in striking. I believe in work.'

Pride begins with the strike being featured on television, with Arthur Scargill, the leader of the National Union of Mineworkers making a speech, individual miners being interviewed, talking about how their 'pride and self-respect' are all they have left, and Margaret Thatcher speaking about the need for tough leadership. *Pride* seeks to go beyond these contemporary television representations of the conflict and to provide an insight into the lives of (in particular) a Welsh village fighting to stave off the closure of its mine. The narrative contrasts two different examples of close-knit communities: the members of the village consisting of (presumed heterosexual) men, women and families, and the LGSM community of youngish gay men and (initially) one lesbian woman, Steph (Faye Marsay). The primary figure in setting up this personal and political alliance between the two communities is Mark Ashton (Ben Schnetzer). At the start, he fails to say goodbye to a young man whom we assume he has spent the night with because his attention is drawn to a TV news programme reporting on the strike. The subsequent headquarters of the LGSM group are in Gethin's (Andrew Scott) gay bookshop in London, and it is Gethin's Welsh origins (and map of Britain) which help to guide the group towards an alliance with a Welsh mining village situated in South Wales as the place to which they will donate the money raised to help support the striking miners and their families. Not everyone in this London-based gay community is supportive of the miners, with some gay men – including one from a Durham mining area – claiming that that the perceived masculine and heterosexual culture of the miners is not one which is sympathetic to or supportive of gay lifestyles or gay culture. Gethin himself has not been back to Wales for sixteen years because his mother's (unspecified) religious beliefs prevent her from accepting his homosexuality ('Let's just say there's not always a welcome in the hillside', he notes wryly). As regards representations of sexuality in the film, it is notable that we do not see any of the gay characters having sex in the film (even when members of the LGSM group are sleeping together on the floor of a miner's house). Nor, one brief scene of pickets clashing with police aside, do we see much of the actual dispute itself. The television news reports of the time were often dominated by scenes of supposed intimidation and harassment carried out by the striking miners against the police and those who refused to join or support the strike, what Raphael Samuel in a 1985 essay, 'Friends and Outsiders', describes as 'TV cameramen' being drawn to the 'theatre of this miners' strike'.[124] With the exception of one character who is at catering college, it is not clear what jobs – if any – the principal members of the LGSM group work at or how they financially support themselves. All we know is that the miners' cause becomes the main activity and concern of their everyday lives. For example, Gethin states that his partner Jonathan (Dominic West) needs something to occupy him – we later learn that this character is HIV-positive.

This illustrates one perceived connection between gay men and striking miners in the mid-1980s. Gay men are shown facing the possibility of debilitation and death from the AIDS virus, and mining men face the possibility of a lifetime without work if the pits in their community are shut down. Both groups face being disapproved of by sectional and sometimes powerful forces within British media culture. *Pride* includes a real television advertisement from the era featuring a voice-over from John Hurt warning of a 'deadly disease' with 'no known cure', posing a 'danger' to lives and a 'threat' to society. This public health warning (promoting the use of condoms and safe sex) with its stonemason imagery and eerie music in the background now appears to be presenting the virus as a kind of force from another galaxy posing a serious threat to humanity.[125] In this mid-1980s scenario, AIDS, the National Coal Board and the Conservative government (in office between 1979 and 1997) are all seen – in one way or another – as threatening sexual liberation, freedom of expression and the future well-being and survival of whole communities.

Pride does not shy away from demonstrating that the gay and lesbian communities are not always well received by some of the younger miners and by one 'respected member of the community', Maureen (Lisa Palfrey), who is never won over. A turning point is Jonathan's striking performance on the dance floor, which impresses the local women who declare that Welsh men don't dance in public. As the narrative unfolds, linguistic definitions based on characters' sexual preferences start to feel somewhat outdated and potentially absurd. 'I'll take an extra gay', declares Cliff (Bill Nighy) when more rooms are needed for the visitors, although he draws the line at taking in lesbians because of their supposed dietary requirements (based around vegetarianism). Cliff also comes out as gay while making sandwiches with Hefina (Imelda Staunton), something he has not publicly announced to his own community. The members of the South Wales mining lodge make a joke (at Gethin's expense) about gays being welcome in the community, but accepting people from North Wales being a step too far (Gethin is from Rhyl), an allusion to perceived social and cultural differences between the two halves of Wales, and playing on the idea promoted in other films studied in this book that certain long-established differences between communal groups in British culture really cannot be transcended or altered.

For all its optimistic spirit and exuberance at depicting people working together to achieve a common goal, this semi-realist, historical comedy-drama, like the 1996 film *Brassed Off* (Mark Herman) about fighting pit closures, finally has to face the historical fact that the miners ended up losing their fight against pit closures and went back to work in March 1985, having gained none of their wished-for concessions or guarantees. ('Nothing worse than a lost cause', Mike (Joseph Gilgun) will wistfully observe at one stage.) A *New Socialist* essay in October 1986 reported grimly that in 'South Wales, ten of the district's 28 pits have been closed since March 1986'.[126] The failure of the strike to achieve its objectives led to reflections by commentators and participants on the significance and implications of the dispute, which lasted over a year.

Margaret Thatcher's account of her time as Prime Minister between 1979 and 1990, *The Downing Street Years* (1993), devotes a whole chapter to the conflict and, as the title of that particular chapter might suggest ('Mr Scargill's Insurrection'), does not mention the kinds of unexpected alliances forged by disparate communities and groups as featured in *Pride*. Her chapter does, though, make reference to what she describes as the 'large-scale intimidation in the mining villages' faced by miners and their families who did not support the strike, claiming that 'The sheer viciousness of what was done provides a useful antidote to some of the more romantic talk about the spirit of the mining communities.'[127] Margaret Thatcher concludes that 'In dealing with the coal industry you must have the mentality of a general as much as that of an accountant', but her own memoirs poignantly acknowledge that by 1993, the 'British coal industry' had 'shrunk far more than any of us thought it would at the time of the strike',[128] ironically illustrating that Arthur Scargill was right to be pessimistic about the future of the British coal industry under a Conservative government. (Mark Fisher concluded that 'Within a decade' of the strike ending in 1985, 'the industry was all but closed down in Britain'.)[129]

In *Chavs: The Demonization of the Working* Class (2011), Owen Jones also sees the defeat of the miners' strike as a decisive turning-point in British social and economic history. His socialistic perspective leads him to be concerned that 'the defeat of the Miners' Strike, meant that class no longer seemed to be a plausible vehicle of change for many leftists. Identity politics, on the other hand, still felt radical and had achievable aims … the emancipation of women, gays and ethnic minorities.' While affirming his commitment to these particular causes and clusters of concerns around sexual and racial identities, Jones laments the subsequent loss of an emphasis on what he terms the 'politics of class' in British culture.[130]

Given the complicated, complex and ultimately rather sad story which *Pride* relates, how does the film choose to conclude its narrative? One member of the group known to the others as 'Bromley' ('My name's Joe', he declares at the close, unconsciously echoing Ken Loach's 1998 film of that name) is initially too young at twenty to legally engage in homosexual intercourse. By the end of the film, Joe (George Mackay) has legally come-of-age and disassociated himself from his family, his mother having warned him that he faces a 'terrible, lonely life' with 'no family' if he pursues a life as a gay man. *Pride* shows him finding a community of people who are, in fact, warmer and more supportive than his own family. At the end, he is sharing a bed with Steph, who declares, 'If we were normal, we'd kiss now' (Steph never seems to find a partner during the course of the film). The narrative finishes with a Gay Pride march in June 1985, which is supported by the mining communities as an acknowledgement of the support given to them by the LGSM.[131] As the marchers cross Westminster Bridge with the Houses of Parliament in the background (and Billy Bragg's *There is Power in a Union* plays on the soundtrack), we learn the fate of certain key characters. Sian (Jessica Gunning), a miner's wife, goes on to become an MP for South Wales in 2005. Jonathan is HIV-positive, but is still alive in 2014. Tragically, however, it emerges that Mark Ashton died of AIDS in 1987 at the age of twenty-six. He is last shown triumphantly alive with his megaphone, being held aloft by miners as the parade proudly marches through London.

While the film stands up for both the cultural and personal identity of the miners and gay and lesbian communities, most of all it celebrates communality over individuality, working actively for others rather than just thinking about oneself, and seeks to affirm Britain as one nation (the frequent journeys between London and South Wales are a testimony to the film's anti-isolationism spirit). Margaret Thatcher declared that the 'coal strike was always about far more than uneconomic pits. It was a political strike.'[132] *Pride* also interprets the term 'political' in the broadest sense as being concerned with the social, economic and psychological arrangements which allow people to live fulfilled lives as both sexualised individuals and valued members of communities and societies. In relating one aspect of the miners' struggle to maintain their way of life, the film juxtaposes this battle with the rights of individuals to pursue their own sexual desires during this time when a terrible and unrelenting disease is also on the march (so to speak). Jeffrey Weeks, writing in the *New Statesman* at the time the miners' strike was drawing to an end in 1985, wondered why 'justice for the sexually oppressed should be so much more controversial than any other cause', and warned that what he termed the 'New Right' was 'increasingly setting the agenda of sexual politics'.[133] Simon Watney wrote in a 1987 issue of *New Socialist* that 'This terrible epidemic should teach us once and for all that if our species has any worth or beauty it lies in our ... capacity to embrace and celebrate all our variously consenting states of desire', adding, 'we might possibly think of Aids as a monstrously ironic means to that end'.[134] In time, the British medical establishment was forced to become more explicit in the language which it deployed to promote the concept of 'safe sex' (sex with a condom), even if the subsequent public health messages were not quite conveyed in the language of *Lady Chatterley's Lover*. (The 1987 short film entitled *AIDS: Iceberg* ominously warned audiences and viewers not to 'die of ignorance'.)

The metaphorical darkness of unemployment (as opposed to the literal darkness of the coalmine) and the awfulness of AIDS converge within the narrative to create a distressing picture of people suffering in bad times. The film's achievement is to formulate positive images of mini-communities working together in a productive fashion for the greater good of all, suggesting that the concept of the exclusive social and sexual couple is not the only way of living. In taking an unblinking view of British society and culture at a crucial transitional moment in its development, *Pride*'s great achievement is to find elements and strands of hope and optimism as issues of sexual politics become embroiled in a wider political and historical struggle which was to end in defeat for mining communities across Britain.

Notes

1 Thomas Carlyle wrote in 1843: 'The condition of England, on which many pamphlets are now in the course of publication … is justly regarded as one of the most ominous, and … strangest, ever seen in this world.' Thomas Carlyle, *Past and Present* (London: Chapman and Hall Limited, 1897 [1843]), p. 1.

2 Raymond Durgnat, *A Mirror for England: British Movies from Austerity to Affluence* (London: Faber & Faber, 1970), pp. 13, 67 and 106.

3 Andrew Marr, *The Day Britain Died* (London: Profile Books, 2000 [1999]), p. 35.

4 Shelagh Delaney, *A Taste of Honey* (London: Bloomsbury, 2015 [1959]), Act 1, Scene 2, p. 27.

5 Pauline Kael, 'Commitment and the Straightjacket' (1961), *I Lost It at the Movies* (London: Jonathan Cape, 1966), p. 74.

6 Geoffrey Nowell-Smith, *Making Waves: New Cinemas of the 1960s* (London: Continuum, 2008), p. 123.

7 Carrie Tarr, '*Sapphire, Darling* and the Boundaries of Permitted Pleasure', *Screen*, 26:1 (January–February 1985), p. 64.

8 Robin Griffiths, 'Sad and Angry: Queers in 1960s British Cinema', in Robin Griffiths (ed.), *British Queer Cinema* (London: Routledge, 2006), p. 85.

9 Alexander Walker, *Hollywood, England: The British Film Industry in the Sixties* (1986), pp. 280–1.

10 Poster for *Accident*, *New Statesman*, 73:1874 (10 February 1967), p. 199.

11 Brian McFarlane, *Twenty British Films: A Guided Tour* (Manchester: Manchester University Press, 2015), p. 135.

12 Walker acknowledged that Bob could be viewed as the most 'progressive'

figure in the narrative, as the only character willing to have sex and enter into relationships with 'both sexes' (p. 235). Alexander Walker, *Double Takes: Notes and Afterthoughts on the Movies 1956–76* (London: Elm Tree Books, 1977).

13 The director and producer of *Pressure* (1975) wrote a letter to the *Daily Mail* in 1976 complaining that 'the public has never had a chance' to see the film, suggesting that this 'premature burial' may have been for 'political' reasons, resulting from the movie having been privately 'shown to Scotland Yard'. Horace Ove, Robert Buckler, 'Unseen film,' *Daily Mail* (4 September 1976), consulted at the British Film Institute Library, Southbank, London, page number not listed.

14 Alexander Walker uses this phrase in his review of *My Beautiful Laundrette* when he describes the film as a 'social comedy about sex, race and class in Thatcher's Britain'. Alexander Walker, 'Taking England to the Wash', *Evening Standard* (14 November 1985), p. 24.

15 For instance, Bart Moore-Gilbert has claimed that *My Beautiful Laundrette* was 'almost certainly the first British film to reach a wide audience which shows a white and a non-white man kissing'. Bart Moore-Gilbert, *Hanif Kureishi* (Manchester: Manchester University Press, 2001), p. 87.

16 Peter Ackroyd, 'Fantasies of Elsewhere', review of *Letter to Brezhnev*, *Spectator*, 255:8210 (16 November 1985), p. 41.

17 Alexander Walker, 'Better Red than Liverpudlian', review of *Letter to Brezhnev*, *Evening Standard* (7 November 1985), p. 24.

18 Sian Barber, 'More than Just a "Nasty" Decade: Classifying the Popular', in Edward Lamberti, Jason Green, David Hyman, Craig Lapper and Karen Myers (eds), *Behind the Scenes at the BBFC: Film Classification From the Silver Screen to the Digital Age* (London: Palgrave Macmillan/the British Film Institute, 2012), p. 119.

19 Hilary Mantel, 'Bonkers in Bradford', review of *Rita, Sue and Bob Too*, *Spectator*, 259:8305 (19 September 1987), pp. 53–4.

20 Walker, 'Taking England to the Wash', *Evening Standard* (14 November 1985).

21 Janie Glen, 'Disposing of the Raj', interview with Hanif Kureishi, *Marxism Today*, 31:1 (January 1987), p. 43.

22 Melanie Williams, *Female Stars of British Cinema: The Women in Question* (Edinburgh: Edinburgh University Press, 2017), p. 135.

23 In a review of Pawel Pawlikowski's *Last Resort* in 2001, Jonathan Romney praised the work of 'foreign' directors making films in and about British society and culture, because, in his view, they did not present a simplified view of Britain as 'one happy nation ... united in love of theme pubs, *Big Brother* and *Bridget Jones*'. Jonathan Romney, 'Welcome to England – a Spiritual Siberia', *Independent on Sunday* (18 March 2001), p. 3.

24 The small and contained role played by Sally Hawkins here is in sharp contrast to her starring and life-affirming performance as the central character in Mike Leigh's *Happy-Go-Lucky* (2008).

25 David Nicholls, *One Day* (London: Hodder, 2011 [2009]), p. 379.

26 Dexter states in the novel that he wishes people would acknowledge that Saddam Hussein 'wasn't a very nice man' and thanks 'God someone's standing up to this fascist dictator'. Nicholls, *One Day*, pp. 374–8.
27 Melanie McDonagh, 'Don't wait for One Day: The perfect soulmate is an illusion that can ruin your life', *Spectator*, 317:9549 (3 September 2011), p. 16. McDonagh felt that watching *One Day* 'must be gratifying' for male viewers because it suggests 'that if you put a decent girl on hold for a decade, she'll still be there for you' (p. 16).
28 David Jenkins, interview with David Nicholls, *Time Out* (25–31 August 2011), p. 78.
29 David Nicholls has stated that the ending in which Emma dies 'was the central idea of the book'. 'Question and Answer session with David Nicholls', in Nicholls, *One Day*, p. 7.
30 Raymond Williams, *Modern Tragedy* (London: Chatto & Windus, 1966), p. 14.
31 Terry Eagleton, *Sweet Violence: The Idea of the Tragic* (Oxford: Blackwell Publishing: 2003), p. 96.
32 *One Day* (the novel) sums up Emma's philosophy in its closing pages as 'Change lives through art maybe. Cherish your friends, stay true to your principles, live passionately … Love and be loved, if you ever get the chance' (p. 433). In the novel, Emma has an affair with her married headmaster: 'Emma Morley lies on her back on the floor of the headmaster's office, with her dress rucked up around her waist' (p. 217), implying that this is one of the reasons why she eventually leaves teaching. The film completely dispenses with this subplot. Nicholls, *One Day*.
33 Hogg argued that being away from home can lead to characters in her films feeling that they are experiencing life in a 'cauldron of insecurity'. Tim Robey, 'Holiday from Hell, Film from Heaven,' *Daily Telegraph* (19 February 2011), pp. 6–7.
34 Dave Calhoun, 'Joanna Hogg', *Time Out* (7–13 October 2010), p. 77.
35 Jonathan Romney, 'Spend an Evening with Unpleasant People being Horrid on Holiday', film review of *Unrelated*, *Independent on Sunday* (21 September 2008), pp. 60–1.
36 Anthony Quinn, 'Tuscan Temptation', film review of *Unrelated*, *Independent* (19 September 2008), Arts and Books Review, pp. 6–7.
37 Sophie Mayer, film review of *Unrelated*, *Sight and Sound*, 18:10 (October 2008), pp. 86–7.
38 Joanna Hogg quoted in Cath Clarke, 'Secrets in the Sun', *Guardian* (11 September 2008), p. 28.
39 Joanna Hogg quoted in Terri White, 'The Viewing Guide': *The Souvenir*, *Empire*, 370 (January 2020), p. 123.
40 Margaret Thatcher, *The Downing Street Years* (London: HarperCollins, 1993), p. 397.
41 Zoe Heller, *Notes on a Scandal* (London: Penguin, 2009 [2003]), p. 1.
42 *Ibid.*, p. 86.

43 Thomas Sutcliffe, 'No Chemistry Lesson with Cate', *Independent* (9 February 2007), Arts and Books Review, p. 5.
44 William Shakespeare, *King Lear* (1608), Act 1, Scene 1, Line 90 (London: The Arden Shakespeare, 2001), p. 164.
45 Philip Larkin's 1955 poem 'Mr Bleaney', about an unfulfilled life, references Stoke in the line about the eponymous lonely lodger spending 'Christmas at his sister's house in Stoke'. Barbara's own rather uninspiring stay with her sister at Christmas inspires her to appreciate the comparatively exciting times she spends with Sheba, which are many things, but never dull. Philip Larkin, *Collected Poems*, edited by Anthony Thwaite (London: The Marvell Press and Faber & Faber, 1988), p. 102.
46 Derek Malcolm, film review of *Notes on a Scandal*, *Evening Standard* (1 February 2007), pp. 34–5.
47 Durgnat, *A Mirror for England*, p. 185.
48 Sutcliffe, 'No Chemistry Lesson with Cate'.
49 In the novel, Barbara worries about how 'desolate' her retirement will possibly be, given that she has 'no husband, very few friends, no children.' Heller, *Notes on a Scandal*, p. 185.
50 *Ibid.*, p. 243.
51 Richard Porton, 'Trusting the Text: An Interview with Cate Blanchett', *Cineaste*, 32:2 (Spring 2007), p. 18.
52 Adam Sonstegard, '*Notes on a Scandal*, Teacher's Edition', in Pamela Demory and Christopher Pullen (eds), *Queer Love in Film and Television: Critical Essays* (Basingstoke: Palgrave Macmillan: 2013), p. 251.
53 Lord Alfred Douglas, *Oscar Wilde: A Summing up* (London: Icon Books, 1962 [1940]), p. 113.
54 Porton, 'Trusting the Text', p. 19.
55 These ages are taken from the published edition of the play, which also informs audiences that events take place in London between 1993 and 1997. Patrick Marber, *Closer*, revised edition (London: Methuen, 1997), p. 5.
56 Graham Saunders, 'Academics', in Mireia Aragay, Hildegard Klein, Enric Monforte and Pilar Zozaya (eds), *British Theatre of the 1990s: Interviews with Directors, Playwrights, Critics and Academics* (Basingstoke: Palgrave Macmillan, 2007), p. 176.
57 Max Stafford-Clark, 'Directors', in *British Theatre of the 1990s*, p. 34. In this interview, the director claims that the role of theatre and playwriting 'is always to respond to the present' (p. 37).
58 Sukhdev Sandhu, film review of *Closer*, *Daily Telegraph* (14 January 2005), p. 21.
59 Robert Hanks, 'A Love Story for our Times', film review of *Closer*, *Independent* (14 January 2005), Review section, pp. 6–7.
60 David Cooke, 'The Director's Commentary', in *Behind the Scenes at the BBFC*, p. 170.
61 John Hazleton, film review of *Closer*, *Screen International*, 1479 (3 December 2004), p. 50.

62 Tom Milne, *Losey on Losey* (London: Secker & Warburg, 1968 [1967]), p. 27.
63 Pierre Macherey, *A Theory of Literary Production* translated by Geoffrey Wall (London: Routledge & Kegan Paul, 1978), p. 63.
64 Kira Cochrane, 'Why porn is the new glamour', *New Statesman* (12 September 2005), p. 34. Cochrane observed, 'Out were the dependability and possible boredom of care work; in were the seedy glamour and possible stardom of the sex industry', before concluding, 'A career in the sex industry remains the deadliest of all ends' (p. 35).
65 Marber, *Closer*, Act Two, Scene Seven, p. 58.
66 Philip Larkin, *High Windows* (London: Faber & Faber, 1974), p. 17.
67 Rebecca Taylor reported that in Peter Stringfellow's Covent Garden Gentlemen's Club, for instance, a customer will pay '£400 an hour for a girl's company, whether she dances [naked] or talks [to him]'. In this article, Stringfellow states, 'People may say what we do is morally wrong' but he argues that 'morals shouldn't come into entertainment' (p. 30). Rebecca Taylor, interview with Peter Stringfellow, *Time Out* (16–29 December 2010), p. 30.
68 Marber, *Closer*, Act Two, Scene Nine, p. 79.
69 Nick Horley, 'They're Brazen, and Coming to a Town near You', *New Statesman & Society* 3:127 (15 November 1990), pp. 32–3.
70 Richard Corliss, 'Best & Worst of 2004', *Time*, 164:25 (27 December 2004/3 January 2005), p. 105.
71 Colin Kennedy, 'Love Hurts', interview with Patrick Marber, *Empire* (February 2005), p. 75.
72 Marber, *Closer*, Act Two, Scene Twelve, p. 105.
73 Kim Newman, 'Movie Trial: *Closer*', *Empire*, 214 (April 2007), p. 149.
74 David Bell and Jon Binnie, *The Sexual Citizen: Queer Politics and Beyond* (Cambridge: Polity, and Malden, MA: Blackwell, 2000), p. 125.
75 Sarah Street, *British National Cinema: Second Edition* (London: Routledge, 2009 [1997]), p. 131.
76 Pawel Pawlikowski admitted in an interview that 'some of the financiers' of *My Summer of Love* would have preferred an ending showing 'Mona enjoying a new life in Paris or somewhere nice', but he insisted on keeping the conclusion open-ended. The director was not sure what would become of Mona, although he felt sure that Tamsin would go on 'to Oxbridge, and have a brilliant career in the media'. Jason Wood, *Talking Movies Contemporary World Filmmakers in Interview* (London: Wallflower Press, 2006), p. 186.
77 Deborah Ross, 'Disappointed of North London', film review of *Disobedience*, 338:9927, *Spectator* (1 December 2018), p. 64. Ross claimed that there was 'little sexual chemistry between the pair'.
78 *Ibid.*
79 Naomi Alderman, *Disobedience* (London: Penguin, 2018 [2006]). 'Dovid is the Rabbi now, although he does not enjoy the title' (p. 254) and 'Those people who remain at the synagogue have come to value Esti and Dovid's continued presence' (p. 253) are key sentences depicting how events conclude in the novel.

80 Lee Edelman, *No Future: Queer Theory and the Death Drive* (Durham, NC, and London: Duke University Press, 2004), pp. 30–1.
81 Andrew Bennett and Nicholas Royle, 'Queer Theory', *An Introduction to Literature, Criticism and Theory*, fifth edition (London: Routledge, 2016), p. 264.
82 Terri White, film review of *God's Own Country*, *Empire*, 340 (September 2017), p. 38.
83 Anna Smith, film review of *God's Own Country*, *Amorist*, 5 (September 2019), p. 65.
84 Clarissa Smith, 'British Sexual Cultures', in Michael Higgins, Clarissa Smith and John Storey (eds), *The Cambridge Companion to Modern British Culture* (Cambridge: Cambridge University Press, 2010), pp. 249–52.
85 Mark Kermode, 'True Romance', film review of *Ae Fond Kiss…*, *New Statesman* (20 September 2004), describes the film as documenting the 'fiery fallout of a Romeo-and-Juliet-style romance between an Irish Catholic and a Glaswegian Muslim', p. 45.
86 Dilys Powell, review of *Poor Cow*, *Sunday Times* (10 December 1967), reprinted in George Perry, ed. *Dilys Powell: The Golden Screen: Fifty Years of Films* (London: Pavilion Books, 1989), pp. 228–9.
87 Editorial, 'Loach in La La Land', *Daily Telegraph* (14 February 2017), p. 17.
88 Ken Loach, interviewed in Graham Fuller (ed.), *Loach on Loach* (London: Faber & Faber, 1998), p. 113.
89 Dominic Sandbrook, 'We've Never Had It So Good', *Daily Mail* (28 December 2019), p. 17.
90 Ryan Gilbey, film review of *Ae Fond Kiss…*, *Sight and Sound*, 14:9 (September 2004), p. 52.
91 Kermode, 'True Romance'.
92 Steve Blandford, '*A Way of Life*, British Cinema and New British Identities', *Journal of British Cinema and Television*, 5:1 (2008), issue editors John Corner and Julian Petley, p. 102. Blandford sees a contrast between the 'bright airy living spaces' in which several scenes of *Ae Fond Kiss…* are set and what he terms the 'old divisions and bigotries' which lead to 'suspicion and division between communities', pp. 101–2.
93 Kermode, 'True Romance'.
94 Tony Padman, 'Kiss and Tell', interview with Ken Loach, *Hampstead and Highgate Express* (10 September 2004), pp. i–ii.
95 Derek Malcolm, film review of *Kidulthood*, *Evening Standard* (2 March 2006), p. 35.
96 Christopher Cauldwell, *Studies in a Dying Culture* (London: John Lane: The Bodley Head, 1951 [1938]), p. 65.
97 Catherine Shoard, 'Street Slang', glossary and interview with Noel Clarke, *Sunday Telegraph* (19 February 2006), consulted at the BFI Library, London, only article page spread details available, pp. 11–15.
98 Alan Franks, 'Too Much Too Young', *The Times Magazine* (25 January 2006), consulted at the BFI Library, London, only article page spread details available, pp. 31–6.

99 Shoard, 'Street Slang'.
100 *Ibid.*
101 F.R. Leavis claimed that Dickens presents London as 'a squalid, gloomy and oppressive immensity, blighting and sinister to the life it swarms with'. Noel Clarke, arguably, presents a not dissimilar view of London at times in his three 'hood' films. F.R. Leavis and Q.D. Leavis, *Lectures in America* (London: Chatto & Windus, 1969), p. 8.
102 This description of the film's thematic landscape is taken from the Pathé *Adulthood* production notes (by Freud Communications) consulted at the BFI Library, London, page numbers not listed.
103 Liz Hoggard, article on *Kidulthood*, *Independent on Sunday* (19 February 2006), p. 51.
104 James Bell, review of *Kidulthood*, *Sight and Sound* (May 2006), p. 58.
105 Nicholas Barber, review of *Adulthood*, *Independent on Sunday* (22 June 2008), p. 63.
106 Alice Thomson, 'A Film to Make Every Mother Shudder', *Daily Telegraph* (1 March 2006), p. 17.
107 Richard Neville, *Play Power* (London: Jonathan Cape, 1970), pp. 15–17.
108 F.R. Leavis, 'The Function of the University at the Present Time', *The Times* (8 October 1968), reprinted in *Letters in Criticism by F.R. Leavis*, ed. John Tasker (London: Chatto & Windus, 1974), p. 130.
109 F.R. Leavis, 'English Studies and Student Unrest', letter to *The Times Literary Supplement* (12 June 1969), reprinted in *Letters in Criticism by F.R. Leavis*, p. 133.
110 Noel Clarke quoted in the production notes for *Adulthood*.
111 Alan Franks reported that Rebecca Martin, who played Katie, had been bullied at a comprehensive school herself: 'she became such a target for bullying that she would regularly find twenty pupils waiting … circling and taunting her'. Apparently, unlike the tragic Katie, 'Rebecca could and did talk to her parents about it, and eventually left to go to a private school.' Franks, 'Too Much Too Young', pp. 31–6.
112 Victoria Segal, 'Young Blood', film review of *Kidulthood*, *New Statesman* (13 March 2006), p. 48.
113 Slavoj Žižek, *The Year of Dreaming Dangerously* (London: Verso, 2012), p. 58.
114 Shoard, 'Street Slang', pp. 11–15.
115 Lexi's tragic tale would seem to be supported by statistical evidence from the Crown Prosecution Service, which stated that 'Fewer than a third of rape prosecutions brought against young men (aged eighteen to twenty-four) in Britain in 2017 resulted in convictions.' Rebecca Watson, 'Only One After: The Prolonged Impacts of Sexual Assault', *The Times Literary Supplement*, 6046 (15 February 2019), p. 3.
116 Derek Malcolm, 'From Bad to Badder', film review of *Adulthood*, *Evening Standard* (19 June 2008), p. 39.
117 Cath Clarke, film review of *Adulthood*, *Guardian* (20 June 2008), film and music section, p. 10.

118 Charles Grant, 'Brotherhood', *Sight and Sound*, 26:9 (September 2016), p. 15.
119 Author not credited, 'Brotherhood', *Screen International*, 1808 (August–September 2016), p. 58.
120 Theodore Dalrymple, 'Appetite for Destruction: Culture and Anarchy in Britain', *Spectator*, 316:9546 (13 August 2011), p. 13. The author bemoaned what he saw as the state of 'contemporary British culture', believing that too often it urged people to indulge their 'baser instincts, desires and urges' (p. 14). An editorial feature in the same issue wrote of 'young men living in workless ghettos … who are failed by the school system and left to fester in welfare slums' (p. 3).
121 Žižek, *The Year of Dreaming Dangerously*, p. 54.
122 Paul Gilroy, *Between Camps: Race, Identity and Nationalism at the End of the Colour Line* (London: Allen Lane, 2000), pp. 249–50.
123 Jeffrey Weeks, 'Putting the Sex into Socialism', *New Socialism*, 109:2812 (8 February 1985), p. 27. Weeks quotes Friedrich Engels as stating 'in all times of great agitation, the traditional bonds of sexual relations, like all other fetters, are shaken off' (p. 27).
124 Raphael Samuel, 'Friends and Outsiders', *New Statesman*, 109:2808 (11 January 1985), p. 14.
125 A 1987 essay on the virus reported that by November 1986 the diagnosed number of AIDS sufferers in Britain was '599, of whom 296 are already dead'. Simon Watney, 'Visual Aids: Right Across the Media Aids is Being Handled with all the Sophistication of the Victorian Age', *New Socialist*, 47 (March 1987), p. 20.
126 Raphael Samuel, 'Doing Dirt on the Miners', *New Socialist*, 42 (October 1986), p. 12. Samuel notes that 'the miners were particularly well supported by gay and lesbian groups during the strike' (p. 16).
127 Thatcher, *The Downing Street Years*, p. 353.
128 *Ibid.*, pp. 686 and 377, respectively.
129 Mark Fisher, 'a world of dread and fear' (2005), republished in Darren Ambrose (ed.), *k-punk: The Collected and Unpublished Writings of Mark Fisher (2004–2016)* (London: Repeater Books, 2018), p. 78.
130 Owen Jones, *Chavs: The Demonization of the Working Class* (London: Verso, 2012 [2011]), p. 255.
131 Robert Stevens, reviewing *Pride* from a Marxist perspective, felt that the film 'seems almost indifferent to the eventual defeat of the miners' strike, ending as it does by depicting a celebratory 1985 Gay Pride march in London'. Robert Stevens, '*Pride*: The UK miners' strike through the distorted mirror of identity politics', *World Socialist Web Site* (29 October 2014). www.wsws.org/en/articles/1014/10/29/prid-o29.html (last accessed November 2019).
132 Thatcher, *The Downing Street Years*, p. 337. Thatcher concluded her account of the 1984–1985 conflict by claiming 'What the strike's defeat established was that Britain could not be made ungovernable by the Fascist Left. Marxists wanted to defy … the laws of economics. They failed' (p. 378).

133 Jeffrey Weeks, 'Putting the Sex into Socialism', *New Statesman*, 109:2812 (8 February 1985), pp. 27–8.
134 Watney, 'Visual Aids', p. 21. Watney noted that the AIDS crisis was resulting in a loss 'of freedoms and friends' (p. 21).

Afterword:
'We must love one another or/and die?'

If *Pride* strives to find some lessons for the future by revisiting the past and a decade haunted by the emergence of the AIDS virus, *Perfect Sense* (David Mackenzie, 2011) identifies a terrifying future lying in wait for humanity in a narrative taking place in a seemingly contemporary (*c.* 2010) timeframe. This film's portrayal of a deadly and unseen virus which breaks up human relationships and the stability of society is a drama which has become more pertinent and disturbing from a post-2020 perspective than it was on its first release. This alarming tale unfolds in a Glaswegian setting, although the virus is depicted as a truly worldwide phenomenon. Short scenes of the havoc unleashed around the world by the virus in the form of news and amateur footage are interwoven with studies of how the disease affects social, sexual and romantic relationships in a particular enclosed part of Glasgow. The film focuses on how chef Michael (Ewan McGregor) and scientist Susan (Eva Green), who researches into the origins and effects of epidemics, begin a relationship just as the virus starts to pervade the city. Michael finds that his work is affected when people lose their senses of smell, taste and hearing. Susan, in turn, experiences professional disappointment when she is unable to make any progress regarding the causes or the likely outcomes of the virus (there are several scenes of her staring intently at rabbits kept in cages as part of her investigations, but no useful information appears to be gleaned from such studies).

Our first glimpse of Susan is of her walking along a bridge during a cloudy and gloomy day and stopping to spit into the sea. A fast edit to images of food can make it appear that she is spitting into food, although this sudden cut serves to introduce the restaurant setting which will be an important feature of the narrative, and the place where Susan and Michael will begin their relationship. Unlike other films discussed in this book, *Perfect Sense* deploys an unseen female narrator to provide an ongoing commentary at various moments throughout the narrative, offering a wider perspective on what is occurring than might be available to Susan and Michael who are in the midst of events. The narrator refers to various possible reasons put forward for the emergence of the virus; ecological harm done to the planet; a 'degenerate capitalist system' bringing about misery and destruction; a Biblical Day of Judgment for sinners and unbelievers unleashed on the world by an angry and disappointed God; terrorist attacks by foes of the Western world. But there appears to be no one reason; the virus is finally a mystery on a par with the question of how and why there is human life and a universe in the first place.

As part of her work, Susan is called in to speak to a Scottish truck driver who has lost his sense of smell and started to doubt whether there is any 'meaning in life'. His wife is concerned because this is not a topic he has previously concerned himself with and is therefore very out of character. Soon afterwards, we see a bus driver uncontrollably breaking down in tears as he drops off his passengers. The virus, it emerges, can cause people to reflect upon their deepest regrets and disappointments in life, bringing to the surface feelings and emotions which are more normally kept under wraps so that people and society can function. When Michael is out on his bike, he is startled to see a fellow bike rider pass by wearing a face mask. Shortly afterwards, another rider goes by, also wearing a face covering. One instance may have no particular significance; two in succession is a sign that something bad is on its way. The virus in the film will go on to demonstrate 'god-like' powers to manipulate and torment human beings seemingly at will. Gradually, people will find that their capacity to taste, smell and hear is taken away, while they are also helpless at times to resist behaving in a disturbing and terrifying fashion – for instance, consuming anything in reach (including flowers) to appease their sudden extreme hunger and loss of taste in ways evoking the desperate devouring of drugs by characters in *Trainspotting* (Danny Boyle, 1995). Another effect of the virus is that characters can become suddenly aggressive, threatening and hurtful to people they like or love. Michael, for instance, dismisses Susan from his life, saying he never wanted 'profound conversations' with her, only sex. For him, he declares, she was simply a female body, interchangeable with other female bodies (our first view of Michael shows him asking a young and (like Susan) dark-haired woman to leave his bed and go home as he cannot sleep with someone lying beside him). He will later claim that it was the disease which made him make such vicious and callous claims, but there is a sense in the film that the virus also succeeds in bringing out and accentuating people's worst instincts and sometimes their ambivalent feelings about their co-workers, partners and loved ones. Michael has previously admitted to having made himself distant from a woman he was due to marry after she became seriously ill and before her untimely death. This scenario has close links with a Scottish character McGregor played for David Mackenzie in the 2003 film *Young Adam,* providing an intertextual reference to *Perfect*

Sense's portrayal of a world where male–female relationships appear to be in a state of turmoil, torment and uncertainty.

Michael and Susan, though, are depicted as succeeding in having passionate and life-affirming sex in one extended sequence, which shows each lover taking it in turns to be on top of the other in a quest for mutual sexual pleasure. A golden glow surrounds the lovers at this moment, in contrast to the film's drained colour palette elsewhere as the virus starts to drain away people's energy and life. Sex in the film is shown as a natural act of progression for a man and a woman interested in and attracted to each other. But for Michael and Susan, conducting a relationship during a pandemic is inevitably problematic and brings to the foreground already existing tensions and uncertainties within their relationship. Susan wonders if Michael is an 'arsehole', similar to other unsatisfactory men whom she has dated in the past. Michael wonders if Susan really is that different from the (unnamed) brunette woman whom he was in bed with at the beginning of the narrative. What do the couple really want (if anything) from each other? The presence of a deadly virus all around them makes it even more important that they try to find meaningful answers to such questions.

In scenes eerily prophetic of how 'real life' would proceed to mirror the art and subject matter of this film from 2019 and 2020 onwards, officials working for the council are shown telling and then forcing infected individuals to stay at home during the pandemic in order to avoid spreading the disease (a generous scheme that provides daily food for the isolated is shown to be authorised and undertaken by the Scottish authorities). Scientists in *Perfect Sense* talk of sticking to the '2006 plan' for dealing with such viral emergencies, but it soon becomes clear that the virus is no respecter of history or pre-planning. New ideas for dealing with it are badly needed, but new technology and concepts are, in fact, shown to be conspicuously absent in the film. Michael and Susan take a picture of themselves as a couple, but the photograph is filmed not on a modern mobile phone, but with an instant camera, an innovation in its time, but one now considered outdated and obsolete. Self-isolating people are told to leave their television screens on for updated information about what to do in the crisis, whereas one might have expected a computer screen to be highlighted as a vital source of information in this multimedia age. The non-diegetic music on the soundtrack of *Perfect Sense* is classical in tone and mood throughout, and this, arguably, helps to create a suitable mood of grandeur and mourning to fit what is happening on screen.

The final images in *Perfect Sense* are of Susan and Michael deciding that they do, in fact, care deeply for each other. If the world is ending and people are about to go blind, a glimpse of each other's face and the feel of each other's bodily warmth are the last sensations and sights they wish to experience and savour. Hence, the film (and, it is implied, life as it has been known) ends with Susan and Michael walking towards each other and smiling that they have – just in time – been able to emotionally reach out to each other. Michael has been able to authentically use that phrase which lovers reach for when they speak of their deepest and most sincere thoughts, saying 'I love you' to Susan as his final utterance within the narrative. Alice in *Closer* (2004) bemoans the sort of love offered by Dan, which she feels cannot be touched or felt. But in the conclusion to *Perfect Sense*, this feeling of love is successfully communicated without words.

This can be viewed as a hopeful conclusion in so far as the ability of human beings to make positive, loving and affirmative commitments to each other will be important if humanity is to be able to rebuild its worlds and societies when the virus has receded and hopefully become less prominent and destructive. Love may not conquer all, but the film suggests that this is a state of being always worth striving for, even if it is elusive. *Perfect Sense* also commemorates the collective efforts of those who work towards keeping society operating and functioning during threats to its safety and well-being (an example being the restaurant workers carrying on cooking for customers and later for those who are self-isolating). Such efforts in the face of all kinds of obstacles and deterrents can be viewed as an example of tangible forms of love in action. The closing credits of *Perfect Sense* carry the standard legal disclaimer that 'This film is a work of fiction and the characters and events portrayed in this film are also entirely fictitious.' For all its fictionality, the film provides some pertinent lessons in how we might seek to conduct ourselves during a pandemic, and how we should learn to value and treat well the people we love and care for, because one day they will be gone for ever.

Perfect Sense provides a timely, disturbing but not entirely pessimistic coda to the concerns and issues explored throughout this study. In conclusion, we can note that Ewan McGregor also appears in *T2 Trainspotting* (Danny Boyle, 2017), in which his character, Renton, arrives home in Scotland from Amsterdam to be greeted at the airport by Eastern European women welcoming him to Edinburgh. Renton is given a keynote speech in the film where he bemoans what he sees as the worst aspects of modern-day Western societies, which involve people choosing to indulge in online 'slut shaming' and 'revenge porn', while being forced to accept 'zero hours' contracts and live lives of 'unfulfilled promise'. His impassioned tirade implicitly suggests that these varied phenomena may be linked in complex and disturbing ways. Larry in *Closer* (2004) had predicted that the internet might end up being used predominantly for the viewing of pornography at the expense of the Worldwide Web's wider social and cultural possibilities, but he, himself, is shown as a willing participant in online sexual fantasy role-playing and of failing (largely) to nurture positive and loving relationships and friendships with those to whom he is close. Larry can diagnose the dangers of online pornography without being able to resist its allure and sensuous appeal. Larry as a dermatologist and Susan as an epidemiologist in *Perfect Sense* have important, well-paid jobs, but other characters in films discussed in the book are less fortunate. Dan in *Closer*, Laura in *Animals* and even Spud (Ewan Bremner) in *T2 Trainspotting* are shown as harbouring literary ambitions, in part to imbue their daily lives with a creative outlet which is not provided by their everyday work-roles in society.

Between the summer of 2016 and the end of 2020, Britain was engaged in the protracted process of ending its membership of the European Union, while striving to obtain some form of workable model and framework for future economic and social relationships and interactions with the European community. In *T2 Trainspotting*, Renton and his accomplice, Simon (Jonny Lee Miller), are shown successfully persuading gullible members of a European Union Small Business Development Loan committee to give them £100,000 to renovate a derelict site which they intend (without the committee's knowledge) to turn into a mini-brothel, with themselves as the owners. The film, in this sense, offers a wry commentary on a Britain moving away from a partnership with European economies and communities and on the ways in which sex in British culture might always take some unusual and morally dubious turns. *T2 Trainspotting* contains a few eye-opening scenes and images of Bulgarian-born escort, Veronika (Anjela Nedyalkova) having sex with male clients in acts which involve her buggering men with a strap-on dildo in rented hotel rooms. Simon (formerly known as 'Sick Boy') secretly films these activities before attempting to blackmail Veronika's male clients with his knowledge of their behaviour and proclivities. Such despicable behaviour trades on the understanding that many men are capable of engaging in sexual activities and fantasies which they would not like to be made public, and Simon seeks to profit from this gap between certain characters' everyday familial and work personas and the sexual desires which they consequently seek to fulfil in private. *T2 Trainspotting* has its own particular version of a happy or morally just ending, as Veronika manages to succeed in prising Simon and Renton's ill-gotten award money from the European Union business fund away from them and returning with the money to her son and mother in Bulgaria. This potentially allows her to embark upon a new and more rewarding way of life, one which does not involve prostitution and blackmailing schemes (her departure evokes memories of Renton's furtive escape from Britain at the close of the first *Trainspotting* film). Simon and Renton are last glimpsed sitting resignedly on Simon's couch in his apartment, their future plans (if any) unclear; a symbolic sign, perhaps, that a particular era in British cinema and cultural history is drawing to a close, with what happens next in a post-Brexit British landscape seemingly still to be determined.

Few of the film-makers discussed in this book have followed Michael Winterbottom's example of producing a film consisting largely of extended explicit sex scenes, but directors and writers now seem more confident about acknowledging the presence and importance of sexuality in their characters' lives. Noel Clarke and Joanna Hogg have sought in their different ways to invest their narratives with a sensuous aura, even if many of the events in their films show characters acting in a harsh and unfeeling manner, unconducive to the promoting of positive loving relationships between men and women. In the work of both writer-directors, the difficulties of attaining sexual and romantic satisfaction for central characters may create situations which cast a disturbing and melancholy shadow over their respective narratives. Neither Clarke nor Hogg suggest that there may be easy answers to the predicaments of their protagonists, but an awareness of the possible reasons why characters act as they do is seen as an important starting point for a possible better future.

This book has sought to demonstrate how these post-2000 diverse and multifaceted films about the changing and recurring faces, symbols and physical manifestations of sex, love and desire have all attempted to explore their subject material from differing perspectives and with emotional depth, intensity, good humour and an awareness that sexual and romantic fulfilment may, sadly, be beyond the grasp of characters and protagonists at the heart of many of the films' narratives. In such instances, despair may constitute the obverse side of desire. The growth of uncensored sexual images on the internet, and an enhanced psychological awareness that sexual desires are potentially infinite and unquenchable, may lead a number of the films examined to imply that stable and contented marriages and relationships may be more difficult to attain for future generations of film viewers and spectators. But if in *9 Songs* (2004) we witness a couple break up after around nine varied sexual encounters during the course of a year, in *45 Years* (Andrew Haigh, 2015) we watch a married couple (Charlotte Rampling and Tom Courtenay) celebrate their lengthy relationship, even if it is revealed to have not been easy or rewarding at times. Several of the films explored have not been straightforwardly classifiable as genre films (*Perfect Sense* draws upon science fiction, social problem and love story narratives), an indication of how British cinema has changed from when films might have been more readily or straightforwardly categorised as social realist narratives or 'sex comedies'. Such generic fluidity and narrative diversity arguably reflects a sense that sexual identities in this modern era are themselves perceived as being of a potentially fluid and unfixed nature, with roots in fictionality as well as reality (Emily Blunt's character in

My Summer of Love is a good example of such features and characteristics in action).

While some of the films examined in this book predominantly move towards the formation of a married heterosexual couple at the close, such relationships are not depicted as necessarily constituting the last word. In *I Give It a Year* (Dan Mazer, 2013), married couple Nat (Rose Byrne) and Josh (Rafe Spall) celebrate the prospect of separating after a year of married life in the film's closing moments, as this allows them the freedom to pursue and embrace another partner. Nat and Josh both agree that they love each other, but are not *in* love with each other; an interesting semantic development from the phrase 'I love you.' This new formulation of what being in love may mean strives to be more precise than its illustrious time-honoured predecessor, although it may end up being somewhat paradoxical and ambivalent as well. Nat and Josh's declarations can be seen as indicative of an increased awareness by film-makers in Britain that sexual and emotional relationships (like the British weather) are capable of sudden and sometimes alarming changes in character, appearance and mood. 'Forever' does not necessarily follow on from, 'I love you' (Nat, in *I Give It a Year*, helpfully goes on to clarify that what she currently feels towards her husband is the 'opposite of love', namely, 'misery').

Many of the relationships depicted are crucially placed in social and economic contexts which are shown as potentially detrimental to the well-being of the romantic partnerships in question. Jobs such as teaching are depicted as rewarding but stressful occupations which are far from secure (Roisin and Esti, for instance, both face losing their jobs for engaging in sexual relationships with partners disapproved of by their schools' governing bodies, as does Sheba, of course, for different reasons). Farming in *God's Own Country* is depicted as a hard and physically demanding way of life which may not offer much in the way of material comfort for those earning their living in this way. A film such as *Pride* indeed suggests that in harsh economic times, couples might do well to situate their relationships within wider communal frameworks, so as not to be left facing potentially difficult situations entirely by themselves. *Pride* also suggests that men and women may be limiting their sexual and emotional life experiences if they are only willing to enter into relationships with members of the opposite sex.

The films as a whole benefit immensely from being able to draw upon a pool of outstanding character actors who invariably play their various roles with precision and sincerity. Colin Firth appears as a loyal friend to Oscar Wilde who is by the author's bedside when he dies, and as Mark Darcy, he is by Bridget Jones's bedside when she has her baby, thus witnessing endings and beginnings, death and the emergence of new life. Evoking Sylvia Syms's memorable portrayals of women characters caught up in complicated tales of sex, love and desire in an earlier era of British cinema, Judi Dench is mesmerising in roles as diverse as Iris Murdoch, Mrs Henderson and Barbara in *Notes on a Scandal*. Jim Broadbent succeeds in bringing to life the characters of Iris Murdoch's husband in *Iris*, Pamela Jones's husband in the Bridget Jones trilogy and Margaret Thatcher's husband in *The Iron Lady*, his performances deftly evoking the pleasures and joys, disappointments and traumas of married life within a British cultural context spanning several decades. Josh O'Connor went on to graduate from playing a homosexual Yorkshire farm worker in *God's Own Country* (2017) to the role of Prince Charles in later seasons of the Netflix historical drama, *The Crown* (2016–), showing that in film and television at least, a 'commoner' may succeed in becoming a 'future king' one day.

Despite the at-times unencouraging weather featured in particular narratives, there always remains the possibility of a 'summer of love' and times of 'disobedience', 'pride' and 'brotherhood', with the possibility of characters finding happiness, hope and contentment if they persevere in their romantic efforts, the only real end of desire being death. Ronit and Esti go their separate ways at the end of *Disobedience*, Sam and Lexi's burgeoning relationship in *Adulthood* ends up being destroyed, Roisin and Casim are (just about) together at the close of *Ae Fond Kiss…* and Johnny and Gheorghe set about embarking on a personal and professional relationship as *God's Own Country* reaches its ending. Each of these romantic and sexual partnerships, in their own particular ways, look forward to a time when the terms 'unlikely' or 'untypical' couples have been rendered redundant and possibly unintelligible. The films as a whole examined in my book also suggest that in seeking love, it may actually be the journey and not the final destination which matters most, and that in looking for possible partners, one should also aim to succeed in finding oneself, whoever that may turn out to be in the end.

In Pawel Pawlikowski's *Last Resort* (2000), Tanya (Dina Korzun) chooses to leave Britain where she is being held in a form of 'house arrest' and return to her native Russia: life in the ironically named 'Stonehaven' (with its hovering 'Ben Dover'-type characters and their seaside-based sex webcam operations) having fallen far short of her romantic hopes and expectations. Kindly Alfie (Paddy Considine), who has fallen somewhat in love with Tanya, facilitates her escape, even though this means losing someone who has given his own somewhat desolate and lonely existence a real sense of purpose and meaning. When he finally says goodbye to Tanya and her son, Artyom (Artyom Strelnikov), he tells Artyom to be a 'good' person and to 'Look after your mum', while hoping that 'everything works out'. Both promise to 'remember' each other, even if it is unlikely that they will ever meet again. As words of wisdom, warmth and hope to conclude this study of love, sex and desire in British cinema and society in a transitional and transformative era, they can scarcely – in the last resort – be improved upon.

Select Bibliography

Ackroyd, Peter, *The Last Testament to Oscar Wilde* (London: Penguin, 1993 [1983]).
Alderman, Naomi, *Disobedience* (London: Penguin, 2018 [2006]).
Alderton, Dolly, *Everything I Know about Love* (London: Fig Tree/Penguin, 2018).
Ambrose, Darren (ed.), *k-punk: The Collected and Unpublished Writings of Mark Fisher (2004–2016)* (London: Repeater Books, 2018).
Amis, Martin, *The Rub of Time: Bellow, Nabokov, Hitchens, Travolta, Trump. Essays and Reportage: 1994–2016* (London: Jonathan Cape, 2017).
Aragay, Mireia, Hildegard Klein, Enric Monforte and Pilar Zozaya (eds), *British Theatre of the 1990s: Interviews with Directors, Playwrights, Critics and Academics* (Basingstoke: Palgrave Macmillan, 2007).
Babington, Bruce (ed.), *British Stars and Stardom from Alma Taylor to Sean Connery* (Manchester: Manchester University Press, 2001).
Bailey, Peter J. and Sam B. Girgus (eds), *A Companion to Woody Allen* (Chichester: Wiley-Blackwell, 2013).
Bayley, John, *The Characters of Love: A Study in the Literature of Personality* (London: Chatto & Windus, 1968 [1960]).
Bayley, John, *Iris: A Memoir of Iris Murdoch* [1998] and *Iris and the Friends: A Year of Memories* [1999] (London: Duckworth, 2002).
Bell, David and Jon Binnie, *The Sexual Citizen: Queer Politics and Beyond* (Cambridge: Polity, and Malden, MA: Blackwell, 2000).
Bennett, Andrew and Nicholas Royle (eds), *An Introduction to Literature, Criticism and Theory*, fifth edition (London: Routledge, 2016).
Bersani, Leo, *A Future for Astyanax: Character and Desire in Literature* (London: Marion Boyars, 1978).
Bloom, Clive, *Bestsellers: Popular Fiction since 1900* (Basingstoke: Palgrave, 2002).
Bourne, Stephen, *Brief Encounters: Lesbians and Gays in British Cinema 1930–1971* (London: Cassell, 1996).
Carlyle, Thomas, *Past and Present* (London: Chapman and Hall Limited, 1897 [1843]).
Cobb, Shelley, 'Adaptable Bridget: Generic Intertextuality and Postfeminism in *Bridget Jones's Diary*', in Jack Boozer (ed.), *Authorship in Film Adaptation* (Austin: University of Texas Press, 2008), pp. 281–304.
Coleman, Rebecca and Debra Ferreday (eds), *Hope and Feminist Theory* (London: Routledge, 2011).
Conradi, Peter J., *Iris Murdoch: A Life* (London: HarperCollins, 2002 [2001]).

Critchley, Simon, *On Humour* (London: Routledge, 2002).
Delaney, Shelagh, *A Taste of Honey* (London: Bloomsbury, 2015 [1959]).
Demory, Pamela and Christopher Pullen (eds), *Queer Love in Film and Television: Critical Essays* (Basingstoke: Palgrave Macmillan, 2013).
Dipple, Elizabeth, *Iris Murdoch: Work for The Spirit* (London: Methuen & Co., 1982).
Dolan, Josephine, '"Old Age" Films: Golden Retirement, Dispossession and Disturbance', *Journal of British Cinema and Television*, 13:4 (2016), pp. 571–89.
Dollimore, Jonathan, *Desire: A Memoir* (London: Bloomsbury, 2017).
Douglas, Alfred (Lord), *Oscar Wilde and Myself* (London: John Long Limited, 1914).
Durgnat, Raymond, *Eros in the Cinema* (London: Calder and Boyars, 1966).
Durgnat, Raymond, *A Mirror for England: British Movies from Austerity to Affluence* (London: Faber & Faber, 1970).
Durgnat, Raymond, *Sexual Alienation in the Cinema* (London: Studio Vista, 1972).
Eagleton, Terry, *William Shakespeare* (Oxford: Blackwell, 1986).
Ellman, Richard (ed.), *The Artist as Critic: Critical Writings of Oscar Wilde* (London: W.H. Allen, 1970).
Fielding, Helen, *Bridget Jones's Diary* (London: Picador, 1997 [1996]).
Fielding, Helen, *Bridget Jones: The Edge of Reason* (London: Picador, 2000 [1999]).
Fielding, Helen, *Bridget Jones: Mad about the Boy* (London: Vintage, 2014 [2013]).
Fielding, Helen, *Bridget Jones's Baby: The Diaries* (London: Vintage, 2017 [2016]).
Frankel, Nicholas, *Oscar Wilde: The Unrepentant Years* (Cambridge, MA, and London: Harvard University Press, 2017).
Frey, Mattias, *Extreme Cinema: The Transgressive Rhetoric of Today's Art Film Culture* (New Brunswick, NJ, and London: Rutgers University Press, 2016).
Frye, Northrop, *Anatomy of Criticism: Four Essays* (Princeton, NJ: Princeton University Press, 1973 [1957]).
Giddens, Anthony, *The Transformation of Intimacy: Sexuality, Love and Eroticism in Modern Sexualities* (Cambridge: Polity Press, 1992).
Greer, Germaine, *The Female Eunuch* (London: Fourth Estate, 2012 [1970]).
Griffiths, Robin (ed.), *British Queer Cinema* (London: Routledge, 2006).
Hallam, Julia, 'Inappropriate Desires? Sex and the (Ageing) Single Girl', *Journal of British Cinema and Television*, 13:4 (2016), pp. 552–70.
Heller, Zoe, *Notes on a Scandal* (London: Penguin, 2009 [2003]).
Higson, Andrew (ed.), *Dissolving Views: Key Writings on British Cinema* (London: Cassell, 1996).
Hill, John, *Sex, Class and Realism: British Cinema 1956–1963* (London: British Film Institute Publishing, 1986).
Hite, Shere, *The Hite Report: A Nationwide Study on Female Sexuality* (London: Talmy Franklin Ltd, 1977 [1976]).
Holbrook, David, *Sylvia Plath: Poetry and Existence* (London: Athlone Press, 1976).
Hosle, Vittorio, *Woody Allen: An Essay on the Nature of the Comical* (Notre Dame, IN: University of Notre Dame Press, 2007).
Hunt, Leon, *British Low Culture from Safari Suits to Sexploitation* (Abingdon: Routledge, 1998).
Hunter, I.Q., *British Trash Cinema* (London: Palgrave Macmillan/British Film Institute, 2013).

Hunter, I.Q., *Cult Film as a Guide to Life: Fandom, Adaptation and Identity* (London: Bloomsbury, 2016).
Illouz, Eva, *Cold Intimacies: The Making of Emotional Capitalism* (Cambridge: Polity Press, 2013 [2007]).
Jeffreys, Sheila, *Anticlimax: A Feminist Perspective on the Sexual Revolution* (London: The Women's Press, 1990).
Jones, Owen, *Chavs: The Demonization of the Working Class* (London: Verso, 2012 [2011]).
Kael, Pauline, *I Lost It at the Movies* (London: Jonathan Cape, 1966).
Kolker, Robert, *The Altering Eye: Contemporary International Cinema* (Oxford: Oxford University Press, 1983).
Krzywinska, Tanya, *Sex and the Cinema* (London: Wallflower Press, 2006).
Kuhn, Annette, 'Women's Genres', *Screen*, 25:1 (January/February 1984), pp. 18–28.
Larkin, Philip, *High Windows* (London: Faber & Faber, 1974).
Leach, Jim, *British Film* (Cambridge: Cambridge University Press, 2004).
Leggott, James, *Contemporary British Cinema: From Heritage to Horror* (London: Wallflower Press, 2008).
Lerner, Lawrence, *Love and Marriage: Literature and Its Social Context* (London: Edward Arnold, 1979).
Lodge, David, *Working with Structuralism: Essays and Reviews on Nineteenth- and Twentieth-Century Literature* (London: Routledge & Kegan Paul, 1981).
Macherey, Pierre, *A Theory of Literary Production*, translated by Geoffrey Wall (London: Routledge & Kegan Paul, 1978).
Magnanti, Brooke, *Belle De Jour: The Intimate Adventures of a London Call Girl* (London: Phoenix, 2007 [2005]).
Malcolm, Janet, *The Silent Woman: Sylvia Plath and Ted Hughes* (London: Picador, 1994 [1993]).
Marber, Patrick, *Closer*, revised edition (London: Methuen, 1997).
Marcuse, Herbert, *The Aesthetic Dimension: Towards a Critique of Marxist Aesthetics* (London: Macmillan, 1979).
McFarlane, Brian, *Twenty British Films: A Guided Tour* (Manchester: Manchester University Press, 2015).
McRobbie, Angela, *The Uses of Cultural Studies: A Textbook* (London: Sage Publications, 2005).
McRobbie, Angela, *The Aftermath of Feminism: Gender, Culture and Social Change* (London: Sage, 2009).
Milne, Tom, *Losey on Losey* (London: Secker & Warburg, 1968 [1967]).
Mortimer, Clare, *Romantic Comedy* (London: Routledge, 2010).
Murdoch, Iris, *A Severed Head* (St. Albans: Triad/Granada, 1981 [1961]).
Murdoch, Iris, *Jackson's Dilemma* (London: Chatto & Windus, 1995).
Murphy, Robert, *Sixties British Cinema* (London: British Film Institute, 1992).
Murphy, Robert (ed.), *British Cinema of the 90s* (London: British Film Institute, 2000).
Murphy, Robert (ed.), *Directors in British and Irish Cinema: A Reference Companion* (London: British Film Institute, 2006).
Murphy, Robert (ed.), *The British Cinema Book*, third edition (London: British Film Institute, 2009).
Newland, Paul, *British Films of the 1970s* (Manchester: Manchester University Press, 2017 [2013]).

Nicholls, David, *One Day* (London: Hodder, 2011 [2009]).
Nowell-Smith, Geoffrey, *Making Waves: New Cinemas of the 1960s* (London: Continuum, 2008).
Penny, Laurie, *Unspeakable Things: Sex, Lies and Revolution* (London and New York: Bloomsbury, 2014).
Plath, Sylvia, *The Bell Jar* (London: Faber & Faber, 1996 [1963]).
Plath, Sylvia, *Crossing the Water* (London: Faber & Faber, 1971).
Plath, Sylvia, *Winter Trees* (London: Faber & Faber, 1971).
Powrie, Phil, Ann Davies and Bruce Babington (eds), *The Trouble with Men: Masculinities in European and Hollywood Cinema* (London: Wallflower Press, 2004).
Rojek, Chris, *Brit-Myth: Who Do the British Think They Are?* (London: Reaktion Books, 2007).
Rolph, C.H. (ed.), *The Trial of Lady Chatterley: Regina v. Penguin Books Ltd* (Place of publication not identified: Privately Printed, 1961).
Sandbrook, Dominic, *State of Emergency: The Way We Were: Britain 1970–1974* (London: Penguin, 2011 [2010]).
Scruton, Roger, *Sexual Desire: A Moral Philosophy of the Erotic* (New York: The Free Press, 1986).
Sheridan, Simon, *Keeping the British End Up: Four Decades of Saucy Cinema* (London: Reynolds & Hearn Ltd, 2001).
Sinfield, Alan, *Literature, Politics and Culture in Postwar Britain* (Oxford: Basil Blackwell, 1989).
Smith, Clarissa, 'British Sexual Cultures', in Michael Higgins, Clarissa Smith and John Storey (eds), *The Cambridge Companion to Modern British Culture* (Cambridge: Cambridge University Press, 2010), pp. 244–61.
Steinberg, Peter K. and Karen V. Kukil (eds), *The Letters of Sylvia Plath Volume II: 1956–1963* (London: Faber & Faber, 2018).
Stevenson, Anne, *Bitter Fame: A Life of Sylvia Plath* (London: Viking, 1989).
Street, Sarah, *British National Cinema: Second Edition* (London: Routledge, 2009 [1997]).
Tarr, Carrie, '*Sapphire, Darling* and the Boundaries of Permitted Pleasure', *Screen*, 26:1 (January–February 1985), pp. 50–65.
Thatcher, Margaret, *The Downing Street Years* (London: HarperCollins, 1993).
Thwaite, Anthony (ed.), *Selected Letters of Philip Larkin 1940–1985* (London: Faber & Faber, 1992).
Townsend, Catherine, *Sleeping Around: Secrets of a Sexual Adventuress* (London: John Murray, 2007).
Townsend, Catherine, *Breaking the Rules: Confessions of a Bad Girl* (London: John Murray, 2008).
Turner, Alwyn W., *Rejoice! Rejoice! Britain in the 1980s* (London: Aurum Press, 2013 [2010]).
Unsworth, Emma Jane, *Animals* (Edinburgh: Canongate Books, 2019 [2014]).
Walker, Alexander, *Hollywood, England: The British Film Industry in the Sixties* (London: Harrap, 1986 [1974]).
Waller-Bridge, Phoebe, *Fleabag* (London: Nick Hern Books, 2017 [2013]).
Walter, Natasha, *The New Feminism* (London: Virago, 2013 [1999]).
Wartenberg, Thomas, *Unlikely Couples: Movie Romance as Social Criticism* (Boulder, CO: Westview Press, 1999).

Weeks, Jeffrey, *Invented Moralities: Sexual Values in an Age of Uncertainty* (Cambridge: Polity Press, 1995).
Wilde, Oscar, 'The Soul of Man Under Socialism' [1891], reprinted in the *Complete Works of Oscar Wilde* with an introduction by Vyvyan Holland (London and Glasgow: Collins, 1988 [1948]).
Williams, Linda, *Screening Sex* (Durham, NC, and London: Duke University Press, 2008).
Williams, Melanie, *Female Stars of British Cinema: The Women in Question* (Edinburgh: Edinburgh University Press, 2017).
Williams, Raymond, *Modern Tragedy* (London: Verso: 1979 [1966]).
Wilson, A.N., *Iris Murdoch as I Knew Her* (London: Arrow Books, 2004 [2003]).
Wolfreys, Julian, *Critical Keywords in Literary and Cultural Theory* (Basingstoke: Palgrave Macmillan, 2004).
Wood, Jason, *Last Words: Considering Contemporary Cinema* (London: Wallflower Press, 2014).
Žižek, Slavoj, *The Year of Dreaming Dangerously* (London: Verso, 2012).

Index

9 Songs 9, 86–7, 88, 105–7, 110–14, 119, 202
45 Years 202

Accident 129–30
Ackroyd, Peter 133
Adulthood 4, 173, 175, 178–80
Ae Fond Kiss… 5, 12, 168–72
Alderton, Dolly 2
Alfie 1
Allen, Woody 5
Amis, Martin 40
Animals 86, 97–101, 119, 120
Archer, Jeffrey 59
Archipelago 4, 145
Auden, W.H. 13, 21–2

Barber, Nicholas 175
Barber, Sian 134
Becoming Jane 19
Beer, Patricia 18
Bell, David 160
Bell, James 175
Bell Jar, The 44
Bennett, Andrew 167
Binnie, Jon 160
Blair, Tony 5, 41, 69, 169
Blanchett, Cate 152–3
Bloom, Clive 52, 61–2
Bourne, Stephen 23
Bradshaw, Peter 55
Bridget Jones's Baby (film) 51, 54–5, 66–72, 74–5, 77
Bridget Jones's Diary (film) 51–2, 55, 56–62, 75
Bridget Jones's Diary (novel) 57

Bridget Jones: Mad about the Boy 53, 66
Bridget Jones: The Edge of Reason (film) 51, 55–6, 63–6, 71–2
Bridget Jones: The Edge of Reason (novel) 75
Brief Encounter 105
Bright Star 19–20
Brotherhood 4, 173, 180–3
Brown, Gordon 5
Bryson, Bill 90

Carlyle, Thomas 126
Carry On Emmannuelle 85
Carry On Loving 85
Cauldwell, Christopher 173
Charles, Prince of Wales 1, 204
Clarke, Cath 180
Clarke, Noel 4, 173–83, 202
Closer 11, 154–61
Cochrane, Kira 157
Coleman, John 38
Conrich, Ian 90
Cooke, David 155
Cool It, Carol! 92–3, 120
Corliss, Richard 159
Critchley, Simon 73
Crompton, Sarah 74
Crosland, Anthony 110
Curtis, Richard 135

Dalrymple, Theodore 181
Darling 73, 129
Deep End 130
Deleuze, Gilles 87
Diana, Princess of Wales 1, 75

Dickens, Charles 20, 174–5
Dipple, Elizabeth 38
Disobedience 5, 11–12, 161–3, 165–6
Dogging – a Love Story 9, 86, 88, 101–3, 120
Dollimore, Jonathan 10
Douglas, Lord Alfred 22, 24, 26, 30, 153
Dover, Ben 113
Durgnat, Raymond 6, 126, 151

Eagleton, Terry 1, 2, 141–2
Edelman, Lee 166
Edge of Love, The 20
Education, An 138–9
Eliot, T.S. 108
Ellen, Barbara 42, 51–2, 55, 118
Escort Girls 93
Eskimo Nell 86, 91–2, 120

Fisher, Mark 11, 41, 186
Fleabag 76–7
Foucault, Michel 93
Four Weddings and a Funeral 135
Fox, Kate 9
Frankel, Nicholas 25–6
Franks, Alan 4, 174
Frey, Mattias 113
Frye, Northrop 70, 71

Georgy Girl 73–4
Gilbey, Ryan 169–70
Gilroy, Paul 183
God's Own Country 5, 12, 167–8, 203
Gold, Tanya 18–19
Gordon, Bryony 52
Greer, Germaine 72
Griffiths, Robin 129
Guattari, Félix 87

Hanks, Robert 154
Happy Prince, The 22–3, 25–31, 42–6
Harvey, David 64
Hazelton, John 155
Here We Go Round the Mulberry Bush 89–90
Hill, Derek 89

Hogg, Joanna 4, 142–7, 202
Hoggard, Liz 175
Holbrook, David 32
Horley, Nick 158
Hudson, Christopher 38
Hunt, Leon 91
Hunter, I.Q. 7, 93, 112, 113
Hussein, Saddam 62, 68–9

I Give It a Year 203
Intimate Games 86
Invisible Woman, The 20
Iris 8, 21, 37–46
Iron Lady, The 183, 204
I Want Candy 86, 88, 103–5, 119, 120

James, Clive 72
Jones, Owen 186

Kael, Pauline 90, 128
Kappeler, Susanne 116
Kermode, Mark 55, 168, 170, 171–2
Kerr, Philip 55
Kidron, Beeban 55–6, 66
Kidulthood 4, 173–9, 182–3
Killing of Sister George, The 131
King, Justine 70
Kuhn, Annette 73
Kureishi, Hanif 135

Lady Chatterley's Lover 7, 89
Landesman, Cosmo 76–7
Larkin, Philip 31, 106, 158
Last Christmas 5, 76
Last Resort 11, 204–5
Lawrence, D.H. 2–3, 7, 35, 74, 118
Leach, Jim 6
Leavis, F.R. 10, 58, 71, 74–5, 175–6
Leggott, James 6–7
Letter to Brezhnev 133–4
Loach, Ken 169, 172
Lodge, David 70
Look of Love, The 6, 9, 87, 88, 114–20
Losey, Joseph 155
Love Actually 136

Macherey, Pierre 155
Maguire, Sharon 55, 66
Malcolm, Derek 150, 173, 180

Malcolm, Janet 31
Manley, Tym 87
Mantel, Hilary 134
Marber, Patrick 159
Marr, Andrew 126
Match Point 5
Mayer, Sophie 143
McDonagh, Melanie 140
McEwan, Ian 111
McFarlane, Brian 130
McLaren, Iona 39
McRobbie, Angela 52, 72, 75
Me Before You 5, 75–6
Medhurst, Andy 90
Military Wives 3, 7
Moore, Caroline 39–40
Mortimer, Clare 53
Mosley, Leonard 88–9
Mrs Henderson Presents 117–18
Muggeridge, Malcolm 107
Muir, Kate 43
My Beautiful Laundrette 134–5
My Name is Joe 169
My Summer of Love 5, 11–12, 161–4

Neville, Richard 85–6, 175
Newland, Paul 91
Newman, Kim 160
Nicholls, David 141
Nighthawks 132, 133, 168
No Sex Please, We're British 90–1
Notes on a Scandal 5, 12, 137, 147–54
Notting Hill 135–6
Nowell-Smith, Geoffrey 128

On Chesil Beach 10, 87, 105–11, 118
One Day 139–42
Oscar Wilde (film) 23–4
O'Sullivan, Charlotte 40

Pelling, Rowan 112–13
Penny, Laurie 1–2, 3–4, 57, 59, 60, 66
Perfect Sense 13, 137, 197–200
Petley, Julian 90
Powell, Dilys 169
Pressure 132–3, 182
Prick Up Your Ears 135
Pride 5, 12, 183–8, 203

Riot Club, The 138
Rita, Sue and Bob Too 74, 133, 134
Romeo and Juliet 168, 182–3
Romney, Jonathan 143
Room at the Top 128
Ross, Deborah 88, 165
Royle, Nicholas 167
Rushdie, Salman 59

Sammy and Rosie Get Laid 135
Samuel, Raphael 184
Sandbrook, Dominic 91, 106, 115, 169
Sandhu, Sukhdev 33–4, 112, 154
Sardar, Ziauddin 9–10
Saturday Night and Sunday Morning 128
Saunders, Graham 154
Segal, Victoria 177
Self, Will 56
Servant, The 128–9
Severed Head, A 38
Sex Lives of the Potato Men 9, 86, 93–7, 118–19, 120, 167
Sexton, David 4
Sheeran, Ed 68
Shoard, Catherine 174, 178–9
Sinfield, Alan 32
Smith, Anna 168
Smith, Clarissa 9, 168
Sonstegard, Adam 153
Sorry We Missed You 172
Souvenir, The 4, 145–7
Spicer, Andrew 54
Stafford-Clark, Max 154
Street, Matthew 90
Street, Sarah 164
Sturges, Fiona 8
Sunday, Bloody Sunday 131–2
Sutcliffe, Thomas 149, 151
Sylvia 7–8, 18–19, 21, 31–7, 42–6
Syms, Sylvia 127–8

T2 Trainspotting 200–2
Tarr, Carrie 129
Thatcher, Margaret 69, 183, 186, 187
Their Finest 138
This Year's Love 1, 136
Thompson, Alice 175
Thomson, David 23

Taste of Honey, A (play) 127
Trials of Oscar Wilde, The 23–4
Two for the Road 130–1

Unrelated 4, 142–5, 146–7
Ups and Downs of a Handyman, The 92

Victim 127

Walker, Alexander 52, 55, 129, 131–2, 133–4
Walter, Natasha 63
Wartenberg, Thomas 3
Watney, Simon 187

Weekend 5, 166, 167
Weeks, Jeffrey 183, 187
Weldon, Faye 53
White, Terri 167
Williams, Linda 113
Williams, Melanie 105, 135
Williams, Raymond 2–3, 141
Wilson, A.N. 18, 39
Winter, Jessica 56
Withnail and I 100
Wood, Robin 35

Žižek, Slavoj 178, 182

EU authorised representative for GPSR:
Easy Access System Europe, Mustamäe tee 50,
10621 Tallinn, Estonia
gpsr.requests@easproject.com

www.ingramcontent.com/pod-product-compliance
Lightning Source LLC
Chambersburg PA
CBHW050925240426
43668CB00021B/2440